EXPERT RESUMES FOR MILITARY-TO-CIVILIAN TRANSITIONS

SECOND EDITION

Wendy S. Enelow and Louise M. Kursmark

jist Works
America's Career Publisher

Expert Resumes for Military-to-Civilian Transitions, **Second Edition**

© 2010 by Wendy S. Enelow and Louise M. Kursmark

Published by JIST Works, an imprint of JIST Publishing
7321 Shadeland Station, Suite 200
Indianapolis, IN 46256-3923
Phone: 800-648-JIST   Fax: 877-454-7839   E-mail: info@jist.com

Visit our Web site at **www.jist.com** for information on JIST, free job search tips, tables of contents, sample pages, and ordering instructions for our many products!

Quantity discounts are available for JIST books. Please call our Sales Department at 800-648-5478 for a free catalog and more information.

Trade Product Manager: Lori Cates Hand
Production Editor: Heather Stith
Cover Designer: Amy Adams
Interior Designer: Trudy Coler
Page Layout: Toi Davis
Proofreaders: Stephanie Koutek, Jeanne Clark
Indexer: Jeanne Clark

Printed in the United States of America

14 13 12 11 10 09   9 8 7 6 5 4 3 2 1

Library of Congress Cataloging-in-Publication Data
Enelow, Wendy S.
     Expert resumes for military-to-civilian transitions / Wendy S. Enelow and
     Louise M. Kursmark. – 2nd ed.
          p. cm.
     Includes index.
     ISBN 978-1-59357-732-2 (alk. paper)
     1. Résumés (Employment)–United States. 2. Career changes–United States.
     3. Retired military personnel–Employment–United States. 4. Veterans–
     Employment–United States. I. Kursmark, Louise. II. Title.
     HF5383.E47885 2010
     650.14′2–dc22
                                   2009038500

We have been careful to provide accurate information in this book, but it is possible that errors and omissions have been introduced. Please consider this in making any career plans or other important decisions. Trust your own judgment above all else and in all things.

Trademarks: All brand names and product names used in this book are trade names, service marks, trademarks, or registered trademarks of their respective owners.

ISBN 978-1-59357-732-2

TABLE OF CONTENTS

ABOUT THIS BOOK

Whether you've been in the military for 2 years, 4 years, 10 years, 20 years, or more, making the transition from a military to a civilian career can be quite a challenge. To begin with, you have a number of very important decisions to make:

- The type or types of positions you want to pursue
- The industry or industries in which you are interested
- The type of company you would like to work for
- Your desired geographic location(s)

Once you have made those decisions, the next step in your job search will be to develop a strong, achievement-focused resume that clearly communicates your skills, knowledge, expertise, and record of performance. The critical challenge you face is to translate those years of military experience into language that "corporate America" understands. Acronyms, abbreviations, and initials that may be a routine part of your vocabulary (for example, FORSCOM, AFB, ECM, DoD, and TRADOC) will most likely *not* be recognizable to these companies and their hiring managers (unless you're targeting your job search to companies that do business specifically with the U.S. government or U.S. Armed Forces).

Learning to write a powerful resume that uses civilian language and positions you as a competitive candidate in the employment market is what this book is all about. As you read through the early chapters, you'll learn that a resume is much more than just your job history, academic credentials, technical skills, and awards. A truly effective resume is a concise, yet comprehensive, document that focuses on your achievements, contributions, and value you bring to a company. Read this book and review the scores of samples, and you'll have the tools you need to create your own winning resume.

Once you have written your resume, this book will instruct you in the methods for preparing resumes for e-mail, scanning, and Web site posting, as well as the traditional printed resume.

By using *Expert Resumes for Military-to-Civilian Transitions* as your professional guide, you will succeed in developing a powerful and effective resume that opens doors, gets interviews, and helps you land a great opportunity!

INTRODUCTION

Unlike some of the other books in the *Expert Resumes* series, which focus on very specific career areas, this book addresses a large and diverse audience: specifically, military personnel who are now pursuing civilian jobs and careers. This unique collection of people represents just about every profession and industry imaginable—from aerospace engineering to logistics management, from airfield operations to software design, from housing to recruitment, and so much more. The *only* thing that each of our readers has in common is the fact that they have decided to leave (or retire from) the military. Beyond that, the range of experiences, qualifications, skills, and expertise that each of our readers has is vastly different.

But that's okay. This book was not written to teach you how to write a resume for a specific industry, profession, or job skill. Rather, this book was written to guide you in translating your military experience into terminology that hiring managers in the corporate world can easily understand. In essence, we want to provide you with the insights you need to translate your military experience into the functions, responsibilities, and skill sets required for a successful career outside the Armed Forces.

To help you use this book wisely, we divided into three parts:

- Part I contains three chapters of critical importance to every reader. These chapters outline important resume-writing strategies, provide instruction on how to write a resume, and explain what you may need to change on your resume depending on how you plan to submit it.

- Part II breaks down the resume samples into chapters based on your current career goals and objectives.

- Part III addresses the critically important document that accompanies your resume just about every time you send it: your cover letter.

Before you start writing a resume, you need to ask yourself some key questions, identify your career objectives, and consider how you will conduct your job search.

The What, How, Which, and Where of Resume Writing

There are four critical questions that you must ask yourself before you ever begin writing your resume:

- **What type of position/career track are you going to pursue?** Your current career goals dictate the entire resume writing and design process. If you're looking for a position where you will have responsibilities similar to what you did in the military, you'll approach your resume one way. On the other hand, if you're now looking to transition your skills into a new career field, your resume should be entirely different.

- **How are you going to paint a picture of your skills and qualifications that will make you an attractive candidate in the civilian world?** What types of information are you going to highlight about your past experiences that tie directly to your current objectives? What accomplishments, skills, and qualifications are you going to "sell" in your resume to support your new civilian career objectives?

- **Which resume format are you going to use?** Is a chronological, functional, or hybrid resume format going to work best for you? Which format will give you the greatest flexibility to highlight the skills you want to bring to the forefront in support of your transition into a civilian career?

- **Where are you going to look for a job?** Once you have decided what type of position and industry you are interested in, how do you plan to identify and approach those companies?

When you can answer the what, how, which, and where, you'll be prepared to write your resume and launch your search campaign. Use chapters 1 through 3 to guide you in developing the content for your resume and selecting the appropriate design and layout. Your resume should focus on your skills, achievements, and qualifications, demonstrating the value and benefit you bring to a prospective employer as they relate to your current career goals. The focus should be on the "civilian" you and not necessarily what you have done in the past in your military career.

Review the sample resumes in chapters 4 through 13 to see what other people have done—people in similar situations to yours who faced similar challenges. You'll find interesting formats, unique skills presentations, achievement-focused resumes, project-focused resumes, and much more. Most importantly, you'll see samples written by the top resume writers in the United States, Canada, and Australia. These are real resumes that got interviews and generated job offers. They're the "best of the best" from us to you.

Finally, review chapters 14 and 15 for best-in-class cover letter strategies and samples. As you'll read, your cover letter is an essential partner to your resume, and that's why we have expanded this edition of *Expert Resumes for Military-to-Civilian Transitions* to include the guidelines and templates you will need for a complete job search campaign.

Determining and Reaching Your Career Objectives

Before you proceed any further with writing your resume, you'll need to begin by defining your career or job objectives—specifically, the types of positions, companies, and industries in which you are interested. This is critical because a haphazard, unfocused job search will lead you nowhere.

KNOW THE EMPLOYMENT TRENDS

One of the best ways to begin identifying your career objectives is to look at what opportunities are available today, in the immediate future, and in the longer-term future. And one of the most useful tools for this type of research and information collection is the U.S. Department of Labor's Bureau of Labor Statistics (www.bls. gov).

According to the Bureau, the employment outlook is optimistic. Consider these findings:

- Service-producing industries and professional occupations will continue to be the dominant employment generators, each with a gain of 16.7 percent.

- Management, business, and financial occupations represent the second largest growing occupational group with 10.4 percent projected growth.

- The 10 industries with the largest wage and salary employment growth are, from first in growth to tenth, management, scientific, and technical consulting; employment services; general medical and surgical hospitals; elementary and secondary schools; local government (excluding education and hospitals); physician offices; limited-service eating establishments; colleges, universities, and professional schools; computer systems design; and home health care services.

- The top 10 occupations with the largest projected employment growth area are, from first in growth to tenth, network systems and data communications analysts; personal and home care aides; home health aides; computer software engineers (applications); medical assistants; computer systems analysts; food preparation and service workers; registered nurses; postsecondary teachers; and management analysts.

- Of all goods-producing industries, the only one projected to grow is the construction industry with a 1 percent gain.

- Transportation and material-moving occupations are projected to grow 10.4 percent.

- Office and administrative support occupations are projected to grow more slowly than average, reflecting the need for fewer personnel as a result of the tremendous gains in office automation and technology.

- Production-related occupations are also projected to grow more slowly as manufacturing automation and technology reduce the need for specific types of employees.

These facts and statistics clearly demonstrate that there are numerous employment opportunities across diverse sectors within our economy, from advanced technology positions to hourly wage jobs in construction and home health care. Although most industries may not be growing at double-digit percentages as in years past, companies continue to expand, and new companies emerge every day. The opportunities are out there; your challenge is to find them and position yourself as the "right" candidate.

MANAGE YOUR JOB SEARCH AND YOUR CAREER

To take advantage of these opportunities, you must be an educated job seeker. That means you must know what you want in your career, where the hiring action is, what qualifications and credentials you need to attain your desired career goals, and how best to market your qualifications. It is no longer enough to have a specific talent or set of skills. Whether you're a programmer for the Army now seeking opportunities in the emerging field of mobile phone applications, a USAF nurse wanting to transfer into medical product sales, a USMC engineer seeking new opportunities as a financial manager, or any one of hundreds of other military-to-civilian career transition targets, you must also be a strategic marketer, able to package and promote your experience to take advantage of this wave of employment opportunity.

There's no doubt that the employment market has changed dramatically from only a few years ago. According to the U.S. Department of Labor, you should expect to hold between 7 and 10 different jobs during your career. No longer is stability the status quo. Today, the norm is movement in a fast-paced and intense employment market where there are many career opportunities. To take advantage of available opportunities, every job seeker—no matter the profession, no matter the industry, no matter the job goal—must proactively control and manage his career.

What's more, you are faced with the additional challenge of positioning yourself for a successful career change into the civilian workforce. In many instances, you may be competing against other candidates who have experience within the industry or profession you are attempting to enter. This can make your job search more difficult than that of the more "traditional" job seeker who moves from one position to another similar position without having to make a significant career transition such as you are facing.

And that is precisely why this book is so important to you. We'll outline the strategies and techniques that you can use to effectively position yourself against other candidates, creating a resume that highlights your skills and qualifications while effectively minimizing the fact that most, if not all, of your experience was acquired through military service. Our goal is to help you appear as a "corporate insider," already possessing the skills and experiences that companies look for in qualified candidates.

> **WARNING:** One of the greatest challenges for anyone making a successful military-to-civilian career transition is to use the "right" language. Chances are that most civilians reviewing your resume will not be familiar with military language, abbreviations, and acronyms. They won't know what FORSCOM means, what an E-5 does, or what a CAC is. As such, it is critical that you translate your military language into civilian language that everyone in the civilian workforce can easily understand. You will read more about this concept in later chapters in this book.

Job Search Questions and Answers

Before we get to the core of this book—resume writing and design—we offer some practical job search advice that is valuable to virtually every job seeker who falls into the military-to-civilian career transition category.

WHAT IS THE MOST IMPORTANT CONSIDERATION FOR A SUCCESSFUL MILITARY-TO-CIVILIAN CAREER TRANSITION?

As outlined previously, the single most important consideration for any candidate who falls into this category is how you're going to highlight your skills, qualifications, and achievements as they relate to and support your current career objectives. Your resume is not a historical document that simply lists your job titles and employers. Rather, a truly effective career transition resume is one that takes all of the skills and experience you have that are relevant to your new career goal and brings them to the forefront in an attempt to create a picture of the "new" you.

Let's use an Army nurse transitioning into the field of medical equipment sales as an example. Nurse Barnes already has extensive experience in the medical and health care fields and has worked closely with physicians and other health care providers throughout her military career. So she is comfortable interacting with them and has a wealth of experience working with a diversity of medical equipment and technology. This is the type of information that will be highlighted in her resume and be of most interest to civilian pharmaceutical companies, *not* her daily nursing and patient care responsibilities at various military installations worldwide.

Another example is Rodney Green, whose entire 20-year military career has been in supply, inventory management, and airfield operations. His goal now is to pursue a career with FedEx, where he can continue to utilize his same core skills and knowledge. When writing his resume, Rodney's goal is to separate his wealth of experience in supply, inventory, and airfield operations from the environment in which it was acquired (the military) so that FedEx can easily "see" that he has all the right qualifications for the company and not focus on the fact that these skills were utilized exclusively during his military service. The moral of the story: Sell the skill and leave the organization behind.

Whatever your situation or objectives, when preparing your resume, you should keep in mind one critical fact:

> *Your resume is a marketing tool written to sell YOU!*

HOW DO YOU ENTER A NEW CAREER?

Entering a new career field is a result of two important factors:

- Highlighting any relevant skills, qualifications, accomplishments, experiences, education, credentials, volunteer work, involvement with professional and/ or civic associations, and other relevant activities and expertise that tie directly into your current career objective.

- Using an integrated job search campaign that will get you in front of decision makers at a wide array of companies in your field of interest. You can read much more about job search strategy in the next few pages of this chapter in the section titled "How Do You Get the Jobs?"

WHAT IS THE BEST RESUME STRATEGY FOR MAKING A SUCCESSFUL MILITARY-TO-CIVILIAN CAREER TRANSITION?

The single most important factor in making a successful career transition is to remember that your resume must *sell* what you have to offer:

- If you're a USCG trainer seeking to transition into a position in corporate training and development, *sell* the fact that you created new curricula, designed new instructional programs, acquired innovative teaching materials, and led new faculty.

- If you're a USMC computer technician now seeking a position marketing new technology products, *highlight* the wealth of your technical expertise, your success in working with and supporting end users, your ability to manage projects, and your strong communication skills.

- If you're a USN budget analyst now pursuing opportunities in general management, *sell* your experience in policy and procedure development, business management, team building and leadership, strategic planning, and organizational development.

When writing your resume, your challenge is to create a picture of knowledge, action, and results. In essence, you're stating "This is what I know, this is how I've used it, and this is how well I've performed." Success sells, so be sure to highlight yours. If you don't, no one else will.

WHERE ARE THE JOBS?

The jobs are everywhere—from multinational manufacturing conglomerates to the small retail sales companies in your neighborhood; from high-tech electronics firms in California to 100-year-old farming operations in rural communities; from banks and financial institutions to hospitals and health-care facilities in every city and town. The jobs are everywhere.

HOW DO YOU GET THE JOBS?

To answer this question, we need to review the basic principle underlying job search:

> Job search is marketing!

You have a product to sell—yourself—and the best way to sell it is to use all appropriate marketing channels just as you would for any other product.

Suppose you wanted to sell televisions. What would you do? You'd market your products using newspaper, magazine, and radio advertisements. You might develop a company Web site to build your e-business, and perhaps you'd hire a field sales representative to market to major retail chains. Each of these is a different marketing channel through which you're attempting to reach your audience.

The same approach applies to job search. You must use every marketing channel that's right for you. Unfortunately, there is no exact formula that works for everyone. What's right for you depends on your specific career objectives—the type of position you want, the industry you're targeting, your geographic restrictions (if you have any), your salary requirements, and more.

Following are the most valuable marketing channels for a successful job search. These are ordered from most effective to least effective:

1. **Referrals.** There is nothing better than a personal referral to a company, either in general or for a specific position. Referrals can open doors that, in most instances, would never be accessible any other way. If you know anyone who could possibly refer you to a specific organization, contact that person immediately and ask for his or her assistance. This kind of connection is particularly critical for military-to-civilian career changers and will be, by far, your single best marketing strategy to land a new position.

2. **Networking.** Networking is the backbone of every successful job search. Although you might consider it an unpleasant or difficult task, it is essential that you network effectively with your colleagues and associates, past supervisors and coworkers, suppliers, neighbors, friends, and others who might know of opportunities that are right for you. Another good strategy is to attend meetings of trade or professional associations in your area. This is a wonderful strategy to make new contacts and start building your network in your new career field. In today's nomadic job market—where you're likely to change jobs every few years—the best strategy is to keep your network "alive" even when you're not searching for a new position.

3. **Responding to newspaper, magazine, and periodical advertisements.** Although, as you'll read later, the opportunity to post job opportunities online has reduced the overall number of print advertisements, they still abound. Do not forget about this "tried-and-true" marketing strategy. If they've got the job and you have the qualifications, it can be a perfect fit.

4. **Responding to online job postings.** One of the most advantageous results of the technology revolution is an employer's ability to post job announcements online and a job seeker's ability to respond immediately via e-mail. In most (but not all) instances, these are bona fide opportunities, and it's well worth your while to spend time searching for and responding to appropriate postings. However, do not make the mistake of devoting too much time to searching the Internet. It can consume a huge amount of your time that you should spend on other job search efforts.

   To expedite your search, here are the largest and most widely used online job-posting sites—presented alphabetically and not necessarily in order of effectiveness or value. We've expanded this list to include some of our favorite sites designed specifically for veterans:

http://careers.msn.com

http://hotjobs.yahoo.com

www.americanjobs.com

www.careerbuilder.com

www.employmentguide.com

www.execunet.com

www.dice.com

www.flipdog.com

www.helmetstohardhats.com

www.hirediversity.com

www.jobcentral.com/vetcentral

www.monster.com

www.net-temps.com

www.netshare.com

www.theladders.com

www.va.gov/jobs

www.veteranemployment.com

www.veteransgreenjobs.org

www.vetjobs.com

5. **Posting your resume online.** The Internet is swarming with reasonably priced (if not free) Web sites where you can post your resume. It's quick, easy, and the only passive thing you can do in your search. All of the other marketing channels require action on your part. With online resume postings, once you've posted, you're done. You then just wait (and hope!) for some response.

6. **Targeted e-mail campaigns (resumes and cover letters) to recruiters.** Recruiters have jobs, and you want one. It's pretty straightforward. The only catch is to find the "right" recruiters who have the "right" jobs. Therefore, you must devote the time and effort to preparing the "right" list of recruiters. There are many resources on the Internet where you can access information about recruiters (for a fee), sort that information by industry (such as banking, sales, manufacturing, purchasing, transportation, finance, public relations, or telecommunications), and then cross-reference it with position specialization (such as management, technical, or administration). This allows you to identify the recruiters who would be interested in a candidate with your qualifications. Because these campaigns are transmitted electronically, they are easy and inexpensive to produce. Examples of such sites are Pro/File Research (www.profileresearch.com) and Kennedy Information (www.kennedyinfo.com).

When working with recruiters, it's important to realize that they do not work for you! Their clients are the hiring companies that pay their fees. They are not in business to "find a job" for you, but rather to fill a specific position with a qualified candidate, either you or someone else. To maximize your chances of finding a position through a recruiter or agency, don't rely on just one or two, but distribute your resume to many who meet your specific criteria.

CAUTION: Most recruiters are looking to fill specific positions with individuals with very specific qualifications. As a military-to-civilian career transition candidate, you may find that recruiters are not your best source of job opportunities because they are not known for "thinking outside the box." If their client (the hiring company) has said that they want a candidate with experience in x, y, and z, they are going to present only those job seekers with precisely that experience. Knowing that you're attempting to change careers and may not have precisely the background that the company is looking for, recruiters may simply pass you by. Don't be alarmed...it's their job!

7. **Targeted e-mail and print campaigns to employers.** Just as with campaigns to recruiters (see item 6 above), you must be extremely careful to select just the right employers that would be interested in a candidate with your qualifications. The closer you stick to "where you belong" in relation to your specific experience, the better your response rate will be. Just as with recruiters, human resource professionals and hiring managers may have difficulty appreciating the unique set of skills and qualifications military candidates bring to a position and to their company. That is why a powerful and effective resume is so very critical for candidates in your situation.

   Targeted letter campaigns can be sent either by e-mail or by traditional U.S. mail. Either can be effective. Keep this in mind when you are gathering contact data for your target companies. Sometimes you won't be able to find e-mail addresses for specific individuals, but you can always find the physical mailing address of the company. In those instances, send your letter by traditional mail to a specific person rather than e-mailing your materials to an anonymous "info" or "jobs" e-mail address. You can then follow up by phone instead of remaining in "e-mail limbo" while waiting for a response from an impersonal corporation.

8. **In-person "cold calls" to companies and recruiters.** We consider this the least effective and most time-consuming marketing strategy. It is extremely difficult to just walk in the door and get in front of the right person or any person who can take hiring action. You will be much better off focusing your time and energy on other, more productive channels.

Conclusion

Career opportunities abound today, even for the military-to-civilian career transition candidate. It has never been easier to learn about and apply for jobs than it is now with all the Internet resources available to all of us. Your challenge is to arm yourself with a powerful resume and cover letter, identify the best ways to get yourself and your resume into the market, and shine during every interview. If you're committed and focused, we can almost guarantee that you'll make a smooth transition into your new career field and find yourself happily employed.

PART I

Resume Writing, Strategy, and Formats

CHAPTER 1

Resume Writing Strategies for Military-to-Civilian Career Transitions

If you're reading this book, chances are that you'll be separating from the military in the near future, if you haven't done so already. It might be that one of the following scenarios applies to you:

- You've served your 20 years and are now retiring.

- You've been passed over several times for a promotion, and you realize that it's time to leave and pursue new career opportunities.

- You've been approached by a company or government contractor and offered an outstanding career opportunity.

- You've decided, after a few years, that the military is not the right career path for you, and you're ready to make a career change.

- You're ready to accept new opportunities and meet new professional challenges.

Whatever the reason, you're faced with some unique challenges in your job search and, more specifically, in how you write your resume and present your qualifications. The critical questions that you must ask yourself include

> "What can I do to capture employers' attention, impress them with my qualifications and achievements, and create a resume that does not put me 'out of the running' because most, if not all, of my experience has been in the Armed Forces?"

And, just as important...

> "How can I write a resume that will clearly communicate how my military experience will fit comfortably into 'corporate America,' using 'corporate lingo' that accurately reflects my military experience?"

The fact that you are seeking to make a career transition will dictate what you write in your resume, how you write it, and where you position it in your resume. Your goal is to paint a picture of a well-qualified candidate who will bring immediate and measurable value to the civilian workplace based on your existing skills, qualifications, competencies, and experiences. How you present those skills, qualifications, competencies, and experiences in your particular resume will depend entirely on your current career goals.

Resume Strategies

For every job seeker—those still on active duty and those not currently working—a powerful resume is an essential component of any successful job search campaign. In fact, it is virtually impossible to conduct a search without a resume. It is your calling card that briefly, yet powerfully, communicates the skills, qualifications, experience, and value you bring to a prospective employer. It is the document that will open doors and generate interviews. It is the first thing people will learn about you when you forward it in response to an advertisement or as the result of a referral, and it is the primary thing they'll remember when they're reviewing your qualifications after an interview.

Your resume is a sales document, and you are the product it is trying to sell! You must identify the *features* (what you know and what you can do) and *benefits* (how you can help an employer) of that product, and then communicate them in a concise and hard-hitting written presentation. Remind yourself over and over, as you work your way through the resume process, that you are writing marketing literature designed to sell a new product—YOU—into a new position.

Your resume can have tremendous power and a phenomenal impact on your job search. So don't take it lightly. Rather, devote the time, energy, and resources that are essential to developing a resume that is well-written, visually attractive, and effective in communicating *who* you are and *how* you want to be perceived.

Now that you understand why your resume is so important, the next step is to learn how to write a good one. Following are the nine core strategies for writing effective and successful resumes.

RESUME STRATEGY #1: WHO ARE YOU AND HOW DO YOU WANT TO BE PERCEIVED?

Now that you're leaving military service, the very first step in making a successful career transition is to identify your career interests, goals, and objectives. *This task is critical,* because it is the underlying foundation for *what* you include in your resume, *how* you include it, and *where* you include it. Knowing that you're leaving the military is not enough. To write an effective and powerful resume, you must know—to some degree of certainty—the type or types of position you will be seeking.

There are two concepts to consider here:

- **Who you are:** This relates to what you have done professionally during your military career. Are you a contract administrator, fleet manager, network administrator, mechanic, training instructor, infantryman, or medical technician? What is it that you have done in the military for all these years? Who are you?

- **How you want to be perceived:** This is critical and relates to your current career objectives. Consider the following scenario: You've been deployed on active duty in Afghanistan and then Iraq, where your Military Occupational Specialty (MOS) has been a Surface Warfare Officer. Now, at this point in your career, you are interested in a position in which you can use the wealth of operations management experience you've acquired—experience in staffing, training, scheduling, resource management, supply chain management, quality assurance, and project management. Rather than focus your resume on your job title and chronological work history with the Navy, you want to highlight all of the relevant skills and experiences you've acquired as an "Operations Manager" (a term that the civilian world can understand and acknowledge). You'll highlight major projects, people, and budgets you've managed; achievements you've delivered; cost savings you've helped deliver; improvements in productivity and efficiency; and everything else that you've done that can meet the needs of a "business" operation. By doing so, you change the perception of who you are from military officer to well-qualified operations manager.

Suppose that you're an experienced software engineer who has worked primarily on the design and development of warfare planning systems for the past 10 years. Now that you're leaving the military, you want to continue in software engineering, but you want employers to understand the scope of your technical expertise without being "turned off" by the nature of the systems (warfare). Be creative in writing your resume. Share the scope of the projects (for example, number of people, budgets, innovative technologies, impact on operations) without referring to each project with its specific name (for example, Strategic Warfare Initiative, SCUD Missile Software Design). You can easily write about the projects, share the quality and depth of your experience, and communicate their critical nature to support operations worldwide while at the same time "demilitarizing" them so that laypeople will understand. If you can accomplish that, you can create a truly effective resume that will help facilitate your successful transition from the military to a civilian career.

Resume Strategy #1 focuses on connecting the two preceding concepts by using the *Who You Are* information that ties directly to the *How You Want to Be Perceived* message to determine what information to include in your resume. By following this strategy, you're painting a picture that allows a prospective employer to see you as you want to be seen—as an individual with the qualifications for the type of position you are pursuing.

> **WARNING:** If you prepare a resume without first clearly identifying what your objectives are and how you want to be perceived, your resume will have no focus and no direction. Without the underlying knowledge of "This is what I want to be," you do not know what to highlight in your resume. As a result, the document becomes a historical overview of your career and not the sales document it should be to facilitate your successful career change.

RESUME STRATEGY #2: SELL IT TO ME...DON'T TELL IT TO ME

We've already established the fact that resume writing is sales. You are the product, and you must create a document that powerfully communicates the value of that product. One particularly effective strategy for accomplishing this is the "Sell It to Me...Don't Tell It to Me" strategy, which impacts virtually every word you write on your resume.

If you "tell it," you are simply stating facts. If you "sell it," you promote it, advertise it, and draw attention to it. Look at the difference in impact between these examples.

Tell it:

> Managed personnel and equipment during 6-month overseas deployment.

Sell it:

> Directed a team of 45 electricians, machinists, and mechanics and maintained more than $30 million in equipment throughout an arduous 6-month overseas deployment. Achieved/maintained 100% inventory accuracy.

Tell it:

> Coordinated all secretarial, clerical, and administrative functions for base commander.

Sell it:

> Implemented a series of process improvements that reduced staffing requirements 20%, increased daily productivity 30%, and reduced reporting errors 14% for the commander of a 12,000-person military installation. Held full decision-making, planning, and scheduling responsibility for all secretarial, clerical, and administrative functions.

Tell it:

> Set up PCs for newly assigned staff at USMC headquarters.

Sell it:

> Installed more than 100 PCs and implemented customized applications to sustain a global technology network supporting more than 200,000 personnel and operations in 42 countries. Surpassed all goals and objectives for technology reliability and performance and reduced PC downtime by 38% over a 6-month period.

What's the difference between "telling it" and "selling it"? In a nutshell...

Telling It	Selling It
Describes features.	Describes benefits.
Tells what and how.	Sells why the "what" and "how" are important.
Details activities.	Includes results.
Focuses on what you did.	Details how what you did benefited your country, branch of service, unit, colleagues, and so on.

RESUME STRATEGY #3: USE KEYWORDS

No matter what you read or who you talk to about searching for jobs, the concept of keywords is sure to come up. Keywords (or, as they were previously known, buzzwords) are words and phrases that are specific to a particular industry or profession. The following paragraphs list a few examples relevant to different career areas:

- Keywords for operations management include production planning and scheduling, materials management, inventory control, quality, process engineering, robotics, systems automation, integrated logistics, product specifications, project management, and many, many more.

- Keywords for training include needs assessment, instructional programming, training program design, testing and evaluation, public speaking, instructional materials design, seminar planning, resource selection, and many, many more.

- Keywords for aircraft maintenance include aircraft electronic systems, fuel handling, hydraulics and braking systems, fixed-wing and rotary, airframe, pyrotechnical equipment, preventive maintenance, and many, many more.

- Keywords for law enforcement include homeland security, emergency response, interrogation, investigation, patrol, criminal justice, search and rescue, suspect apprehension, security procedures, inspections, and many, many more.

When you use these words and phrases—in your resume, in your cover letter, or during an interview—you are communicating a specific message. For example, when you include the words *supply chain* in your resume, your reader will most likely assume that you have experience in inventory planning and control, purchasing, vendor selection, pricing, contract negotiations, requisitioning, warehousing, distribution, and more. As you can see, people will make inferences about your skills based on the use of just one or two specific words.

Keywords are also an integral component of the resume-scanning process, whereby employers and recruiters electronically search resumes for specific terms to find candidates with the skills, qualifications, and credentials for their particular hiring needs. Over the past several years, keyword scanning has dramatically increased in popularity because of its ease of use and efficiency in identifying prime candidates (see chapter 3 for more on creating "scannable" resumes). Every job seeker today must stay on top of the latest trends in technology-based hiring and employment to ensure that their resumes and other job search materials contain the "right" keywords to capture the interest of prospective employers.

In more and more organizations, electronic scanning has replaced the more traditional method of an actual person reading your resume (at least initially). Therefore, to some degree, the *only* thing that matters in this instance is that you have included the "right" keywords to match the company's or the recruiter's needs. Without them, you will most certainly be passed over.

Of course, in virtually every instance, your resume will be read at some point by human eyes, so it's not enough just to throw together a list of keywords and leave it at that. It's not even necessary to include a separate "keyword summary" on your resume. A better strategy is to incorporate keywords naturally into the text within the appropriate sections of your resume.

For transitioning military personnel, keywords are particularly relevant and require a good deal of thought, because you do not necessarily want to include keywords that are descriptive of your past experiences. Rather, you want to include keywords that reflect your current career goals so that your resume will be noticed and not ignored. There are basically two ways to accomplish this:

- In sections throughout your resume, integrate keywords from your past experiences that relate directly to your current career goals. The Surface Warfare Officer who was seeking a civilian position in operations management in our previous example had experience in staffing, training, scheduling, resource management, supply chain management, quality assurance, project management, and the like. Those keywords should be highlighted on that job seeker's resume. Even though these tasks might have been only a small part of that soldier's experience, they are the type of information that should be highlighted in the resume because they are relevant to his current career goals.

- Include an Objective section on your resume that states the type of position that you are seeking and the associated responsibilities. For example, "Seeking a position in purchasing management where I can utilize my strong skills in research, analysis, negotiations, vendor selection, and inventory management." This is an excellent strategy for integrating keywords that instantly will be noticeable at the beginning of your resume, particularly when you do not have a great deal of supporting work experience.

Keep in mind, too, that keywords are arbitrary; there is no defined set of keywords for a human resources manager, aircraft mechanic, recruiter, engineer, military police officer, finance officer, or any other position. Employers searching to fill these positions develop a list of terms that reflect the specifics they desire in a qualified candidate. These might be a combination of professional qualifications, skills, education, technology expertise, length of experience, and other easily defined criteria, along with "soft skills," such as organization, time management, team building, leadership, problem-solving, and communication. Be certain that your resume includes all the necessary keywords so that you will get noticed and not passed over, regardless of whether a computer or a human reviews your resume.

NOTE: Because of the complex and arbitrary nature of keyword selection, we cannot overemphasize how vital it is to be certain that you include in your resume *all* of the keywords that summarize your skills *as they relate to your current career objectives.*

How can you be sure that you are including all the keywords, and the *right* keywords, for the position you want? Just by describing your work experience, achievements, educational credentials, technical qualifications, objective, and the like, you may naturally include most of the terms that are important in your new career field. However, military-to-civilian career changers must pay special attention to including keywords that will be recognizable by civilian employers. Keywords that might be used daily within a military organization are often not the same words used in the civilian workplace. Be sure to take the time to translate your military keywords to civilian keywords so that you're certain to position yourself well against others competing for the same positions.

TIP: To translate your military occupation to equivalent civilian job titles, here's a great resource. Go to http://online.onetcenter.org/crosswalk and enter your MOC in the box. Instantly you will see a list of equivalent job titles and their descriptions! Our thanks to Janet Farley, author of the JIST book *Military-to-Civilian Career Transition Guide,* for this information.

To cross-check what you've written, review online or newspaper job postings for positions that are of interest to you. Look at the precise terms used in the ads and be sure you have included them in your resume (as appropriate to your skills and qualifications).

Another great benefit of today's technology revolution is our ability to find instant information, even information as specific as keywords, for hundreds of different industries and professions. Refer to the appendix for some Web sites that list thousands of keywords, complete with descriptions. These are outstanding resources.

NOTE: If you are planning to pursue a civilian career with an organization closely aligned with the Armed Forces or U.S. government, you may want to keep much of the insider's military language within your resume because it will be recognizable to this audience. Remember, keywords are intended to capture the attention of prospective employers, so it is important to use their language. Know who you are writing to and then select your keywords wisely!

RESUME STRATEGY #4: USE THE "BIG" AND SAVE THE "LITTLE"

When deciding what you want to include in your resume, try to focus on the big things, such as new programs, special projects, cost savings, productivity and efficiency improvements, technology implementations, and staff/team performance. Give a good, broad-based picture of what you were responsible for and how well you did it. Here's an example:

> Supervised daily airfield and maintenance shop operations at a large facility in Northern Italy. Managed a team of 89 personnel and an annual operating budget of $3.5 million for supplies and materials. Consistently achieved/surpassed all productivity, efficiency, readiness, and personnel objectives.

Then save the little stuff—the details—for the interview. With this strategy, you will accomplish two things:

- You'll keep your resume readable and of a reasonable length (while still selling your achievements).

- You'll have new and interesting information to share during the interview, rather than merely repeating what is already on your resume.

Using the preceding example, when discussing this experience during an interview, you could elaborate on your specific achievements—namely, improving productivity and efficiency ratings, reducing annual operating and material costs, improving employee training, strengthening relationships with support organizations, introducing new technologies, upgrading performance ratings, and managing facility upgrades.

RESUME STRATEGY #5: MAKE YOUR RESUME "INTERVIEWABLE"

One of your greatest challenges is to make your resume a useful interview tool. After the employer has determined that you meet the primary qualifications for a position (you've passed the keyword scanning test or initial review) and you are contacted for a telephone or in-person interview, your resume becomes all-important in leading and prompting your interviewer during your conversation.

Your job, then, is to make sure the resume leads the reader where you want to go and presents just the right organization, content, and appearance to stimulate a productive discussion. To improve the "interviewability" of your resume, consider these tactics:

- Make good use of Resume Strategy #4 (Use the "Big" and Save the "Little") to invite further discussion about your experiences.

- Be sure your greatest "selling points" are featured prominently, not buried within the resume.

- Conversely, don't devote lots of space and attention to areas of your background that are irrelevant or about which you feel less than positive; you'll only invite questions about things you really don't want to discuss. This is particularly true for military-to-civilian career changers who want their resumes to focus on the skills that will be needed in their new profession, not necessarily on skills they acquired in past positions.

- Make sure your resume is highly readable—this means plenty of white space, an adequate font size, and a logical flow from start to finish.

RESUME STRATEGY #6: ELIMINATE CONFUSION WITH STRUCTURE AND CONTEXT

Keep in mind that your resume will be read *very quickly* by hiring authorities! You may agonize over every word and spend hours working on content and design, but the average reader will skim quickly through your masterpiece and expect to pick up important facts in just a few seconds. Try to make it as easy as possible for readers to grasp the essential facts.

- Be consistent: for example, put job titles, company/organization names, and dates in the same place for each position.

- Make information easy to find by clearly defining different sections of your resume with large, highly visible headings.

- If relevant to your new career path, define the context in which you worked (for example, the organization, your department, and the specific challenges you faced) before you start describing your activities and accomplishments.

RESUME STRATEGY #7: USE FUNCTION TO DEMONSTRATE ACHIEVEMENT

When you write a resume that focuses only on your job functions, it can be dry and uninteresting and will say very little about your unique activities and contributions. Consider the following example:

> Responsible for all aspects of housing and welfare at the base level.

Now, consider using that same function to demonstrate achievement and see what happens to the tone and energy of the sentence. It comes alive and clearly communicates that you deliver results:

> Led a team of 35 responsible for all aspects of housing and welfare for 2,000 soldiers and more than 4,000 family members at Fort Dix, New Jersey. Fully accountable for more than $30 million in assets, a $10 million annual operating budget, and a series of innovative programs to enhance soldier/family morale and retention within the Armed Forces. Achieved retention rates 12% higher than the nationwide norm during a period of massive reduction in force.

Try to translate your functions into achievements, and you'll create a more powerful resume presentation.

RESUME STRATEGY #8: REMAIN IN THE REALM OF REALITY

We've already established that resume writing is sales. And, as any good salesperson does, one feels somewhat inclined to stretch the truth, just a bit. However, be forewarned that you must stay within the realm of reality. Do not push your skills and qualifications outside the bounds of what is truthful. You never want to be in a position where you have to defend something that you've written on your resume. If that's the case, you'll lose the opportunity before you ever get started.

RESUME STRATEGY #9: BE CONFIDENT

You are unique. There is only one individual with the specific combination of employment experience, qualifications, achievements, education, and special skills that you have. In turn, this positions you as a unique commodity within the competitive job search market. To succeed, you must prepare a resume that is written to sell *you* and highlight *your* qualifications and *your* successes as they relate to your current career goals. If you can accomplish this, you will have won the job search game by generating interest, interviews, and offers.

Resume Standards

One of the greatest challenges in resume writing is that there are no rules to the game. However, there are certain expectations about information that you will include: principally, your primary skills, employment history, and educational qualifications. Beyond that, what you include is entirely up to you and what you have done in your career. What's more, you have tremendous flexibility in determining how to include the information you have selected. In chapter 2, you'll find a wealth of information on each possible category you might include in your resume, the type of information to be placed in each category, preferred formats for presentation, and lots of other information and samples that will help you formulate *your* best resume.

Although there are no rules, there are a few standards to live by as you write your resume. The following sections discuss these standards in detail.

CONTENT STANDARDS

Content is, of course, the text that goes into your resume. Content standards cover the writing style you should use, information you should be sure to include, information you should avoid including, and the order and format in which you list your qualifications.

Writing Style

Always write in the first person, but drop the word *I* from the beginning of each sentence. This style gives your resume a more assertive and professional tone than the passive third-person voice. The following examples illustrate the difference.

Here is a description written in first person:

> Manage 122-person team in the design and development of next-generation avionics tracking software. Serve as project manager for initiatives representing $70 million in multiyear investments and ensure the on-time, on-budget completion of each project deliverable.

This is the same description in third person:

> Manages a 122-person team in the design and development of next-generation avionics tracking software. Serves as project manager for initiatives representing $70 million in multiyear investments and ensures the on-time, on-budget completion of each project deliverable.

By using the first-person voice, you are assuming "ownership" of that statement. You did such-and-such. When you use the third-person voice, "someone else" did it. Can you see the difference?

Phrases to Avoid

Steer clear of phrases such as "responsible for" or "duties included." These words create a passive tone and style. Instead, use active verbs to describe what you did.

Compare these two ways of conveying the same information:

> Responsible for all marketing, advertising, and public speaking programs to encourage enlistment in all four branches of the U.S. Armed Forces.

or

> Orchestrated a series of innovative marketing, advertising, and public speaking programs to encourage enlistment in all four branches of the U.S. Armed Forces. Created energy and enthusiasm throughout the local community, sponsored community-based programs, and built relationships with community leaders. Results included a 42% increase in number of enlistments over two years.

Resume Style

The traditional *chronological* resume lists work experience in reverse chronological order (starting with your current or most recent position). The *functional* style deemphasizes the "where" and "when" of your career and instead groups similar experience, talents, and qualifications regardless of when they occurred.

Today, however, most resumes follow neither a strictly chronological nor strictly functional format; rather, they are an effective mixture of the two styles usually known as a *combination* or *hybrid* format.

Like the chronological format, the hybrid format includes specifics about where you worked, when you worked there, and what your job titles were. Like a functional resume, a hybrid emphasizes your most relevant qualifications—perhaps within chronological job descriptions, in an expanded summary section, in several "career highlights" bullet points at the top of your resume, or in project summaries. Most of the examples in this book are hybrids and show a wide diversity of organizational formats that you can use as inspiration for designing your own resume.

We strongly recommend the hybrid format for military-to-civilian career transitions. This format allows job seekers to begin their resume with an intense focus on skills, competencies, experience, and accomplishments that are directly related to their new career objectives. Then, to substantiate their solid work experience, job seekers can briefly list employment history with a focus on specific achievements, responsibilities, and projects that again relate to current career goals.

Resume Formats

Resumes, principally career summaries and job descriptions, are most often written in a paragraph format, a bulleted format, or a combination of both. Following are three job descriptions, all very similar in content, yet presented in each of the three different writing formats. We also review the advantages and disadvantages of each format.

Paragraph Format

Department Head—Marine Avionics Squadron   20XX to 20XX

Managed and led staff of handpicked officers who provided advanced training in ground and aviation tactics for 600 prospective Marine Corps instructors. Developed and monitored course objectives. Created training materials and course syllabi. Worked directly with prospective instructors to teach them leadership by example in addition to advanced tactical and management principles.

Planned and coordinated large-scale, high-risk combat exercises involving more than 100 aircraft and 3,000 personnel. Instructed 120 elite personnel, recognized among the best in the world (equivalent to "Top Gun" status). Led team of instructors to analyze and refine procedures, yielding insights that became official Marine Corps doctrine. Created training methods adopted throughout the Marine Corps, markedly improving trainees' ability to manage complex, faster-paced combat operations.

Advantages

Requires the least amount of space on the page. Brief, succinct, and to the point.

Disadvantages

Achievements get lost in the text of the paragraphs. They are not visually distinctive, nor do they stand alone to draw attention to them.

Bulleted Format

Department Head—Marine Avionics Squadron   20XX to 20XX

- Managed and led staff of handpicked officers who provided advanced training in ground and aviation tactics for 600 prospective Marine Corps instructors.

- Developed and monitored course objectives.

- Created training materials and course syllabi.

- Worked directly with prospective instructors to teach them leadership by example in addition to advanced tactical and management principles.

- Planned and coordinated large-scale, high-risk combat exercises involving more than 100 aircraft and 3,000 personnel.

- Instructed 120 elite personnel, recognized among the best in the world (equivalent to "Top Gun" status).

- Led team of instructors to analyze and refine procedures, yielding insights that became official Marine Corps doctrine.

- Created training methods adopted throughout the Marine Corps, markedly improving trainees' ability to manage complex, faster-paced combat operations.

Advantages

Quick and easy to peruse.

Disadvantages

Responsibilities and achievements are lumped together, with everything given equal value. In turn, the achievements get lost and are not immediately recognizable.

Combination Format

Department Head—Marine Avionics Squadron   20XX to 20XX

Managed and led staff of handpicked officers who provided advanced training in ground and aviation tactics for 600 prospective Marine Corps instructors. Developed and monitored course objectives. Created training materials and course syllabi. Worked directly with prospective instructors to teach them leadership by example in addition to advanced tactical and management principles.

- Planned and coordinated large-scale, high-risk combat exercises involving more than 100 aircraft and 3,000 personnel.

- Instructed 120 elite personnel, recognized among the best in the world (equivalent to "Top Gun" status).

(continued)

(continued)

> - Led team of instructors to analyze and refine procedures, yielding insights that became official Marine Corps doctrine.
> - Created training methods adopted throughout the Marine Corps, markedly improving trainees' ability to manage complex, faster-paced combat operations.

Advantages

We recommend this format because it clearly presents overall responsibilities in the introductory paragraph and then accentuates each achievement as a separate bullet.

Disadvantages

If you don't have clearly identifiable accomplishments, this format is not effective. It also may shine a glaring light on the positions where your accomplishments were less notable. For career changers, past accomplishments may not be relevant to current career objectives and, therefore, this format may be less appropriate.

You'll find numerous other examples of how to best present your employment experience in the resume samples that follow in chapters 4 through 13. Chapter 2 discusses formats you can use to highlight your skills and achievements more prominently than your work history. In many military-to-civilian career transition situations, this approach is critical to get yourself noticed and not passed over.

E-mail Address and URL

As we all know, e-mail has become the preferred method of communication between employers and job seekers. Therefore, be sure to include your e-mail address prominently at the top of your resume. If you don't yet have an e-mail address, visit www.gmail.com or www.yahoo.com, where you can get a free e-mail address that you can access through the Web.

In addition to your e-mail address, if you have a URL (Web site address) where you have posted your Web resume, be sure to also display that prominently at the top of your resume. For more information on Web resumes, refer to chapter 3.

PRESENTATION STANDARDS

Presentation focuses on the way your resume looks. It relates to the fonts you use, the paper you print it on, any graphics you might include, and the number of pages in your resume.

Typestyle

Use a typestyle (font) that is clean, conservative, and easy to read. Stay away from anything that is too fancy, glitzy, curly, and the like. Here are a few recommended typestyles:

Tahoma	Times New Roman
Arial	Bookman
Krone	Book Antiqua
Soutane	Garamond
CG Omega	Century Schoolbook
Century Gothic	Lucida Sans
Gill Sans	Verdana

Although Times New Roman is extremely popular, it is not our preferred typestyle simply because it is overused. More than 90 percent of the resumes we see are typed in Times New Roman. Your goal is to create a competitive, distinctive document. In order to achieve that, we recommend an alternative typestyle.

Your choice of typestyle should be dictated by the content, format, and length of your resume. Some fonts look better than others at smaller or larger sizes; some have "bolder" boldface type; some require more white space to make them readable. Once you've written your resume, experiment with a few different typestyles to see which one best enhances your document.

Type Size

Readability is everything! If the type size is too small, your resume will be difficult to read and difficult to skim for essential information. Interestingly, a too-large type size, particularly for senior-level professionals, can also give a negative impression by conveying a juvenile or unprofessional image.

As a general rule, select type from 10 to 12 points in size. However, there's no hard-and-fast rule, and a lot depends on the typestyle you choose. Take a look at the following examples.

Very readable in 9-point Verdana:

Staff officer responsible for research, analysis, and presentation of Marine Corps critical long-range planning and policy development issues in support of the intelligence community.

Difficult to read in too-small 9-point Gill Sans:

Staff officer responsible for research, analysis, and presentation of Marine Corps critical long-range planning and policy development issues in support of the intelligence community.

Concise and readable in 12-point Times New Roman:

Developed and implemented a comprehensive training program that resulted in 60% increase in number of certified personnel.

A bit overwhelming in too-large 12-point Bookman Old Style:

Developed and implemented a comprehensive training program that resulted in 60% increase in number of certified personnel.

Type Enhancements

Bold, *italics*, underlining, and CAPITALIZATION are ideal to highlight certain words, phrases, achievements, projects, numbers, and other information to which you want to draw special attention. However, do not overuse these enhancements. If your resume becomes too cluttered with special formatting, nothing stands out.

> **NOTE:** Resumes intended for electronic transmission and computer scanning have specific restrictions on typestyle, type size, and type enhancements. We discuss these details in chapter 3.

Page Length

For most industries and professions, the "one- to two-page rule" for resume writing still holds true. Keep it short and succinct, giving just enough to entice your readers' interest. However, there are many instances when a resume may be longer than two pages. For example:

- You have an extensive list of technical qualifications that are relevant to the position for which you are applying. (You may consider including these on a separate page as an addendum to your resume.)

- You have extensive educational training and numerous credentials/certifications, all of which are important to include. (You may consider including these on a separate page as an addendum to your resume.)

- You have an extensive list of special projects, task forces, and committees to include that are important to your current career objectives. (You may consider including these on a separate page as an addendum to your resume.)

- You have an extensive list of professional honors, awards, and commendations. This list is tremendously valuable in validating your credibility and distinguishing you from the competition.

If you create a resume that's longer than two pages, make it more reader-friendly by carefully segmenting the information into separate sections. Your sections may include a career summary, work experience, education, professional or industry credentials, honors and awards, technology and equipment skills, publications, public-speaking engagements, professional affiliations, civic affiliations, technology skills, volunteer experience, foreign-language skills, and other relevant information you want to include. Put each into a separate category so that your resume is easy to peruse and your reader can quickly see the highlights. You'll read more about each of these sections in chapter 2.

Paper Color

Be conservative. White, ivory, and light gray are ideal. Other "flashier" colors are inappropriate for most individuals unless you are targeting jobs in a highly creative industry and your paper choice is part of the overall design and presentation of a creative resume.

Graphics

An attractive, relevant graphic, table, or chart can enhance your resume. When you look through the sample resumes in chapters 4 through 13, you'll see some excellent examples of the effective use of graphics to enhance the visual presentation of a resume. Just be sure not to get carried away; be tasteful and relatively conservative, and don't insert graphs just for the sake of creating a visual. Be certain they add value to your resume and clearly support your expertise and qualifications as they relate to your current objectives.

White Space

We'll say it again—readability is everything! If people have to struggle to read your resume, they simply won't make the effort. Therefore, be sure to leave plenty of white space. It really does make a difference.

ACCURACY AND PERFECTION

The very final step, and one of the most critical in resume writing, is the proofreading stage. It is essential that your resume be well-written, visually pleasing, and free of any errors, typographical mistakes, misspellings, and the like. We recommend that you carefully proofread your resume a minimum of three times, and then have two or three other people also proofread it. Consider your resume an example of the quality of work you will produce on a company's behalf. Is your work product going to have errors and inconsistencies? If your resume does, it communicates to a prospective employer that you are careless, and this is the "kiss of death" in job search. Take the time to make sure that your resume is perfect in all the little details that do, in fact, make a big difference to those who read it.

CHAPTER 2

Writing Your Resume

For many job seekers, resume writing is *not* at the top of the list of fun and exciting activities. How can it compare to leading a successful military campaign, cutting mission costs, introducing new technologies, streamlining operations, or protecting a nation and its people? We're sure that it can't!

Yet resume writing can be an enjoyable and rewarding task. When your resume is complete, you can look at it proudly, reminding yourself of all that you have achieved. It is a snapshot of your career and your success. When it's complete, we guarantee you'll look back with tremendous self-satisfaction as you launch and successfully manage your job search.

As the first step in your transition to a civilian career, resume writing can be the most daunting of all tasks in your job search. If writing is not one of your primary skills or a past job function, it might have been years since you've sat down and written anything other than notes to yourself. Even for people who write on a regular basis, resume writing is unique. As with any specialty document, a resume has its own style and a number of peculiarities.

Recommended Resume Strategies and Formats for Military-to-Civilian Career Transitions

Writing career-transition resumes is a particularly unique challenge, and many of the strategies and formats that the more "typical" job seeker uses are generally not applicable for many job seekers transitioning from military to civilian employment. "Typical" formats most often put an emphasis on past work experience and employers, along with the responsibilities and achievements of each of those positions. If you're transitioning from the military sector to the civilian sector, most likely your goal is to downplay your specific employer and job titles on your resume, while highlighting your skills and core competencies as they relate to your current objectives.

As we discussed in chapter 1, before you even begin to start writing your career-transition resume, you must know the specific type(s) of position(s) you are going after. This will give your resume a theme around which you can build the entire document. Your theme (or objective) should dictate what you include on your resume, how you include it, and where. Writing a career-transition resume is all about creating a picture of how you want to be perceived by a prospective employer—a picture that closely mirrors the people who are hired in that career field.

Assuming that you have researched the type of career you want to pursue, you should have collected a great deal of information about the duties and responsibilities for positions in that field. You should then carefully review your past employment experience, job responsibilities, special project assignments, educational background, training qualifications, technical competencies, volunteer work, professional affiliations, civic affiliations, and other activities and qualifications to identify skills you've acquired that are transferable to your new career. These, then, are the items that become the foundation of your resume.

> **NOTE:** Transferable skills are the foundation of every successful military-to-civilian career transition resume.

If you're not sure how to identify your transferable skills, here's an easy way to do just that. First, review advertisements for positions that are of interest to you. You can get this information from newspapers, professional journals, and hundreds of online resources. You can also talk to and network with people who are already working in your new career field and ask them to give you feedback regarding their specific responsibilities, the challenges they face, the opportunities that are available, and how to get into the field.

Once you've collected this information, make a detailed list of the specific requirements for these jobs (for example, budgeting, staff training, staff supervision, project management, statistical analysis, customer relationship management, supply chain management, operations management, and field operations supervision). Be as comprehensive as possible, even if the list goes on and on for pages. Then, go through the list and highlight each of the skills in which you have some experience from your work, education, or outside activities. Now you can use those skills and competencies as the foundation for your new career-transition resume.

It is important to remember that when you are writing a career-transition resume and focusing on your transferable skills, your entire background counts—everything that you've ever done, from your 10-year infantry career with the U.S. Army to your six years as a volunteer for the local Special Olympics. Just think of the great skills you acquired in event planning, logistics, volunteer training, fundraising, media affairs, contract negotiations, and more from the Special Olympics experience. Those skills are just as important to include in your career-transition resume as any other skills you acquired in a paid position.

> **WARNING:** If you don't know what your objective is—you only know that you want to leave the military and pursue opportunities in the private sector—we strongly urge that you spend some time investigating potential career tracks to determine your overall areas of interest. Without this knowledge, you cannot focus your resume in any one particular direction, and as a result, it simply

becomes a recitation of your past work experience. This, as we've already discussed, is not the strategy for a successful career-transition resume. Your resume must have a theme and a focus to effectively position you for new civilian career opportunities. If you're having difficulty determining your objective, you might want to consider hiring a career coach who can help you critically evaluate your skills and qualifications, assess potential career opportunities, and explore new professions to guide you in setting your direction.

INSIDER ADVICE FOR MILITARY-TRANSITION RESUMES

Chris Hale is General Manager of *G.I. Jobs* magazine, a publication devoted to helping transitioning military as well as veterans find civilian employment. We asked Chris what are the most-asked questions and most-noted problems with regard to resumes and transitions for military personnel.

> "One of the biggest problems we see is too much military jargon in a resume. We also see a lot of military titles that don't mean much in the corporate world. Military need to translate their experience to civilian job skills. I like to refer to it as the 'Aunt Jane' test. If you can hand your resume to Aunt Jane and she can understand what you do, then you can use it in your job search. If she's confused, you need to spell out more clearly what you do and 'civilianize' it so that your military experience is translated to civilian experience."

Another critical shortcoming that Chris often notices is that military personnel, being team-oriented, tend to downplay their notable achievements.

Finally, there are some organizational issues that Chris sees on many military resumes. For example, it might be more beneficial to group early training under one heading with a synopsis of what you learned rather than spelling out three-month or six-month deployments that will make you look like a "job hopper" to a civilian hiring manager who doesn't understand the military training model.

In a nutshell, Chris recommends that transitioning military strive to understand the corporate or government environment they seek to join and use their resume and other documents to clearly communicate how they can benefit that organization.

You can find out more about *G.I. Jobs* and other military-transition resources in the appendix.

CHOOSE THE RIGHT FORMAT AND PAINT THE RIGHT PICTURE

To see just how important choosing the right format is to the success of your resume and job search, carefully review the following two resumes. They are prime examples of how critical it is for job seekers in career transition to give careful thought to *how* they want to be perceived in the job market and then create a resume that supports that specific objective.

Both resumes are for the same job seeker—Rees Donovan—but each uses a different format and strategy. In turn, they create an entirely different perception of *who* Rees Donovan is and the value he can bring to two totally different types of organizations—a college/university and a corporation.

Rees's first resume (for a position with a college/university) begins with a strong and detailed Career Summary, followed by a chronological review of his Career History (work experience). As we mentioned in Chapter 1, this format is called a *hybrid resume*. It uses the skills and qualifications focus of a functional resume to create his Career Summary and adds a step-by-step review of his chronological work experience, including all of his positions, responsibilities, and achievements. In fact, the first job you see on Rees's resume is as Department Head of the Naval Science Department at Drake University. This resume clearly supports his objective for a position in career development, educational counseling, or admissions.

Now take a look at Rees's second resume, which was written to support his objective for a position in logistics and transportation management with a private-sector company. This resume also begins with a comprehensive Career Summary, but this time it focuses on his skills, qualifications, and achievements as they relate to this objective. Then, instead of continuing with a chronological work history, Rees's resume transitions to a functional format where he highlights his most notable achievements in cost reduction and savings, process and inventory improvements, and team building and training. Note that this resume does include a chronological listing of Rees's experience, just more briefly and only on page 2.

The writer of both of these resumes (Marcy Johnson, NCRW, CPRW, CEIP) did an excellent job in creating two entirely different perceptions of *who* Rees Donovan is and what types of positions he is qualified for.

Rees T. Donovan

reestdonovan@msn.com

11805 Northshore Drive • Des Moines, Iowa 50314
Phone: (515) 545-1515 • Cell: (515) 230-3366

Career Focus: Career Development • Educational Counseling • Admissions

Proactive, highly organized administrative professional with more than two years of experience providing academic advisement, recruitment, mentoring, orientation, and retention activities for diverse students at a Division I university. A diplomatic, people-oriented advisor who builds rapport, extracts maximum effort, and enables students to succeed. More than 10 years of additional experience recruiting and mentoring other professionals. Accomplished written and oral communicator with training in media relations.

Notable:

▸ Helped guide students through academic cycle, achieving 100% success rate during first formal schooling assignments.

▸ Actively interpreted requirements; counseled and supported almost 200 future leaders through the academic process.

▸ Assimilated college freshmen quickly by reinstituting freshman orientation, mentoring program, and team activities.

▸ Designed curriculum and initiated senior-level professional development class offering "real-life" applications.

▸ Developed positive, educated, and well-rounded students and citizens with strong commitment to community.

▸ Used analysis and problem-solving skills to elicit high levels of productivity and success from teams up to 1,000.

Competencies:

Academic Advising... Recruitment... Orientation... Educational Planning... Transfer Credits and Requirements... Application Procedures... Counseling... Graduation Requirements... Academic Skills... Career Planning... Career and Interest Assessments... Budgeting Experience... Event Planning... Goal Setting...

CAREER HISTORY

UNITED STATES MARINE CORPS, 1981–Present

Career in increasingly responsible positions as a Commissioned Marine Corps Officer, including these recent assignments:

Department Head, Naval Science Department • Drake University, Des Moines, Iowa   **2006 to Present**

Professor of Naval Science leading nine-member department training 65 junior executives for positions with joint, multinational, and high-level service organizations. Forecast, track, analyze, and manage university, federal, and alumni budgets simultaneously, balancing dynamic organizational mission with small operating budget. Develop and modify curricula to meet standards of leadership development and succession planning.

- Created and implemented professional development class focused on real-life applications. Lent active hand to guiding next-generation leaders through training cycle, achieving 100% success rate in first assignments.

- Conducted assessment of existing Naval Science Department program. Changed purchasing process from inventory-based model to information-based model, with the goal of reducing inventory by $100,000.

Director, Force Protection Development, U.S. Second Fleet • Norfolk, Virginia   **2005 to 2006**

Assembled team of cross-functional experts to conduct survey, analyze information, and initiate actions to develop effective tactics, doctrine, and exercises for improving U.S. Navy security. Served as member of senior management team and liaison to help plan and execute three joint and NATO combined initiatives, earning Legion of Merit Award.

- Developed multinational logistic program and helped lead organization through its most significant logistic restructuring in 50 years.

(continued)

Rees Donovan's resume in a hybrid chronological format to support his career goal for a position in career development, educational counseling, and/or admissions with a college/university.

CAREER HISTORY

- Noted as one of the single most important players in dramatic shift and improvement plan for U.S. Second Fleet. Created detailed system for review and personally assembled expert team to revise plans.

- Ensured solid working relationships at all levels. Served as liaison to procure equipment and develop standard operating procedures enhancing defense of U.S. Second Fleet.

- Led transformation of traditional logistics exercise into premier NATO joint venture. Coordinated 96 NATO and U.S. senior officers from 21 nations in first-ever combined exercise conducted in Ukraine.

Director, Logistics, Plans & Exercises • Norfolk, Virginia   **2003 to 2005**

Developed budget and initiated multinational planning and coordination for expansion of NATO exercise, including joint logistics for cross-functional teams. Coordinated initial development of standard operating procedures (SOPs) and reprogrammed logistic training objectives. Participated in development of first agreement between United States Joint Forces and NATO forces exercising on U.S. soil. Served as Logistics Division representative between review board and executive team. Chaired NATO Logistics Syndicate and co-chaired Western European Union Logistics Syndicate for logistics exercise.

- Reduced expenses $1.5 million by making significant contributions to logistics system and tactical vehicle readiness of multimillion-dollar fleet.

Chief Operating Officer, 7th Motor Transport Battalion • Camp Pendleton, California   **2000 to 2002**

Administered $265 million budget and directed 1,000-member team while managing life cycle of complex logistics system, including long-term planning, funding, testing, quality control, contract administration, and logistic support.

- Reduced vehicle repair cycle 60% initially, continuing to implement process improvements for 70% total reduction. Won National Defense Transportation Association Award and recognized as top transportation unit.

Early career: Senior Management Positions in Procurement and Logistics

Fielded a 945-vehicle fleet valued in excess of $302 million. Saved $1.49 million by negotiating an innovative lift program from United States to Okinawa on space-available basis vs. exclusive transportation reservation system. Benchmarked truck acquisition project, creating a 20-year plan for rebuilding and using fleet. Integrated logistics support and operational requirements, saving thousands of dollars on multiyear contract worth more than $300 million. Ensured a high state of motor transport readiness and reorganized five-ton truck fleet.

EDUCATION AND TRAINING

MA — **National Security and Strategic Studies,** College of Naval Warfare, Newport, Rhode Island • 2003
MBA — **Logistics,** Florida Institute of Technology, Melbourne, Florida • 1993
BA — **Business Management,** University of Northern Iowa, Cedar Falls, Iowa • 1981

Additional Training: Numerous leadership, business management, media training, and strategic planning courses
Computer Skills: Microsoft Word, Excel, PowerPoint

HONORS AND AWARDS

Meritorious Service Medal (with Gold Star) • Navy Commendation Medal • Numerous Other Awards

Rees T. Donovan

reestdonovan@msn.com

11805 Northshore Drive • Des Moines, Iowa 50314
Phone: (515) 545-1515 • Cell: (515) 230-3366

LOGISTICS, TRANSPORTATION MANAGEMENT, AND TRAINING
Supply Chain Management • Integrated Logistics Management
Employee Empowerment • Leadership Development

Dedicated logistics professional combining initiative and integrity to direct expansive international transportation systems. Strategic, big-picture thinker readily assimilating into new environments and ensuring continuous process improvements / multimillion-dollar cost reductions. Solid track record eliciting high levels of productivity, loyalty, and success from cross-functional teams of 9 to 1,000 people. Accomplished written and oral communicator with training in media relations. Demonstrated success in

- Cradle-to-Grave Procurement
- Carriage / Fleet Management
- Staff Development / Training

- Strategic Planning / Process Improvement
- Inventory Optimization / Planning
- Asset Management / Vendor Alliance

- Acquisition Management
- Cost Savings and Reductions
- Precision Logistics

MBA in Logistics • Florida Institute of Technology

CAREER HIGHLIGHTS

Cost Reductions and Savings

- Saved $1.49 million by negotiating an innovative vehicle lift program from the United States to Okinawa. Managed life cycle of complex logistics system and fielded a 945-vehicle fleet valued in excess of $302 million.

- Reduced expenses $1.5 million by making significant contributions to the logistics system and tactical vehicle readiness of multimillion-dollar fleet.

Process and Inventory Improvements

- Reduced vehicle repair cycle 60% initially, continuing to implement process improvements for 70% total reduction. Won National Defense Transportation Association Award and recognized as top transportation unit.

- Developed multinational logistic program and helped lead organization through its most significant logistic restructuring in 50 years.

- Created system for fleet review of every ship's force protection plan for non-Navy port visits. Noted as one of the single most important players in a dramatic improvement for force protection of the U.S. Second Fleet.

- Conducted complete assessment of existing Naval Science Department program. Changed purchasing process from inventory-based model to information-based model, with goal of reducing inventory by $100,000.

Team Building and Training

- Ensured solid working relationships at all levels. Served as liaison to procure equipment and develop standard operating procedures enhancing defense of U.S. Second Fleet against asymmetrical threat.

- Led transformation of traditional logistics exercise into premier NATO joint venture. Coordinated participation of 96 NATO and U.S. senior officers from 21 nations in first-ever combined exercise conducted in Ukraine.

- Designed training curriculum to prepare senior managers for operational and tactical leadership in joint or multinational environments. Reestablished mentoring program and team-building activities.

- Created and implemented professional development class focused on real-life applications. Lent active hand to guiding next-generation leaders through the training cycle, achieving 100% success rate in first assignments.

Endorsement: "Through [Rees Donovan's] positive leadership, the department has been a "can-do" organization...People orientation, sincerity, and rapport enables him to extract maximum efforts while maintaining a high state of morale."
—R.C. Hill, Deputy Director of Logistics

Rees Donovan's resume in a hybrid functional format to support his career goal of a position in logistics and/or transportation management in the civilian workforce.

CAREER PROGRESSION

UNITED STATES MARINE CORPS, 1981–Present

Career in increasingly responsible positions as a Commissioned Marine Corps Officer, including these recent assignments:

Department Head, Naval Science Department • Drake University, Des Moines, Iowa   **2006–Present**

Professor of Naval Science leading nine-member department training 65 junior executives for positions with joint, multinational, and high-level service organizations. Forecast, track, analyze, and manage university, federal, and alumni budgets simultaneously, balancing dynamic organizational mission with small operating budget. Develop and modify curricula to meet standards of leadership development and succession planning.

Director, Force Protection Development, U.S. Second Fleet • Norfolk, Virginia   **2005–2006**

Assembled team of cross-functional experts to conduct a survey, analyze information, and initiate actions to develop effective tactics, doctrine, and exercises for improving U.S. Navy security. Served as member of senior management team and liaison to help plan and execute three joint and NATO combined initiatives, earning Legion of Merit Award.

Director, Logistics, Plans & Exercises • Norfolk, Virginia   **2003–2005**

Developed budget and initiated multinational planning and coordination for expansion of NATO exercise, including joint logistics for cross-functional teams. Coordinated initial development of standard operating procedures (SOPs) and reprogrammed logistic training objectives. Participated in development of first agreement between United States Joint Forces and NATO forces exercising on U.S. soil. Served as Logistics Division representative between review board and executive team. Chaired NATO Logistics Syndicate and co-chaired Western European Union Logistics Syndicate for logistics exercise.

Chief Operating Officer, 7ᵗʰ Motor Transport Battalion • Camp Pendleton, California   **2000–2002**

Administered $265 million budget and directed 1,000-member team while managing life cycle of complex logistics system. Conducted long-term planning, funding, quality control, contract administration, and logistic support.

Early career: Senior Management Positions in Procurement and Logistics

Fielded a 945-vehicle fleet valued in excess of $302 million. Saved $1.49 million by negotiating an innovative lift program from the United States to Okinawa on space-available basis vs. exclusive transportation reservation system.

Benchmarked truck acquisition project, creating a 20-year plan for rebuilding and using fleet. Integrated logistics support and operational requirements, saving thousands of dollars on a multiyear contract worth more than $300 million. Ensured a high state of motor transport readiness and reorganized five-ton truck fleet.

EDUCATION & TRAINING

MA — **National Security and Strategic Studies,** College of Naval Warfare, Newport, Rhode Island • 2003
MBA — **Logistics,** Florida Institute of Technology, Melbourne, Florida • 1993
BA — **Business Management,** University of Northern Iowa, Cedar Falls, Iowa • 1981

Computer Skills: Microsoft Word, Excel, PowerPoint

Additional Training:

- Leadership / Business Management Training
- Motor Transport Maintenance Training
- Supply Chain Management Training
- Advanced Logistics Training
- Media Training Seminar
- Numerous Management / Strategic Planning Courses

AWARDS AND HONORS

Meritorious Service Medal (with Gold Star) • Navy Commendation Medal • Numerous Other Awards

Endorsement: "Intelligent. Aggressive. Considerate. [Rees Donovan] has distinguished himself in all areas with exceptionally sound performance and absolute integrity. He has demonstrated unusual sensitivity and rare people skills.
—*Jonathan T. Williams, Director Logistic Plans and Readiness*

Step-by-Step: Writing the Perfect Resume

This section is a detailed discussion of the various sections that you might include in your resume (for example, Career Summary, Professional Experience, Education, Technical Qualifications, Professional Memberships, Public Speaking, Publications, Honors and Awards, and Volunteer Experience), what each section should include, and where to include it.

CONTACT INFORMATION

Before we get into the major sections of the resume, let's briefly address the very top section: your name and contact information.

Name

You'd think writing your name would be the easiest part of writing your resume! But there are several factors you might want to consider:

- Although most people choose to use their full, formal name at the top of a resume, it has become increasingly more acceptable to use the name by which you prefer to be called.

- It's to your advantage that readers feel comfortable calling you for an interview. If your name is gender-neutral, difficult to pronounce, or unusual, employers might feel uncomfortable because they don't know who they're calling (a man or a woman) or how to ask for you. You can make it easier for them by following these examples:

> Lynn T. Cowles (Mr.)
>
> (Ms.) Michael Murray
>
> Tzirina (Irene) Kahn
>
> Ndege "Nick" Vernon

As a member or officer in the military, you are probably quite proud of the rank you have attained. And if you were seeking advancement in the military, that rank would be an all-important credential. But when writing your resume for a civilian audience, it is best not to include your rank, especially right up top with your name. Not only are military ranks not well understand by the civilian audience, but including your rank will pigeonhole you as a military person, whereas now you wish to be perceived as a corporate employee.

Address

You should always include your home address on your resume. If you use a post-office box for mail, include both your mailing address and your physical residence address if possible. We understand that this might not be possible for some departing military personnel and the only address you will have is a post-office box. If that's the case, simply include that contact information only.

Telephone Number(s)

We recommend that you include just one phone number on your resume—the number where you can be reached most readily and where callers can leave a voice mail message for a speedy return call. For many people, this number is a cell phone number; for others, it is a home number.

In certain cases, you will want to include more than one number on your resume. If cell coverage is spotty or you are often unable to take calls on your cell phone, include your home as well as your cell number. Be sure to have a brief, professional-sounding voice mail greeting for all phone numbers that appear on your resume and to regularly monitor your messages.

E-mail Address

Always include your e-mail address on your resume. E-mail is often the preferred method of communication in job search, particularly in the early stages of each contact. If you do not have an e-mail account, you can obtain a free, accessible-anywhere address from a provider such as Yahoo! (www.yahoo.com) or Google (www.gmail.com).

As you look through the samples in this book, you'll see how resume writers have arranged the many bits of contact information at the top of a resume. You can use these as models for presenting your own information. The point is to make it as easy as possible for employers to contact you!

Page 2

We strongly recommend that you include your name, phone number, and e-mail address at the top of the second page of your resume and any additional pages. If, by chance, the pages get separated, you want to be sure that people can still contact you, even if they have only page 2 of your resume.

Now, let's get into the nitty-gritty of the core content sections of your resume.

CAREER SUMMARY

The Career Summary is the section at the top of your resume that summarizes and highlights your knowledge and expertise. You might be thinking, "But shouldn't my resume start with an objective?" Although many job seekers still use objective statements, we believe that a Career Summary is a much more powerful introduction. The problem with objectives is that they are either too specific (limiting you to a "position as a Network Administrator") or too vague (doesn't everyone want "a challenging opportunity with a progressive organization offering the opportunity for growth and advancement"?). In addition, objective statements can be read as self-serving because they describe what *you* want rather than suggesting what you have to offer an employer.

In contrast, an effective Career Summary allows you to position yourself as you want to be perceived. This is particularly important for people transitioning to new careers. A Career Summary allows you to immediately paint a picture of yourself that directly supports your current career objective in the civilian workforce.

It is critical that this section focus on the specific skills, qualifications, and achievements of your career that are related to your objectives. Your summary is *not* a historical overview of your career. Rather, it is a concise, well-written, and sharp presentation of information designed to *sell* you into your next position.

What to Call It

This section can have various titles, such as the following:

Career Summary	Management Profile
Career Achievements	Professional Qualifications
Career Highlights	Professional Summary
Career Synopsis	Profile
Skills Summary	Summary
Executive Profile	Summary of Achievements
Expertise	Summary of Qualifications
Highlights of Experience	

Or, as you will see in the Headline Format example shown later, your summary does not have to have any title at all.

Why the Summary Is So Important

The Career Summary section of the resume can be the single most important section on any career-transition resume because of its content—the skills, qualifications, achievements, technical competencies, and other unique expertise and value you offer that are in line with your current career objectives. Your goal is to capture your reader's attention and immediately communicate the value you bring to the organization. If you are able to bring your relevant skills to the forefront, you will have favorably positioned yourself before a prospective employer. The fact that your prior work experience has been with the military becomes much less significant. This is precisely what you want to accomplish with your Career Summary.

A Career Summary is a great thing because it allows you to include skills and competencies that you've acquired not only through your work experience, but also through your volunteer experience, education, training, internships, memberships, community service, and more. The skills you include in your Summary *do not* have to be only a direct result of paid work experience. This is wonderful news if you are making a career transition because it may very well be that you want to draw special attention to projects and activities that are not associated with your military service. Remember, a summary is just that—a summary—of the things that you do best, and it doesn't matter where you learned to do them.

For most people making a military-to-civilian career transition, the Career Summary will be the focal point of your resume. Be sure to package and sell all of your qualifications as they relate to your current career goals in the civilian workplace. Don't be concerned if your Career Summary is longer than normal. This section is the foundation for your entire resume. Be thorough so that you're sure to sell yourself into your next job.

Sample Career Summary Sections

Here are five sample Career Summary sections. Consider using one of these as the template for developing your Career Summary, or use them as the foundation to create your own presentation. You will also find some type of Career Summary in just about every resume included in chapters 4 through 13. Closely review them as well to find a format and style that's in line with your specific needs.

Bullet Format

Career Transition: 20-year career in Special Warfare Operations with the Navy, now transitioning to a position in security and counterterrorism in the private sector.

SUMMARY

Strong qualifications relating to Personal Security and Force Protection Consulting, Counterterrorism, and Security Operations developed through extensive Naval Surface Warfare experience and advanced training.

- Subject-matter expert on Force Protection and Special Operations. Level II Force Protection Officer; conduct routine analysis, escape and evasion planning, and tactical studies in advance of deployments. Consult with Navy SEAL Teams, Special Boat Units, Army and Air Force Special Operations, DEA, CIA, and Coast Guard on all aspects of mission planning, special operations, and clandestine operations.

- Expert knowledge of land-based and special warfare combatant craft (SWCC) operations, including threat assessment, strategic and tactical planning, situational analysis, combatant craft tactics, small-boat handling, seamanship, navigation, engineering, weapons proficiency, and boarding procedures.

- Combat-tested leadership, judgment, teaching, and team-building activities. Possess the initiative, adaptability, and motivation to meet any challenge; able to instill these qualities in others as an instructor and leader.

- Outstanding initiative and decision-making skills; proven ability to take effective action in rapidly changing, chaotic situations.

- Consulted with private-industry engineers and elite military personnel about technical aspects of special warfare operations.

- Conversant in Spanish (level 2+2) and Thai (1+0) as well as English. Highly effective liaison with senior military and civilian officials, including personnel from countries throughout South America and the Pacific.

This military officer had a wealth of experience in security, counterterrorism, and other activities that tied directly into his current objectives for a civilian career. By presenting his qualifications in a skills-based format, it was readily apparent to anyone reading the resume that this candidate had the qualifications to support his current objectives.

Headline Format

Career Transition: Administrative Supervisor for the U.S. Navy seeking a new career as a Senior Executive Assistant/Administrative Manager in the civilian work-force.

SENIOR EXECUTIVE ASSISTANT / ADMINISTRATIVE MANAGER
Business Administration / Logistics / Project Management
Program Administration / Budgeting & Cost Control / Organizational Development

Although this individual's work experience was principally with the Armed Forces, her professional skills and qualifications were identical to those used by her civilian counterparts. As such, they were the foundation for her Career Summary and her entire resume.

Paragraph Format

Career Transition: Aircraft Equipment Maintenance Technician seeking new career in automotive maintenance and repair.

CAREER SUMMARY

MAINTENANCE TECHNICIAN with 10 years of experience in the maintenance, repair, troubleshooting, and operation of highly complex electronics equipment. Technical skills include maintaining hydraulic, pneumatic, mechanical, electrical, and electronic systems. Demonstrated ability to train and lead others to perform productively and efficiently. Comfortable in fast-paced, high-stress environments requiring attention to detail, ability to meet stringent deadlines, and quick adaptation to constantly changing priorities.

Although this individual's primary job responsibilities had been in the maintenance and operational readiness of aircraft, his transferable skills in maintenance, repair, troubleshooting, and the like were highlighted in support of his transition into automotive maintenance.

Core Competencies Summary Format

Career Transition: Senior Instructor and Operations Manager with the USMC seeking a mid-level general management position with a multinational corporation.

OPERATIONS MANAGER
12 Years of Experience Building Top-Performing Operations

- Vision & Mission Planning
- Budgeting & Financial Reporting
- Process Development
- High-Impact Presentations
- Project Administration
- Operations Planning & Management
- Strategic Problem-Solving
- Team Building & Leadership
- Logistics Planning
- Policy & Procedure Development

With 12 years of experience in general business affairs and operations management, this candidate had precisely the qualifications that many civilian companies seek in their management candidates. The resume was written to allow the candidate to pursue a number of related opportunities, all under the umbrella of general management/operations management.

Project Highlights Format

Career Change: Programmer with the U.S. Coast Guard transitioning into a Programming/Software Development position in the private sector.

PROJECT HIGHLIGHTS & ACCOMPLISHMENTS:

Programmer / Technologist with 5+ years of experience with C/C++, Java, Visual Basic, Oracle (SQL, SQL*Plus, PL/SQL), DataEase, Windows, and UNIX. Major projects have included

- ✓ **Cost Reporting System.** Created a normalized relational database (using DataEase on a Windows XP network) to provide complete invoicing, billing, accounts receivable, and accounts payable management for more than $200 million in inventory dispersed throughout more than 20 sites worldwide.

- ✓ **Client-Service Resource Management Module in Java.** Using TCP/IP sockets, connected GUI front end to console application, allowing users to query server for price, availability, and delivery status.

- ✓ **Training Module in Visual Basic.** Created GUI front end to Access database, allowing input of training information for more than 2,000 personnel.

- ✓ **Airfield Management System in Oracle.** Generated users, tables, views, sequences, and triggers using SQL, SQL*Plus, and PL/SQL to create Oracle database. Imported data and used Oracle Developer Suite to create forms.

Because of this job seeker's advanced technology qualifications, he is already a hot commodity in the civilian market. By highlighting his major technology projects, he further positions himself for an immediate civilian career opportunity.

PROFESSIONAL EXPERIENCE

As a career-transition candidate, how much information you include in your Professional Experience section will depend entirely on how relevant that experience is to your current career objectives. If it's relevant (or if just parts of it are relevant), you'll want to be sure to highlight that information—in detail—on your resume. If it's irrelevant, you'll want to be very brief with your job descriptions, if you include them at all. As discussed previously, the best strategy for a career transition may be a functional resume that focuses on skills and qualifications while downplaying work experience. Read further and you'll understand why.

The Most Time-Consuming Section to Write

Writing your Professional Experience section might take you the longest of any section of your resume. Suppose that you had the same types of positions for 10 years. How can you consolidate all that you have done into one short section? If, on the opposite end of the spectrum, you've had several short-term assignments over the past several years, how can you make your experience seem substantial, noteworthy, and relevant? If your experience is in between, what should you include and how should you present it?

These are not easy questions to answer. In fact, the most truthful response to each question is, "it depends." It depends on you, your experience, your achievements and successes, your current career objectives, and how closely your past experience ties into and supports those objectives.

Sample Professional Experience Sections

Here are five samples of Professional Experience sections. Review how each individual's unique background is organized and emphasized, and consider your own background when choosing one of these as the template or foundation for developing your Professional Experience section. To get even more ideas, be sure to review all of the resume samples in this book.

Achievement Format

Career Transition: Aircraft Maintenance Supervisor seeking a similar position with a major air carrier. The format emphasizes rapid promotion through each position, overall scope of responsibility, and resulting achievements that are particularly relevant to his new civilian career objective.

PROFESSIONAL EXPERIENCE

AIR NATIONAL GUARD—Field Maintenance Division

▶ **Aircraft Systems Maintenance Supervisor** (2004 to Present)
▶ **Aircraft Maintenance Lead** (2001 to 2004)
▶ **Aircraft Maintenance Mechanic/Engineer** (1997 to 2001)

Manage aircraft maintenance operations and inspections with accountability for strategic and financial planning, recruitment, training and development, purchasing, ground equipment, and resources. Lead a team of 6 supervisors, 50 technicians, and 100 weekend Air Guard personnel. Plan and administer $800,000 annual budget to support operations. Instrumental member of continuous improvement and other initiatives impacting daily operations.

Achievements:

- Significantly improved staff performance and skills by revamping the training and development program; passing rate on courses jumped from 74% in prior years to 94% in 2009.
- Consistently led unit to achieve top ratings from Air Force inspection team and increased division output 10% by introducing quality-assessment program.
- Increased efficiency in aircraft inspection preparation process by restructuring workflow, cutting prep time from 60 days to 8 days; commended as the "best seen to date" by inspection team.
- Created an evaluation rating system resulting in the selection of top-tier employees; program was adopted by other supervisors with similar positive results in candidate quality.
- Cited by the state Department of Environmental Protection for having *"the best safety program in the state."*

Challenge, Action, and Results (CAR) Format

Career Transition: Operations Manager with the U.S. Army seeking to transition into a general management or executive management position in the civilian workforce. Format emphasizes the challenge of each position, the action taken, and the results delivered.

Professional Experience

Operations Manager—Ft. Tarpton/Arabia, United States Army   *2007 to Present*

Challenge: To plan and execute a complete turnaround and revitalization of a 900-person operational force suffering from severe personnel problems, huge cost overrides, an uncontrollable inventory-management program, and a total lack of communication.

Action: Launched a massive reorganization of the entire operation and all personnel assignments. Reallocated budgets and resources to meet actual operating needs, retrained technical staff and management teams, and launched a massive cost-containment initiative. Rewrote operating policies and procedures, introduced new technologies, and created a structured communication channel to ensure cooperation among operating units, divisions, and commands.

Results:
- Achieved/surpassed all turnaround objectives and restored the operation to full productivity and accountability in first year. Delivered strong and sustainable gains:
  - 100% elimination of cost overrides.
  - $1.8 million budget savings through efficient resource allocation.
  - $2.4 million reduction in annual supply and inventory costs.
- Awarded commendation medal for exemplary leadership achievement and operational improvements.
- Achieved 100% graduation rate from all technical training courses.
- Developed and taught the flagship Leadership Development program.
- Introduced PC-based technology to enhance communications flow and increase the accuracy of reporting and recordkeeping.
- Guided development of standard operating procedures subsequently adopted by other units worldwide.
- Restructured and streamlined the entire supply chain management process.

Functional Format

Career Transition: Maintenance Technician seeking maintenance management position in the civilian workforce. Format emphasizes the functional areas of responsibility within his job and associated achievements—both technical and leadership—that position him for a technical management position.

EMPLOYMENT EXPERIENCE

Aircraft Maintenance Technician   UNITED STATES NAVY, Norfolk, VA   2003 to 2009

Promoted through a series of increasingly responsible positions in aviation equipment operation, maintenance, quality assurance, and safety. Selected by supervisor (out of 22 technicians) to handle one of the most complex assignments in the entire division.

Equipment Repair & Maintenance

- Experienced in the operation and maintenance of multimillion-dollar aircraft launching and recovery equipment.
- Performed troubleshooting and/or repair of electrical, electronic, hydraulic, pneumatic, and mechanical systems.
- Ensured and documented safe equipment operation and work practices; oversaw proper handling, storage, and disposal of hazardous materials to meet compliance standards.

Quality Assurance & Inspection

- Accurately calibrated and installed 70+ precision-measurement tools valued at more than $250,000.
- Accountable for quality assurance of all tools, parts, and materials to maximize safety of all personnel and equipment.
- Supervised all maintenance checks to monitor accuracy and adherence to precision procedures.

Training & Team Leadership

- Trained and oversaw 40-member work center in the operation, maintenance, and repair of various equipment.
- Trained and advanced the skills of new personnel, quickly advancing the qualifications of more than 15 team members who subsequently contributed to 15,000+ safe, error-free aircraft operations.
- Coordinated technical reference manuals on electrical and hydraulic systems and mechanical operations of equipment to upgrade staff on new parts, materials, and maintenance procedures.

Project Highlights Format

Career Transition: An experienced, senior-level Technology Engineer seeking a civilian career in infrastructure development, solutions, and applications. This format highlights her special projects and activities as they relate to infrastructure, solutions, and applications, although this was a small component of her actual job responsibilities.

Information Technology Engineer, 12/2005 to 12/2009   U.S. COAST GUARD, Galveston, TX

Fast-paced advanced-technology position working with a team of systems developers to design state-of-the-art infrastructure, systems, applications, software, telecommunications, and networks in support of USCG operations nationwide.

INFRASTRUCTURE DEVELOPMENT:
- Partnered with MIT, Cisco, and an independent software company to develop high-speed WAN technology. Developed a 20-node T1/T3 WAN within 2 years and achieved/maintained 99.9% uptime.
- Built data center from start-up into a 24x7 operation supporting high-end Sun UNIX systems and an NT platform primarily hosting Oracle databases (ERP applications).
- Designed LAN models and standardized voice communications using a mix of open-standard PBXs, voice mail, and voice over IP. Built MCI back-up ISDN network and multiple secure Internet protocols.

SOLUTIONS & APPLICATIONS:
- Revitalized fledgling Oracle implementation and took project "live" in less than 10 months. Modules included AP, AR, GL, Purchasing, Inventory, Project Management, and HR.
- Designed "new" Internet computing architecture, migrating Oracle applications onto a 3-tier Web-based environment. Delivered 100% migration of 92 customizations within 60 days.
- Integrated 13 e-mail systems (Lotus Notes, Eudora) into one system (Microsoft Exchange) to facilitate collaborative participation among all ABC companies and operating sites.
- Led the selection and implementation of AT&T's VPN solution for direct access to ABC's private network.

Experience Summary Format

Career Transition: Housing Manager seeking new career in hotel management with a nationwide hotel chain. Format briefly emphasizes relevant highlights of each position because the bulk of this individual's experience in housing will have been summarized at length in his Career Summary.

EXPERIENCE SUMMARY

Housing Manager, Fort Dix, NJ—2004 to 2009
- ✓ Directed operations for the housing of more than 3,000 military and civilian personnel.
- ✓ Controlled $260,000 annual operating budget and millions of dollars allocated for housing renovation and new construction projects.
- ✓ Negotiated multimillion-dollar contracts for facilities maintenance and repair with local companies.
- ✓ Coordinated site remediation of 50,000 tons of lead-contaminated soil from 150 residential sites two weeks ahead of schedule and $56,000 under budget.

Bakeshop Supervisor, USS *Theodore Roosevelt*—2002 to 2004
- ✓ Managed and trained 10 pastry chefs serving a crew of 3,200.
- ✓ Planned and managed all bakery production, scheduling, and delivery operations.
- ✓ Coordinated menus, supplier relationships, and on-board transactions.

Bakeshop Watch Captain, U.S. Navy Hospital, Camp Lejeune, NC—2000 to 2002
- ✓ Managed one supervisor and nine support personnel responsible for daily bakeshop operations supporting more than 3,000 personnel.

EDUCATION, CREDENTIALS, AND CERTIFICATIONS

Your Education section should include college, certifications, credentials, licenses, registrations, and continuing education. For career changers whose greatest selling point for their new career is education, this section is extremely important and will, most likely, be placed on your resume immediately following your Career Summary. Be sure to display your educational qualifications prominently if they are a key selling point for you in helping to facilitate your transition into your new career track.

The following five sample Education sections illustrate a variety of ways to organize and format this information.

Academic Credentials Format

EDUCATION

MBA, Emphasis in Supply Chain Logistics, Fairleigh Dickinson University, 2008

BS, Major in Mechanical Engineering, magna cum laude, Rutgers University, 2000

Highlights of Continuing Professional Education:
- Command and General Staff College, Fort Covey, KS, 2006
- Leadership Development, Purdue University, 2005
- Financial Management for Non-Financial Managers, Purdue University, 2005
- Conflict Resolution & Violence Management in the Workplace, Institute for Workplace Safety, 2002

Executive Education Format

————————————————————*Education*————————————————————

Executive Leadership Program	STANFORD UNIVERSITY
Executive Development Program	NORTHWESTERN UNIVERSITY
Master of Business Administration (MBA) Degree	NORTHWESTERN UNIVERSITY
Bachelor of Science Degree	UNITED STATES NAVAL ACADEMY

Certifications Format

TECHNICAL CERTIFICATIONS & DEGREES

Registered Nurse, University of Maryland, 2006
Certified Nursing Assistant, University of Maryland, 2004
Certified Nursing Aide, State of Maryland, 2000
Bachelor of Science in Nursing, University of Maryland, 2006
Associate of Arts in General Studies, Plymouth Community College, Plymouth, Delaware, 2004

Specialized Training Format

TECHNICAL LICENSES & CERTIFICATIONS

- Certified Health & Safety Manager, OSHA, 2008
- Maintenance Supervisor Certification, USAF, 2007
- Primary Leadership Certification, USAF, 2006
- Impact Training, Motor Control Seminar, 2006
- CAT-5 Certification, 2005
- Variable Speed Drive Certification, 2004
- SOARS Grounding of Electrical Systems for Safety Certification, 2003
- Graduate, Jefferson Forest High School, Lynchburg, VA, 2000

Non-degree Format

TRAINING & EDUCATION—————————————————————

▶ UNIVERSITY OF FLORIDA, Tampa, Florida
B.S. Candidate—Business Administration (Senior class status)

▶ UNIVERSITY OF OREGON, Portland, Oregon
Dual Majors in Business Administration & Computer Science (2 years)

▶ Completed 100+ hours of continuing professional education offered by the USMC, University of Michigan, Dell, and Microsoft. Topics included business administration, finance, strategic planning, organizational development, team building, and various PC technologies and software programs.

THE "EXTRAS"

The primary focus of your resume is on information that is directly related to your career goals, whether from your paid work experience, volunteer experience, education and training, affiliations, or someplace else. However, you also should include things that will distinguish you from other candidates and clearly demonstrate your value to a prospective employer. Not surprisingly, it is often the "extras" that get the interviews.

Following is a list of the other categories you might or might not include in your resume depending on your particular experience and your current career objectives. Review the information. If it's pertinent to you, use the samples for formatting your own data. Remember, however, that if something is truly impressive, you might want to include it in your Career Summary at the beginning of your resume to draw even more attention to it. If this is the case, it's not necessary to repeat the information at the end of your resume.

Technology Skills and Qualifications

Many technology professionals have a separate section on their resumes for technology skills and qualifications. It is here that you will summarize all the hardware, software, operating systems, applications, networks, and additional technology-related information that you know and that are relevant to your current career objectives.

You'll also have to consider placement of this section in your resume. If the positions for which you are applying require strong technical skills, we recommend you insert this section immediately after your Career Summary (or as a part thereof). If, on the other hand, your technical skills are more of a plus than a specific requirement, the preferred placement is further down in your resume.

Either way, these skills are vital in virtually any technology-related position. As such, this is extremely important information to a prospective employer, so be sure to display it prominently.

Here are two different ways to format and present your technical qualifications.

TECHNOLOGY PROFILE	
Operating Systems:	Windows 7/Vista/XP, NetWare, MS-DOS
Protocols/Networks:	TCP/IP, IPX/SPX, Ethernet 10/100Base-T
Hardware:	Hard drives, printers, scanners, fax/modems, CD-ROMs, Cat5 cables, hubs, NIC cards
Software:	Microsoft Office, Microsoft Exchange, Microsoft Project, FileMaker Pro, pcAnywhere, ARCserve

TECHNOLOGY SKILLS SUMMARY		
Windows 7/Vista/XP	SAP	TCP/IP
NetWare	MRP	IPX/SPX
Microsoft Office	DRP	ARCserve
pcAnywhere	Microsoft Exchange	FileMaker Pro

If your goal is to simply mention the fact that you are proficient with specific PC software, a quick line or two at the end of your Career Summary should cover this information. For example:

> PC proficiency with Word, Excel, Access, Adobe InDesign, and WordPerfect. Extensive experience in Internet research and benchmarking.

Equipment Skills and Qualifications

Many people whose background is in facilities, construction, engineering, automotive and aircraft maintenance, and other technical fields have a unique portfolio of equipment skills and knowledge. If these skills are relevant to your current career goals, it is critical that you communicate them in your resume, highlighting all the equipment with which you are proficient or familiar. Consider this format for an individual with extensive experience in the installation, maintenance, repair, and support of avionics technology:

Perform on- and off-equipment inspections and repairs of avionics systems, including

Fuel Quantity Indication	Pilot-Static	Engine Indication
Flight Management	Inertial Navigation	Color Weather Radar
Flight Control Augmentation	Flight Director	Digital Autopilot
Digital Interphone	Global Positioning	Traffic Collision Avoidance
Flight Data Recorder	Magnetic Compass	Turbine Engine Management

Honors and Awards

If you have won honors and awards, you can either include them in a separate section near the end of your resume or integrate them into the Education or Professional Experience section if they are particularly noteworthy and related to your current career objectives. If you choose to include them in a separate section, consider this format:

- Three Army Achievement Medals
- Two Army Commendation Medals
- Overseas Service Ribbon (Peacekeeping Mission)
- Outstanding Volunteer Service Award, U.S. Army
- Cum Laude Graduate, Southern Illinois University

Public Speaking

Experts are the ones who are invited to give public presentations at conferences, seminars, workshops, training programs, symposia, and other events. So if you have public-speaking experience, others must consider you an expert. Be sure to include this very complimentary information in your resume. Here's one way to present it:

- **Keynote Speaker,** "Preparedness in Today's Armed Forces," Army National Guard Annual Conference, New York City, 2009
- **Panel Presenter,** "Maximizing Resource Utilization & Deployment," Army Staff College Conference, 2006
- **Session Leader,** "Planning for Our Military's Future," NATO Conference, 2005

Publications

If you're published, you must be an expert (or at least most people will think so). Just as with your public-speaking engagements, be sure to include your publications. They validate your knowledge, qualifications, and credibility. Publications can include books, articles, online Web site content, manuals, and other written documents. Here's an example:

- ✓ Coauthor, *Computer-Aided Design of Hybrid Microcircuits,* National Electronic Packaging Association Newsletter, 2009.
- ✓ Author, *Subtle Aspects of Microcircuit Technology,* Product Assurance Newsletter, 2008.
- ✓ Author, *Microcircuit Technology Practices, Policies, and Processes,* USMC Training Manual, 2005.

Teaching and Training Experience

Many professionals, regardless of their industry or profession, also teach or train at colleges, universities, technical schools, and other organizations in addition to training that they offer on the job. If applicable to you and your current objectives, you will want to include that experience on your resume. If someone hires you (paid or unpaid) to speak to an audience, it communicates a strong message about your skills, qualifications, knowledge, and expertise. Here's a format you might use to present that information:

Adjunct Faculty, Department of Chemical Engineering, Texas A&M University, 2006 to Present. Teach Introductory and Advanced Chemical Engineering.

Guest Lecturer, Department of Statistics, Reynolds Community College, 2003 to 2006. Provided semiannual, daylong lecture series of the applications of statistics and statistical theory in the workplace.

Trainer, Macmillan School of Engineering, 2001 to 2003. Taught Chemical Engineering 101 and Chemical Lab Analysis to first-year students.

Committees and Task Forces

Many professionals serve on committees, task forces, and other special project teams either as part of, or in addition to, their full-time job responsibilities. Again, this type of information further strengthens your credibility, qualifications, and perceived value to a prospective employer when it is related to your current objectives. Consider a format such as this:

- Member, 2009–2010 Strategic Planning & Reorganization Task Force, U.S. Army Command
- Member, 2007 Study Team on "Redesigning Training Systems to Maximum Productivity," U.S. Army Command
- Chairperson, 2002–2003 Committee on "Safety & Regulatory Compliance in the Workplace," Fort Dix

Professional Affiliations

If you are a member of any educational, professional, or leadership associations, be sure to include that information on your resume. It communicates a message of professionalism, a desire to stay current with the industry, and a strong professional network. What's more, if you have held leadership positions within these organizations, be sure to include them. Here's an example:

ASSOCIATION OF THE INDUSTRIAL COLLEGE OF THE ARMED FORCES

- Professional Member (2003 to Present)
- Program Committee Member (2005 to 2009)
- Curriculum Committee Member (2004 to 2006)

AMERICAN SOCIETY FOR QUALITY

- Professional Member (2001 to Present)
- Technology Task Force Member (2001 to 2003)

NATIONAL SAFETY COUNCIL

- Professional Member (2001 to 2006)
- Health Physics Committee Member (2003 to 2004)

Civic Affiliations

Civic affiliations are fine to include if they fit into one of the following categories:

- Are with a notable organization.
- Demonstrate leadership experience.
- Are of interest to a prospective employer.

However, noting roles such as being treasurer of your local condo association or a singer with your church choir are not generally of value in marketing your qualifications unless, of course, that experience is directly relevant to your current career objectives. Here's an example of what to include and how:

- Volunteer Chairperson, United Way of America, Detroit Chapter, 2007 to Present
- President, Greenwood Environmental District, 2006 to Present
- Treasurer, Habitat for Humanity, Memphis Chapter, 2003 to 2004

Personal Information

We do not recommend that you include such personal information as birth date, marital status, number of children, and related data. However, including a little bit of personal information is sometimes appropriate. If this information will give you a competitive advantage or answer unspoken questions about your background, then by all means include it. Here's an example:

- ➤ **Born in Belgium. U.S. Permanent Residency Status since 2004.**
- ➤ **Fluent in English, French, German, Flemish, and Dutch.**
- ➤ **Competitive triathlete. Top-5 finish, 2007 Midwest Triathlon and 2010 Des Moines Triathlon.**

Note in the above example that the job seeker is multilingual. This is a particularly critical selling point, and although it is listed under Personal Information in this example, it is usually more appropriately highlighted in the Career Summary.

Consolidating the Extras

Sometimes you have so many extra categories at the end of your resume, each with only a handful of lines, that spacing becomes a problem. You certainly don't want to have to make your resume a page longer to accommodate five lines, nor do you want the "extras" to overwhelm the primary sections of your resume. Yet you believe the information is important and should be included. Or perhaps you have a few small bits of information that you think are important but don't merit an entire section. In these situations, consider consolidating the information using one of the following formats. You'll save space, avoid overemphasizing individual items, and present a professional, distinguished appearance. Here are two examples of how to consolidate and format your "extras":

PROFESSIONAL PROFILE

Technology Qualifications	Microsoft Office Suite, SAP, MRP, DRP, LAN, WAN, Lotus Notes, Novell NetWare
Affiliations	Association of Quality Control Institute of Electrical & Electronic Engineers American Electrical Association
Public Speaking	Speaker, IEEE Conference, Chicago, 2009 Presenter, AEA National Conference, Miami, 2006 Panelist, IEEE Conference, Detroit, 2004
Languages	Fluent in English, Spanish, and German

ADDITIONAL INFORMATION

- Co-Chair, Education Committee, Detroit Technology Association.
- PC literate with MRP, DRP, SAP, and Kaizen technologies.
- Available for relocation worldwide.
- Eagle Scout … Boy Scout Troop Leader.

Writing Tips, Techniques, and Important Lessons

At this point, you've done a lot of reading, probably taken some notes, highlighted samples that appeal to you, and are ready to plunge into writing your resume. To make this task as easy as possible, we've compiled some "insider" techniques that we've used in our professional resume-writing practices. These techniques were learned the hard way through years of experience! We know they work; and they will make the writing process easier, faster, and more enjoyable for you.

GET IT DOWN—THEN POLISH AND PERFECT IT

Don't be too concerned with making your resume "perfect" the first time around. It's far better to move fairly swiftly through the process, getting the basic information organized and on paper (or on screen), rather than agonizing about the perfect phrase or ideal formatting. When you've completed a draft, we think you'll be surprised at how close to "final" it is, and you'll be able to edit, tighten, and improve formatting fairly quickly.

WRITE YOUR RESUME FROM THE BOTTOM UP

Here's the system:

1. **Start with the easy things**—Education, Technology, Professional Affiliations, Public Speaking, Publications, and any other extras you want to include. These items require little thought and can be completed in just a few minutes.

2. **Write short job descriptions for your older positions, the ones you held years ago.** Be very brief and focus on highlights such as rapid promotion, achievements, innovations, honors, or any other notable items.

   NOTE: Even if you plan to create a functional resume that combines job achievements in one "front-and-center" location, we recommend that you first draft these descriptions in a chronological format. It will be easier to remember what you did if you take each of your jobs in turn. Later you can regroup your statements to emphasize related skills and abilities, and leave your employment history as a simple list or brief description to support your career-transition objectives.

   Once you've completed job descriptions for your older positions, look at how much you've written in a short period of time! Then move on to the next step.

3. **Write the job descriptions for your most recent positions.** This will take a bit longer than the other sections you have written. Remember to focus on the overall scope of your responsibility, major projects and initiatives, and significant achievements as they relate directly to your current objectives. Tell your reader what you did and how well you did it. You can use any of the formats recommended earlier in this chapter, or you can create something that is unique to you and your career.

    Now, see how far along you are? Your resume is 90 percent complete with only one section left to do.

4. **Write your career summary.** Before you start writing, remember your objective for this section. The summary should not simply rehash your previous experience. Rather, it is designed to highlight the skills and qualifications you have that are most closely related to your current career objective(s). The summary is intended to capture the reader's attention and "sell" your expertise and is *the* most important section for any career-transition resume.

That's it. You're done. We guarantee that the process of writing your resume will be much, much easier if you follow the "bottom-up" strategy. Now, on to the next tip.

INCLUDE NOTABLE OR PROMINENT "EXTRA" STUFF IN YOUR CAREER SUMMARY

Remember the "extra" sections that are normally at the bottom of your resume? If this information is particularly significant or prominent—you won a notable award, spoke at an international conference, developed a new training methodology, or designed a new process that slashed inventory costs—you might want to include that information at the top of your resume in your Career Summary. Remember, the summary section is written to distinguish you from the crowd of other qualified candidates. As such, if you've accomplished anything that clearly demonstrates your knowledge, expertise, and credibility, consider moving it to your Career Summary for added attention. Refer to the sample Career Summary sections earlier in this chapter for examples.

USE RESUME SAMPLES TO GET IDEAS FOR CONTENT, FORMAT, AND ORGANIZATION

This book is just one of many resources where you can review sample resumes to help you in formulating your strategy, writing the text, and formatting your resume. These books are published precisely for that reason. You don't have to struggle alone. Rather, use all the available resources at your disposal.

Be forewarned, however, that it's unlikely you will find a resume that fits your life and career to a *t*. It's more likely that you will use pieces from different samples to create a resume that is uniquely you.

HANDLE DATES EFFECTIVELY

Unless you are over age 50, we recommend that you date your work experience and your education. Without dates, your resume becomes vague and difficult for the typical hiring manager or recruiter to interpret. Leaving off dates often communicates the message that you are trying to hide something. By including the dates of your education and your experience, you create a clean and concise picture that one can easily follow to track your career progression.

If you want your dates to be prominent, consider putting them at the right margin. Conversely, if you want to downplay your dates, put them in small type immediately after the name of your company or the title of your position, or even at the end of the descriptive paragraph for each position.

How Should You Present Early Job Experience?

If you are over age 50, dating your early positions must be an individual decision. On the one hand, you do not want to "date" yourself out of consideration by including dates from the 1970s and 1980s. On the other hand, those positions might be worth including for any one of a number of reasons. Further, if you omit those early dates, you might feel as though you are misrepresenting yourself (or lying) to a prospective employer.

Here is a strategy to overcome those concerns while still including your early experience: Create a separate category titled "Previous Professional Experience" in which you summarize your earliest employment. You can tailor this statement to emphasize just what is most important about that experience.

If you want to capitalize on the good reputation of your past employers, include a statement such as this:

> • Prior to military career, held several key supervisory positions with IBM, Dell, and Xerox.

If you want to focus on the rapid progression of your career, consider this example:

> • Promoted rapidly through a series of increasingly responsible operations and resource management positions with the U.S. Air Force.

If you want to focus on your early career achievements, include a statement such as this:

> • Member of 16-person task force credited with the strategic planning, design, and launch of the Army's first-ever PC training program.

By including any one of the preceding paragraphs, under the heading "Previous Professional Experience," you are clearly communicating to your reader that your employment history dates further back than the dates you have indicated on your resume. In turn, you are being 100 percent above-board and not misrepresenting yourself or your career. What's more, you're focusing on the success, achievement, and prominence of your earliest assignments.

Should You Include Dates in the Education Section?

If you are over age 50, we generally do not recommend that you date your education or college degrees. Simply include the degree and the university with no date. Why exclude yourself from consideration by immediately presenting the fact that you earned your college degree in 1972, 1976, or 1980—perhaps the year the hiring manager was born? Remember, the goal of your resume is to share the highlights of your career and open doors for interviews. It is *not* to give your entire life story. As such, it is not mandatory to date your college degree.

However, if you use this strategy, be aware that the reader is likely to assume there is *some* gap between when your education ended and your work experience started. Therefore, if you choose to begin your chronological work history with your first job out of college, omitting your graduation date could actually backfire, because the reader might assume that you have experience that predates your first job. In this case, it's best either to include your graduation date or omit dates of earliest experience, using the summary strategy discussed earlier.

ALWAYS SEND A COVER LETTER WHEN YOU FORWARD YOUR RESUME

Sending a cover letter every time you send a resume is expected and is appropriate job search etiquette. For all military-to-civilian career transition job seekers, your cover letter is *vital* to the success of your job search campaign.

Consider the following: When you write a resume, you are writing a document that you can use for every position you apply for, assuming that the requirements for all of those positions will be similar. You invest a great deal of time and effort in crafting just the "right" resume for you, but once it's done, it's done.

Your cover letter, however, is a document that is constantly changing to meet the needs of each individual situation for which you apply. In essence, it is the tool that allows you to customize your presentation to each company or recruiter, addressing their specific hiring requirements. Use your cover letter to highlight the most important qualifications, experiences, and achievements you bring to that specific company so that a prospective employer doesn't have to search through your resume to find what is most important. It is also the appropriate place to include any specific information that has been requested, such as salary history or salary requirements (see the following section for more on including salaries).

Your cover letter will allow you to briefly address why you're making a career transition. Here are three examples of such explanations:

> After years of career success managing large-scale airfield operations for the United States Air Force, I have decided to leave the military and transition into the private sector. My goal is an airfield management position with a major airport in the Southwest where I can continue to direct ground operations while achieving new career milestones.

> Although my career with the Marine Corps has been exceptional and presented me with opportunities I never imagined possible, my real passion has always been product marketing. As such, I have resigned and will be leaving my leadership position in June to begin interviewing with product marketing firms throughout New York to identify entry-level professional opportunities where I can begin to establish my new career track.

> My 7-year military career has been an extraordinary experience, highlighted by rapid promotions and numerous commendations. However, the time has now come to transition my years of experience into the civilian market as an automotive mechanic and/or maintenance engineer. Aware of the quality of your company and your interest in hiring departing military professionals, I am submitting my resume for your consideration.

See chapters 14 and 15 for a more in-depth discussion of cover letters and strategies for creating interesting, relevant, and compelling letters of your own.

NEVER INCLUDE SALARY HISTORY OR SALARY REQUIREMENTS ON YOUR RESUME

Your resume is *not* the proper forum for a salary discussion. First of all, you should never provide salary information unless a company has requested that information and you choose to comply. (Studies show that employers will look at your resume anyway, so you might choose not to respond to this request, thereby avoiding pricing yourself out of the job or locking yourself into a lower salary than the job is worth.)

When contacting recruiters, however, we recommend that you do provide salary information, but again, only in your cover letter. With recruiters you want to "put all of your cards on the table" and help them make an appropriate placement by providing information about your current salary and salary objectives. For example, "Be advised that my most recent compensation was $55,000 annually and that I am interested in a position starting at a minimum of $65,000 per year." Or, if you would prefer to be a little less specific, you might write, "My annual compensation over the past three years has averaged $50,000+."

ALWAYS REMEMBER THAT YOU ARE SELLING

As we have discussed over and over throughout this book, resume writing is sales. Understand and appreciate the value you bring to a prospective employer, and then communicate that value by focusing on your achievements. Companies don't want to hire just anyone; they want to hire "the" someone who will make a difference. Show them that you are that candidate.

CHAPTER 3

Printed, Scannable, Electronic, and Web Resumes

After you've worked so tirelessly to write a winning resume, your next challenge is the resume's design, layout, and presentation. It's not enough for it to read well; your resume must also have just the right look for the right audience.

The Four Types of Resumes

In today's employment market, job seekers use four types of resume presentations:

- Printed
- Scannable
- Electronic (e-mail attachments and ASCII text files)
- Web

The following sections give details on when you would need each type, as well as how to prepare these types of resumes.

THE PRINTED RESUME

We know the printed resume as the "traditional resume," the one that you mail to a recruiter, take to an interview, and forward by mail or fax in response to an advertisement. When preparing a printed resume, you want to create a sharp, professional, and visually attractive presentation. Remember, that piece of paper conveys the very first impression of you to a potential employer, and that first impression goes a long, long way. Never be fooled into thinking that just because you have the best qualifications in your industry, the visual presentation of your resume does not matter. It does, a great deal.

THE SCANNABLE RESUME

The scannable resume can be referred to as the "plain-Jane" or "plain-vanilla" resume. All of the things that you would normally do to make your printed resume look attractive—bold print, italic, multiple columns, sharp-looking typestyle, and more—are stripped away in a scannable resume. You want to present a document that can be easily read and interpreted by scanning technology.

Although the technology continues to improve, and many scanning systems in fact can read a wide variety of type enhancements, it's sensible to appeal to the "lowest common denominator" when creating your scannable resume. Follow these formatting guidelines:

- Choose a commonly used, easily read font such as Arial or Times New Roman.

- Don't use bold, italic, or underlined type.

- Use a minimum of 11-point type size.

- Position your name, and nothing else, on the top line of the resume.

- Keep text left-justified, with a "ragged" right margin.

- It's okay to use common abbreviations (for instance, scanning software will recognize "B.S." as a Bachelor of Science degree). But, when in doubt, spell it out.

- Eliminate graphics, borders, and horizontal lines.

- Use plain, round bullets or asterisks.

- Avoid columns and tables, although a simple two-column listing can be read without difficulty.

- Spell out symbols such as % and &.

- If you divide words with slashes, add a space before and after the slash to be certain the scanner doesn't misread the letters.

- Print using a laser printer on smooth white paper.

- If your resume is longer than one page, be sure to print on only one side of the paper; put your name, telephone number, and e-mail address on the top of page two; and don't staple the pages together.

- For best possible results, mail your resume (don't fax it), and send it flat in a 9 × 12 envelope so that you won't have to fold it.

Scannable resumes are becoming less common and less in demand as the majority of career documents are transmitted by e-mail or pasted into online applications. It is only when your resume pages need to physically pass through a scanner that you will need a scannable resume. We recommend that you not worry about this format until and unless you are required to produce one for a specific company. For electronic resume guidelines, see the next section.

THE ELECTRONIC RESUME

Your electronic resume can take two forms: e-mail attachments and ASCII text files.

E-mail Attachments

When including your resume with an e-mail, simply attach the word-processing file of your printed resume. Because a vast majority of businesses use Microsoft Word, it is the most acceptable format and will present the fewest difficulties. However, given the tremendous variety in versions of software and operating systems, not to mention printer drivers, it's quite possible that your beautifully formatted resume will look quite different when viewed and printed at the other end. To minimize these glitches, use generous margins (at least 0.75 inch all around). Don't use unusual typefaces, and minimize fancy formatting effects.

Test your resume by e-mailing it to several friends or colleagues, and then having them view and print it on their systems. If you use WordPerfect, Microsoft Works, or another word-processing program, consider saving your resume in a more universally accepted format such as RTF or PDF. Again, try it out on friends before sending it to a potential employer.

Although employers can easily open, view, and print a PDF (Portable Document Format) file, we do not recommend this as your primary electronic format. A PDF file is viewed as a graphic rather than an editable file, and therefore the data from your resume cannot be read into a company's resume-storage system unless it is printed and physically scanned. PDF is an excellent option if your resume has an unusual design, and especially if design skills are an important part of your qualifications. But for the most part, the PDF format will be less useful than a word-processing file format (such as .doc) for the companies receiving your resume.

ASCII Text Files

You'll find many uses for an ASCII text version of your resume:

- To avoid formatting problems, you can paste the text into the body of an e-mail message rather than send an attachment. Many employers actually prefer this method. Pasting text into an e-mail message lets you send your resume without the possibility of also sending a virus.

- You can readily copy and paste the text version into online job application and resume bank forms, with no worries that formatting glitches will cause confusion.

- Although it's unattractive, the text version is 100 percent scannable.

To create a text version of your resume, follow these simple steps:

1. Create a new version of your resume using the Save As feature of your word-processing program. Select "text only" or "ASCII" in the Save As option box.

2. Close the new file.

3. Reopen the file, and you'll find that your word processor has automatically reformatted your resume into Courier font, removed all formatting, and left-justified the text.

4. To promote maximum readability when sending your resume electronically, reset the margins to 2 inches left and right, so that you have a narrow column of text rather than a full-page width. (This margin setting will not be retained when you close the file, but in the meantime you can adjust the text formatting for best screen appearance. For instance, if you choose to include a horizontal line to separate sections of the resume, by working with the narrow

margins you won't make the mistake of creating a line that extends past the normal screen width. Plus, you won't add hard line breaks that create odd-length lines when seen at normal screen width.)

5. Review the resume and fix any "glitches" such as odd characters that may have been inserted to take the place of "curly" quotes, dashes, accents, or other nonstandard symbols.

6. Remove any tabs and adjust spacing as necessary. You might add a few extra blank lines or move text down to the next line.

7. If necessary, add extra blank lines to improve readability.

8. Consider adding horizontal dividers to break the resume into sections for improved skimmability. You can use any standard typewriter symbols such as *, -, (,), =, +, ^, or #.

To illustrate what you can expect when creating these versions of your resume, on the following pages are some examples of the same resume in traditional printed format, scannable version, and electronic (text) format.

THE WEB RESUME

This newest evolution in resumes combines the visually pleasing quality of the printed resume with the technological ease of the electronic resume. You host your Web resume on your own Web site (with your own URL), to which you refer prospective employers and recruiters. Now instead of seeing just a "plain-Jane" version of your e-mail resumes, with just one click an employer can view, download, and print your Web resume—an attractive, nicely formatted presentation of your qualifications.

What's more, because the Web resume is such an efficient and easy-to-manage tool, you can choose to include more information than you would in a printed, scannable, or electronic resume. Consider separate pages for project highlights, achievements, technology qualifications, equipment skills, honors and awards, management skills, volunteer contributions, professional memberships, civic memberships, publications, public speaking, international travel and foreign languages, and anything else you believe will improve your market position. Remember, you're working to sell yourself into your next job!

If you are in a technology-related position, you can take it a step further and create a virtual multimedia presentation that not only tells someone how talented you are, but also visually and technologically demonstrates it. Web resumes are an outstanding tool for people seeking jobs in technologically or visually related professions.

Your Web resume can also include all of the items that you would include in a professional portfolio, such as photographs of your work, writing samples, designs, or job evaluations. Testimonials and letters of reference can be another powerful part of your Web resume.

Depending on your technology skills, you might decide to create and manage your own Web resume/portfolio. We suggest visiting www.visualcv.com, where you can enhance your traditional resume with a full selection of add-ons. This service is free to individuals and is a versatile tool for job search and lifelong career management. Another option is to outsource this project to a firm that specializes in career portfolios. We like Blue Sky Portfolios (www.blueskyportfolios.com).

An online version of your Microsoft Word resume can also serve as a simple Web resume. Instead of attaching a file to an e-mail that you send to an employer, you can include a link to the online version. This format is not as graphically dynamic as a full-fledged Web resume, but it can be a very useful tool for your job search. For instance, you can offer the simplicity of text in your e-mail, plus the instant availability of a printable, formatted word-processing document for the interested recruiter or hiring manager.

T. RICHARD POLAWSKI
5252 Memory Lane — Shuffletown, NC 28217 — 704-365-1818 — trpolawski@carolina.rr.com

CAREER GOAL

Position as Instructor in an environment focused on education, enlightenment, and encouragement.

KEY BENEFITS

- Exceptional ability to communicate technical information to end users. Have provided end-user training and ongoing support in network, Internet/Web, and various Microsoft applications (Windows, Outlook, Exchange).
- Offer a unique, valuable perspective gained from longevity in the field (11 years with Microsoft Corporation), complemented by a passion for technology, an enjoyment of training delivery, and an inner drive to remain on the cutting edge.
- Expertise in systematically troubleshooting network messaging problems, upgrading hardware/ software, and performing service work; received superlative grades in computer programming courses.

INFORMATION TECHNOLOGY COMPETENCIES

- ***Microsoft Certified Systems Engineer (MCSE), Microsoft Certified Professional (MCP):*** Design, install, maintain, troubleshoot, test, and repair computer systems. Experienced in building and rebuilding computers and related peripherals.
- Strong background in developing and evaluating new products and implementing "best practices." Extensive experience in writing technical (including user-training) procedures.

RECENT EMPLOYMENT HISTORY

MICROSOFT CORPORATION — Charlotte, NC   1999–Present
Product Support Engineer

Currently provide product support for MS Exchange: Troubleshoot message-flow problems across various networks and the Internet, to include interfacing with Lotus Domino and Novell GroupWise servers. Previously provided support for MS Word for Windows and Macintosh. **Wrote technical procedures for user functions,** including repair, optimization, and other customer requirements.

A section of the print version of the resume.

T. Richard Polawski
5252 Memory Lane, Shuffletown, NC 28217
704-365-1818 — trpolawski@carolina.rr.com

CAREER GOAL
Position as Instructor in an environment focused on education, enlightenment, and encouragement.

KEY BENEFITS
- Exceptional ability to communicate technical information to end users. Have provided end-user training and ongoing support in network, Internet/Web, and various Microsoft applications (Windows, Outlook, Exchange).
- Offer a unique, valuable perspective gained from longevity in the field (11 years with Microsoft Corporation), complemented by a passion for technology, an enjoyment of training delivery, and an inner drive to remain on the cutting edge.
- Expertise in systematically troubleshooting network messaging problems, upgrading hardware/software, and performing service work; received superlative grades in computer programming courses.

INFORMATION TECHNOLOGY COMPETENCIES
- Microsoft Certified Systems Engineer (MCSE), Microsoft Certified Professional (MCP): Design, install, maintain, troubleshoot, test, and repair computer systems. Experienced in building and rebuilding computers and related peripherals.
- Strong background in developing and evaluating new products and implementing "best practices." Extensive experience in writing technical (including user-training) procedures.

RECENT EMPLOYMENT HISTORY
MICROSOFT CORPORATION, Charlotte, NC, 1999–Present
Product Support Engineer
Currently provide product support for MS Exchange: Troubleshoot message-flow problems across various networks and the Internet, to include interfacing with Lotus Domino and Novell GroupWise servers. Previously provided support for MS Word for Windows and Macintosh. Wrote technical procedures for user functions, including repair, optimization, and other customer requirements.

A section of the scannable version of the resume.

```
T. Richard Polawski
5252 Memory Lane, Shuffletown, NC 28217
704-365-1818 — trpolawski@carolina.rr.com

==========================================
CAREER GOAL

Position as Instructor in an environment focused on education, enlightenment, and
encouragement.

==========================================
KEY BENEFITS

* Exceptional ability to communicate technical information to end users. Have
provided end-user training and ongoing support in network, Internet/Web, and various
Microsoft applications (Windows, Outlook, Exchange).
* Offer a unique, valuable perspective gained from longevity in the field (11 years
with Microsoft Corporation), complemented by a passion for technology, an enjoyment
of training delivery, and an inner drive to remain on the cutting edge.
* Expertise in systematically troubleshooting network messaging problems, upgrading
hardware/software, and performing service work; received superlative grades in
computer programming courses.


==========================================
INFORMATION TECHNOLOGY COMPETENCIES

* Microsoft Certified Systems Engineer (MCSE), Microsoft Certified
Professional (MCP): Design, install, maintain, troubleshoot, test, and repair
computer systems. Experienced in building and rebuilding computers and related
peripherals.
* Strong background in developing and evaluating new products and implementing
''best practices.'' Extensive experience in writing technical (including user-
training) procedures.


==========================================
RECENT EMPLOYMENT HISTORY

MICROSOFT CORPORATION, Charlotte, NC, 1999-Present
------------------------------
Product Support Engineer
------------------------------
Currently provide product support for MS Exchange: Troubleshoot message-flow
problems across various networks and the Internet, to include interfacing with Lotus
Domino and Novell GroupWise servers. Previously provided support for MS Word for
Windows and Macintosh. Wrote technical procedures for user functions, including
repair, optimization, and other customer requirements.
```

A section of the electronic version of the resume.

The Four Resume Types Compared

This chart quickly compares the similarities and differences between the four types of resumes we've discussed in this chapter.

	PRINTED RESUMES	SCANNABLE RESUMES
TYPESTYLE/ FONT	Sharp, conservative, and distinctive (see our recommendations in chapter 1).	Clean, concise, and machine-readable: Times New Roman, Arial, Helvetica.
TYPESTYLE ENHANCEMENTS	**Bold,** *italic,* and <u>underlining</u> for emphasis.	CAPITALIZATION is the only type enhancement you can be certain will transmit.
TYPE SIZE	10-, 11-, or 12-point preferred; larger type sizes (14, 18, 20, 22, and even larger, depending on typestyle) will effectively enhance your name and section headers.	11- or 12-point or larger.
TEXT FORMAT	Use centering and indentations to optimize the visual presentation.	Type all information flush left.
PREFERRED LENGTH	1 to 2 pages; 3 if essential.	1 to 2 pages preferred, although length is not as much of a concern as with printed resumes.
PREFERRED PAPER COLOR	White, ivory, light gray, light blue, or other conservative background.	White or very light with no prints, flecks, or other shading that might affect scannability.
WHITE SPACE	Use appropriately for best readability.	Use generously to maximize scannability.

ELECTRONIC RESUMES	WEB RESUMES
Courier.	Sharp, conservative, and distinctive… attractive onscreen and when printed from an online document.
CAPITALIZATION is the only enhancement available to you.	**Bold,** *italic,* and <u>underlining</u>, and color for emphasis.
12-point.	10-, 11-, or 12-point preferred; larger type sizes (14, 18, 20, 22, and even larger, depending on typestyle) will effectively enhance your name and section headers.
Type all information flush left.	Use centering and indentations to optimize the visual presentation.
Length is immaterial; almost definitely, converting your resume to text will make it longer.	Length is immaterial; just be sure your site is well organized so viewers can quickly find the material of greatest interest to them.
N/A.	Paper is not used, but do select your background carefully to maximize readability.
Use white space to break up dense text sections.	Use appropriately for best readability, both onscreen and when printed.

Are You Ready to Write Your Resume?

To be sure that you're ready to write your resume, go through the following checklist. Each item is a critical step that you must take in the process of writing and designing your own winning resume.

- ☐ Clearly define "who you are" and how you want to be perceived.

- ☐ Document your key skills, qualifications, and knowledge.

- ☐ Document your notable career achievements and successes.

- ☐ Identify one or more specific job targets or positions.

- ☐ Identify one or more industries that you are targeting.

- ☐ Research and compile key words for your profession, industry, and specific job targets.

- ☐ Determine which resume format suits you and your career best.

- ☐ Select an attractive font.

- ☐ Determine whether you need a print resume, a scannable resume, an electronic resume, a Web resume, or all four.

- ☐ Secure a private e-mail address.

- ☐ Review resume samples for up-to-date ideas on resume styles, formats, organization, and language.

PART II

Sample Resumes for Military-to-Civilian Transitions

CHAPTER 4

Resumes for Careers in Administration, Accounting, and Finance

- Administrative Support Professionals

- Executive Assistants

- Administrative Assistants/Clerks/Computer Specialists

- Administrative Managers

- Information Technology Managers

- Finance Managers

The primary concern when writing resumes for this type of position is to translate military language to business terms. The resumes in this chapter highlight specific job duties as well as significant career achievements. Many of these resumes are detail-rich to correspond with the detail-oriented nature of administrative, accounting, finance, and insurance positions. Both functional and chronological styles are used effectively.

Barbara Brandon   ◆   7979 Marshall Street   ◆   Brighton, CA 92700   ◆   **Cell: 760-525-0055**

ADMINISTRATIVE SUPPORT PROFESSIONAL

- Disciplined, enthusiastic, and goal-oriented.
- Extensive training in client service and satisfaction. Good listener; capable communicator; quick learner.
- Courteous, respectful, hardworking, and well-organized; effective at balancing workplace priorities.
- Computer skills: MS Office (Word, Excel, Access, and Outlook); basic knowledge of PowerPoint.

RELATED PROFESSIONAL EXPERIENCE

U.S. Navy   5/05–5/09
Administrative Assistant, San Diego, CA (7/08–4/09)
Progressed steadily, reaching the rank of E-5 within the shortest possible time frame.

Developed, updated, and disseminated training schedule. Coordinated class schedules with
instructors. Created/updated Excel spreadsheets to track and maintain records of required
certifications. Tracked qualification requirements for all training officers. Published PQS (personnel
qualification standards) reports for each workcenter and division, detailing mandatory deadlines for
personnel training. Conducted research; printed/distributed reports. Maintained contact database in
MS Outlook. Composed and proofread shipwide correspondence. Answered telephones; delivered
messages. Previously, performed additional activities including navigation, general maintenance, and
food service.
- Commended by officers for courtesy and professionalism.
- Earned Navy Good Conduct Medal, Navy Unit Commendation, and Sea Service medals.
- Deployed in support of Operation Enduring Freedom (Afghanistan) and Operation Iraqi Freedom.
- *"Petty Officer Brandon has established herself as a hard worker and her efforts have allowed her to excel as
  the command's Training Petty Officer." ~* Senior Supervisor

The Main Office, Brighton, CA   2000–Present
Office Assistant (per diem, vacations)
   Developed 100+-page catalog in MS Word. Performed general office tasks. Proofread book manuscript.

EDUCATION

Central Texas College (U.S. Navy—at sea)   2007–2008
Courses: Public Speaking, Introduction to Biology, Introduction to Psychology, Advanced Psychology
- Earned top grades in every class.
- Additional U.S. Navy studies: navigation and computer basic training (including math, binary to
  base 32).

University of Massachusetts   2004–2005
Courses: Historical Geology, History of Western Theater, Russian 101, Music History, and Theater
Workshop
- Recruited as a freshman for varsity volleyball team.

ETC.

Selected as lead singer for ship's band during deployment.
Helped to refurbish children's playground in Cabo San Lucas, Mexico (U.S. Navy).

This job seeker trimmed details and used civilian language to highlight just the activities she wants
to pursue in her civilian job. As the resume writer puts it, "There is no need to tell the reader that
she swabbed decks."

LARRY GLASS

433 Crescent Street, #100 • Oakland, CA 94601 • (510) 249-5125 • lglass@aol.com

Executive Assistant with 9 years of experience and outstanding organizational, training, and computer skills.

SUMMARY OF QUALIFICATIONS

- Consistent and thorough in completion of complex administrative assignments.
- Proficient in Microsoft Office, graphics, and database applications.
- Able to maintain extensive files, including personnel folders and medical reports.
- Familiar with military administrative procedures and reporting formats.
- Possess excellent interpersonal skills.

EMPLOYMENT HISTORY

U.S. NAVY, Pearl Harbor, HI   *2005–2010*
Administrative Technician supporting all administrative functions of busy on-base dental clinic.
- Improved efficiency of human resources administration by establishing employee assignment and leave-tracking system.
- Managed front-desk reception area, routing incoming calls, greeting visitors, distributing mail, and performing various administrative tasks, including copying and faxing.
- Scheduled conference rooms in Microsoft Outlook and administered database.
- Maintained office equipment inventory and troubleshot operating problems.
- Generated confidential correspondence and documents.
- Arranged conferences, travel, and accommodations for senior management, and maintained calendars for staff.
- Recorded minutes of management and steering committee meetings.

U.S. NAVY, Twentynine Palms, CA   *2003–2005*
Program Specialist for base chapel.
- Answered busy phones and set appointments for head chaplain.
- Updated and maintained personnel records in database.
- Transcribed pastoral counseling notes and performed all word processing, including correspondence, memoranda, and reports.
- Trained volunteer personnel in office procedures.
- Made travel arrangements and produced various presentations.

RICHARD ALLEN INSTITUTE, Oakland, CA   *2001–2003*
Administrative Assistant to Executive Director in research facility.
- Transcribed and processed confidential documents and reports.
- Handled multiline switchboard.
- Coordinated volunteer services, ordered supplies, and arranged meetings and travel for senior management.

COMPUTER SKILLS

Microsoft Office, Microsoft Access, WordPerfect

KEYWORDS

Administration, word processing, personnel, equipment, switchboard, program management

Bullet points highlight relevant experience and achievements during this person's stint in the Navy. Earlier corporate experience is also included.

Emilie Geoffreys

206 Leonard Street
North Bay, ON P1B 5K2

E-mail: emilieg@rogers.com

Home: (613) 687-5871
Cell: (613) 732-5217

Administrative Assistant • Clerk • Computer Specialist
Extensive knowledge within top-secret security settings

Consummate professional utilizing vast experience within military circles including all levels of hierarchy to achieve innovative projects. Consistently successful in forging alliances, supervising administration programs, and instituting superior customer services. Excellent leadership, communication, management, and human relationship skills. Core competencies include

- Project & Team Management
- Communication Tracking & Control
- Top Secret Classification

- Computer Knowledge & Support
- Superior Typing Speed—70WPM
- Troubleshooting, Research & Analysis

Experience within international security agencies and governmental departments

TECHNICAL ACUMEN

- Basic UNIX
- Microsoft Office (Word, Excel, PowerPoint)
- Government Research Database

- UNIX Administrator
- PC / UNIX System
- Local & Wide Area Networks (LAN/WAN)

RELATED WORK EXPERIENCE

CANADIAN ARMED FORCES—*Serving Member of Military*   1994–2010

Dynamic and motivated expert within the field of communication research, reaching the rank level of Master Corporal within a highly specialized office environment. Promoted through increasingly responsible positions based on superior leadership qualities and ability to adapt to any challenge quickly and effectively. Ability to maintain discretion and professionalism throughout all assignments, even involving life-and-death scenarios. Highlights of positions include

WATCH CENTER SUPERVISOR—*CFB North Bay, Ontario* (2007–2010)

Essential member of the process and reporting message center servicing the entire Canadian Forces. Charged with the supervision of a team of operators while accomplishing the mission management role. Helped accomplish center aims and duties, which encompassed 24/7 manning. Tour included a Persian Gulf deployment.

SIGNALLER—*CFB Toronto, Ontario* (2001–2007)

Charged with the establishment of communication webs throughout all training/deployments.

-- Continued --

Highlighting this individual's experience within top-secret communications environments helped her to position herself for administrative jobs within the government sector.

Emilie Geoffreys

(613) 687-5871   Page 2   emilieg@rogers.com

COMMUNICATION OPERATOR—*U.S. Naval Exchange Program, California* (1998–2001)

Handpicked to represent Canada within this highly sought-after communication industry program. Interacted with the Search and Rescue operations of the United States Coast Guard. Superior ability to maintain detailed records and publications while utilizing complex leading-edge technology, including unique software packages specific to operational environments.

EARLY CAREER PROGRESSION

Assigned within communication field as intercept operator at message centers throughout Canada, maintaining signals collection and dissemination. Performed diverse research and office tasks. Interacted with all rank levels. Progression:

Signals Development Operator—*Vancouver, British Columbia* (1996–1998)
Intercept Operator—*Goose Bay, Labrador* (1996)
Intercept Operator—*Vancouver, British Columbia* (1994–1996)

AWARDS/RECOGNITION

➢ Received numerous Letters of Appreciation for volunteer work.
➢ Earned Top Student Award (Military Training).
➢ Awarded a BZ (Bravo Zulu = tremendous job) from the Processing and Reporting Section for identifying and reporting unique and very important activity.
➢ Received CO's Commendation for performing first aid on Detachment Commander when he was found unconscious and bleeding.

EDUCATION/PROFESSIONAL DEVELOPMENT

Junior Leadership course, *Department of National Defense (DND)*	2009
Basic French course, *DND*, Canadian Second Language Training	2007
Computer courses (Microsoft Office), *Toronto School of Business*	2006
High School Diploma, *Widdifield Secondary School, North Bay, Ontario*	1993

Various military and civilian professional courses including WHMIS Training, First Aid Certification, Assistant Range Safety Officer, Signals Development Operator, and Qualified Instructor.

Marcus L. Valentino

P.O. Box 853198 ▪ San Diego, California 92137
Home: (858) 654-4693 ▪ E-mail: mlvalentino@hotmail.com ▪ Cell: (858) 423-5416

ADMINISTRATIVE MANAGER

**Business Operations ▪ Project Management ▪ Staff Training & Leadership ▪ Program Administration
Process & System Improvements ▪ Event Coordination ▪ Budgeting ▪ Organizational Development**

Twenty-year record of excellence in administrative and executive support in the U.S. Navy. Strong contributions in managing a full scope of support operations in high-profile settings. Exceptional organizational skills and a flair for multi-tasking projects and events. Expert communication skills across diverse groups and at all corporate levels. Reputation for delivering world-class customer care. Top Secret security clearance.

Consistent high achiever who thrives in high-pressure, deadline-sensitive environments that demand a rapid learning curve, resourceful problem solving, and uncompromised integrity.

CAREER OVERVIEW

United States National Support Element, Naples, Italy   **2008–2010**
ADMINISTRATIVE SUPERVISOR / TRAVEL AND BUDGET COORDINATOR

Managed 7 junior administrative and logistics personnel with oversight for support of more than 75 combined military staff across all U.S. military services. Served as travel coordinator for 176 NATO personnel, 300+ international military staff, and family members. Nearly single-handedly managed all aspects of travel, including transportation coordination, orders preparation, and travel claim processing. Administered $200,000+ annual travel budget. Controlled quality assurance and timeliness of administrative actions and processes. Maintained administrative files.

- Recognized as a moving force in the administration department, positively impacting daily operations and influencing process improvements throughout.
- Conducted specialized correspondence training for administrative staff.
- Identified and corrected travel claim discrepancies, resulting in thousands of dollars in cost savings and dramatically improved quality assurance.
- Established detailed guidelines for the travel/budget position, creating repeatable processes for future incumbents.

Commander Fleet Air / Navy Region Europe, Madrid, Spain   **2005–2008**
EXECUTIVE ASSISTANT / DEPARTMENT SUPERVISOR / PROGRAM INSTRUCTOR

Direct assistant to senior executive management, ensuring provision of top-flight administrative and technical support to more than 15,000 personnel spread across 6 international locations. Trained and supervised 45 administrative and program staff. Overhauled entire awards department, creating a sharp, professional office with focus on total customer care.

- Automated process to produce more than 1,500 staff awards with the highest degree of accuracy and timeliness.
- Dramatically increased morale and motivation throughout entire organization as Morale, Welfare, and Recreation President. Built solid foundation for program through functions and fundraisers.
- Built highly successful Fitness Enhancement Program from the ground up. Led more than 80% of program participants to meet stringent standards within 6 months.

U.S. Pacific Fleet, Commander Forces, Alameda, California   **2000–2005**
OFFICE MANAGER / EXECUTIVE ASSISTANT / PROGRAM COORDINATOR

High-level supervisory role in Administration Office that delivered administrative support and customer services to more than 30,000 Navy personnel throughout the West Coast. Trained and supervised 30 administrative personnel. Maintained audiovisual equipment for use in daily operations, training, and conferences. Managed database for certified mail.

- Tracked supply requests for 6 offices and maintained $24,000 annual supply budget.
- Maintained sensitive data for 150 senior managers and ensured accountability of 2,500+ classified documents.
- Single-handedly tracked and distributed 200 pieces of outgoing and incoming mail daily for Pacific Fleet Command, a task formerly handled by 3 people.
- Handpicked to assist in annual inventory of top-secret classified material. Completed inventory with zero discrepancies.
- Flawlessly planned, scheduled, and managed the fleet's first Senior Enlisted Management Conference.

This resume is detail-rich and contains numerous examples of specific contributions the candidate made during a military career in administrative management.

Marcus L. Valentino ▪ Page 2

(858) 654-4693   mlvalentino@hotmail.com

CAREER OVERVIEW, CONTINUED...

USS Abraham Lincoln (CVN 72), Moffat Field, California   **1996–2000**
EXECUTIVE ASSISTANT / DEPARTMENT ADMINISTRATOR / SUPPLY MANAGER

Provided administrative support to approximately 600 officers and 4,400 enlisted personnel. Ensured smooth daily operations of the administration office during a 6-month deployment. Served as direct assistant to top executives. Supervised as many as 8 direct reports; trained 2 junior staff in all facets of the administration office. Administrative authority for training operations, budgets, travel arrangements, personnel awards, communications, and supplies.

- Catalyst for numerous improvements in administrative processes and record levels of productivity.
- Maintained impeccable records and total accountability of the $120,000 annual supply budget.
- Reorganized and updated the training department's entire filing system. Established a quick-access inventory database for confidential executive files.
- Coordinated and processed awards for entire group of 5,000 personnel with zero error rate.
- Cultivated an environment of high morale, team cohesion, and excellent rapport across all levels.
- Prepared 1,300+ sets of cost and no-cost orders during intense in-port and deployed period.

Helicopter Anti-Submarine Squadron Light, Montgomery, Alabama   **1994–1996**
EXECUTIVE ASSISTANT / DEPARTMENT SUPERVISOR / PROGRAM ADMINISTRATOR

Served as executive assistant to the top division executive. Provided administrative support to 145 staff members. Administrator for the training and budget departments with oversight of a $50,000+ budget. Coordinated funding, emergency preparation, transportation, and travel orders. Managed sponsorships, special programs, and fundraisers.

- Built reputation for handling all assigned tasks efficiently and ahead of deadlines.
- Received outstanding grade on training and budget records during a management inspection.
- Orchestrated a highly successful sponsor program that garnered elite Bravo Zulu recognition.
- Participated in the administrative preparation that enabled a flawless change in management.

Patrol Squadron, Montgomery, Alabama   **1990–1994**
JUNIOR ADMINISTRATOR / SYSTEM ADMINISTRATOR

Dual roles in the Administration and Operations Departments. Provided administrative support and customer services to 145 staff at all levels. Operated office equipment, computers, and software programs.

- Stepped into additional role of managing the critical communication/cryptological billet. Pivotal contributor to an exceptionally well-run communications office.
- Garnered praise from several squadron navigators/communicators for efficient preparation of communication boxes and secure handling of classified material.
- Change agent for process improvements that enhanced the tracking of supply part component turn-ins and cut supply issue response time from 65% to 85%.

EDUCATION, TRAINING & AWARDS

Business & Communications Degree Coursework (3 credit hours)—Navy Leadership Course (2006–2008)
Business Management Coursework (15 credits from A.S. Degree)—Mississippi State University
Certification in Administration—Naval Technical Training Center, Meridian, Mississippi

Computer Skills: Expert-level knowledge in Windows, Microsoft Office (Word, Excel, PowerPoint, Access, Outlook), e-mail, Internet research, and scheduling/calendar

Sampling of Special Recognition:

- Unrivaled performance marked by 3 Navy Achievement Medals, 3 Navy Commendation Medals, various letters of commendation and appreciation, verbal accolades, and 2 Military Outstanding Volunteer Service Awards.
- Sustained superior performance recognized with administration department's Employee of the Month award, Employee of the Quarter nomination, and Junior Employee of the Month nomination.

JOSLYN F. TIMBERS   1298 Green Post Lane * Columbia, Maryland 21045
                                          410-765-9034 * jft@yahoo.com

ADMINISTRATIVE MANAGER

Personnel Administration ▪ Employee Development ▪ EEO Compliance ▪ Office Management

Developed, implemented, evaluated, and monitored administrative policies, procedures, and guidelines.
Directed day-to-day administration support operations.
Controlled, trained, tasked, and evaluated large staffs.
Managed budgets, purchasing, and ledgers.

❑ Consistently progressed to more senior positions with consequential responsibility for personnel, budgets, resources, and schedules. Managed budget changes that affected the workforce.

❑ Managed myriad administrative requirements. Coordinated the work of clerical and secretarial staffs required to implement administrative policies, personnel actions, and academic or legal activities.

❑ Contracted for supplies, services, and equipment. Reviewed contract terms to ensure compliance.

❑ Designed and oversaw personnel management information systems.

❑ Rallied team members to reach established goals. Managed planning efforts and organizational structures to support quality control and administrative functions. Established work schedules, assigned tasks, and advised subordinates. Planned, developed, and conducted training.

❑ Analyzed plans to determine the impact on administrative processes and the feasibility of making modifications to accomplish assigned projects.

❑ Tracked and inventoried office equipment; managed and executed a $1 million budget.

❑ Established file systems and filing procedures. Managed and maintained databases.

▪ Liaison & Rapport Building	▪ Supervision & Training
▪ Policies & Procedures Implementation	▪ Project Management
▪ Recruiting & Selection	▪ Oral & Written Communications
▪ Resource Allocation	▪ Interpersonal & Communications Skills
▪ Purchasing & Inventory Management	▪ Employee Development & Training
▪ Contracting & Acquisitions	▪ Employee Relations & EEO Compliance
▪ Budgets & Fiscal Policy Development	▪ Research & Analysis

EMPLOYMENT

United States Army, 1990 to present (available for employment 04/2010), Secret security clearance

Administrative Manager/Personnel Services Supervisor, Italy, 12/2006–present
❑ Supervise an administrative manager and a staff who provide administrative support to more than 3,000 personnel in geographically dispersed offices. Prepare evaluation reports and recommend military awards.
❑ Orchestrate first-rate, monthly newcomer and departures briefings supporting 3,000 personnel.
❑ Serve as point of contact between subordinate units and divisions.

Page 1 of 2

A strong summary highlights both achievements and skills/knowledge. Military job titles have been changed to make them understandable to a nonmilitary audience.

Joslyn F. Timbers, Page 2   410-765-9034 * jft@yahoo.com

Administrative Manager, continued
- ❏ Manage fiscal control of accounting and analysis of financial data for the decision-making process. Review policy to formulate and establish accounting policies and procedures.
- ❏ Work with transportation offices to plan, procure, and coordinate relocating personnel and personal property. Negotiate travel requirements and rates.
- ❏ Evaluate resources and missions to determine organizational effectiveness and efficiencies. Improved the timeliness and effective processing of personnel actions with a 98% success rate.

Senior Executive Assistant, Fort Meade, Maryland, 12/2002–12/2006
- ❏ Promoted over six colleagues to serve as Senior Executive Assistant to the Secretary of the General Staff (SGS). Supervised, trained, and evaluated 22 staff responsible for administration and logistics.
- ❏ Monitored that tasks were completed according to schedule; ensured adequate staffing. Supervised the accountability of 2,000 general office documents with an automated tracking system.
- ❏ Maintained direct oversight and strict accountability of the operational budget worth $2 million.
- ❏ Implemented a rigorous staff training program, increasing personnel proficiency by 25%.
- ❏ Initially took charge of a $1.5 million inventory and property book. Applied sound fiscal policy and supply discipline, and regained accountability for a deficient supply process, recouping $4 million in lost items.

Administrative Manager, 244th Quartermaster BN, Korea, 12/1999–12/2002
- ❏ Managed a personnel operations office supporting personnel actions, awards, and performance evaluations for more than 2,000 personnel.

Postal Operations Supervisor/Post Locator, Hawaii, 12/1996–12/1999
- ❏ Managed postal operations and served as post locator for an installation.

Installation Security Clerk, Department of Plans, Training and Mobilizations, Seattle, Washington, 12/1994–12/1996
- ❏ Processed Top Secret security clearances. Reviewed personnel records for current security clearance level. Initiated new clearances. Fingerprinted applicants and made security photos.

EDUCATION AND PROFESSIONAL DEVELOPMENT

- ❏ 70 credits toward a Bachelor's Degree in HR Administration, 2000, Saint Leo College, Florida
- ❏ Basic Noncommissioned Officers Course, 1999 (Management)
- ❏ Primary Leadership Development Course, 1993

Completed hundreds of hours of training in computer operations, administrative procedures, sexual harassment issues, management and leadership, and personnel operations.

~ Received numerous awards for exemplary performance and professionalism. ~

David Jones

Telephone: (02) 2390 0404
Mobile: 0417 2234 567

20 Sabina Crescent
Williamstown NSW 2314

e-mail: davj@hotmail.com

—Administrative Manager—

QUALIFIED BY

Eight years of service in the Air Force leading to the rank of Corporal with responsibility for supervising technical and customer-service teams from 5 to 25 people. Bachelor of Information Management in Office Management.

KEY COMPETENCIES

• Supervising • Organising • Communicating • Training • Leading Teams
• Analysing • Assessing • Decision Making • Customer Liaison

COMPETENCY AREAS

- Supervision and training of personnel to ensure functional effectiveness
- Organisation of daily operations, including rostering personnel and assigning tasks
- Oral presentations to all levels of management and staff
- Clear and concise instructions to subordinates
- Creation of letters, reports, minutes, and manuals
- Staff performance assessment
- Decision-making in a high-stress environment
- Liaison with external clients, partners, and other stakeholders
- Provision of customer service and resolution of complaints
- Staff training for effective operations in high- or low-tech environments
- Fluency in word-processing packages, spreadsheets, databases, e-mail, and Internet

PERFORMANCE HIGHLIGHTS

- Gained rapid promotion in the Air Force to rank of Corporal after relatively short period, demonstrating high levels of presentation, professionalism, technical competence, and the ability to supervise and lead others.
- Demonstrated commitment to adult learning by achieving high results in a number of University and College units leading to the award of Bachelor of Information Management in Office Management, and maintaining a 100% success record in all training outcomes over the whole period of military service.

EXPERIENCE

Air Surveillance Supervisor: Royal Australian Air Force Base, Williamstown, NSW   2005–current
Air Surveillance Operator: Royal Australian Air Force, Darwin, NT   2001–2005

EDUCATION AND TRAINING

Certificate III in Government: *Canberra Adult Education College, ACT*   2008
Certificate III in Aviation: *Royal Australian Air Force*   2008
Bachelor of Information Management in Office Management: *University of Canberra, ACT*   2004

Experience is presented in general terms to avoid too strong an emphasis on the high-tech environments in which this person worked.

ANDREW T. ROBERTS

1001 Penderbrook Terrace, Fairfax, VA 22030
Mobile: (703) 549-1442, E-mail: atroberts@aol.com

QUALIFICATIONS SUMMARY

Results-oriented manager with 20+ years of international and domestic experience in the fields of finance and information technology (IT). Demonstrated success in directing multimillion-dollar financial systems serving thousands of customers in deadline-focused environments. Skilled at managing an array of IT professionals to provide help-desk services, support network operations, direct enterprise resource management (ERM), maintain Internet and intranet Web servers, and build and configure workstations. Adept at creating strategic and tactical solutions for various IT challenges, having developed and implemented operating policies and procedures throughout the U.S. Navy. **Certified A+ Technician.** Hold **active Top Secret security clearance.**

- AREAS OF EXPERTISE -

- Leadership / Supervision
- Strategic Planning
- Product Development
- Resource Alignment & Utilization

- Financial Systems Operations
- Staff Training & Development
- Technical Communications
- Organizational Partnerships

PROFESSIONAL EXPERIENCE

UNITED STATES NAVY, Washington, DC 1989–Present
Chief, Information Technology (IT) Division (2004–Present)

Supervise 100+ people among 6 teams to provide an extensive range of workstation / network / Web monitoring services to 9,400+ users. Oversee operations of the Headquarters Help Desk to provide user support 5 days per week, 12 hours per day. Conduct annual hardware evaluations to select PC and laptop purchases, amounting to approximately $8 million annually, for internal customers.

Key Achievements

- Guided the division in achieving "the highest customer satisfaction rating to date in government or industry," as evaluated by a performance metrics study.
- Implemented controls to ensure continuous network operation without interruption due to viruses.
- Standardized hardware and software purchases, allowing the help-desk staff to develop extensive expertise for a specific range of products.

Account Representative (Liaison Officer) (2003–2004)

Selected for this newly created position to oversee the support of the customer services infrastructure, which provides decision-support systems to the headquarters staff. Coordinated system changes and upgrades and assessed the impact on 230+ customers.

Key Achievements

- Created a customer support model that was adopted organization-wide.
- Reengineered and implemented a transition network, saving several million dollars and improving the headquarters' support functions.
- Guided an IT team to rapidly develop a testing methodology for all supported software.

- Continued -

Solid management experience and accomplishments in finance and IT are highlighted in this resume. Because the candidate is also considering government positions, his highly desirable security clearance is also featured.

ANDREW T. ROBERTS   Mobile: (703) 549-1442

Chief, Compensation Management, Financial Services Division (FSD), Chicago, IL (2000–2003)

Managed 293 people among 6 divisions to ensure the integrity of 1.3 million pay accounts for active and reserve personnel. Directed all aspects of a $16 billion payroll system.

Key Achievements

- Instituted employee training in Total Quality Management (TQM), forming process action teams that improved communication and morale. FSD was subsequently awarded an Organizational Excellence Award.
- Established an information system (IS) security officer position to increase security and improve the integrity of payroll data.
- Implemented innovative operating procedures that reduced overtime without increasing processing time and resulted in a $12 million refund to the government.

Deputy Finance Manager, Finance Support Unit, Frankfurt, Germany (1998–2000)

Served as the Commander overseeing unit and individual training, supply, morale, discipline, unit administration, and wartime readiness. Provided military pay, travel, disbursal, and banking liaison services to 17,000+ soldiers and civilians.

Chief, System Support, U.S. Navy Information Technology Command, Annapolis, MD (1996–1998)

Developed, maintained, and supported the Standard Financial System, which automated all Navy installation finance and accounting offices, accounts payable (AP), and travel and disbursal activities. Achieved 100% compliance with all configuration management regulations and guidelines.

Previous Professional Experience with the U.S. Navy includes the following:
- **Chief, Plans and Operations,** Software Development Center, Washington, DC 1994–1996
  U.S. Navy IT Command, Annapolis, MD
- **Assistant Finance Officer** 1989–1994
  U.S. Navy, Finance and Accounting Office, Springfield, IL

PROFESSIONAL DEVELOPMENT

Certified A+ Technician 2007
Local Area Networks (LANs) 2004
Introduction to the Internet and Intranets for Business 2004
Labor Relations for Supervisors & Managers 2001

Additional Professional Development includes courses in **systems automation, management, and advanced finance and accounting** at the U.S. Navy Finance School.

EDUCATION

M.S., Information Systems (Cum Laude Graduate), George Mason University, Fairfax, VA 1997
B.S., Business Administration, James Madison University, Harrisonburg, VA 1987

- Page 2 -

Jordan Cravett

548 Jefferson Drive ■ Junction City, KS 66441 ■ (785) 210-3822 ■ jcravett@hotmail.com

FINANCE & OPERATIONS MANAGER

Accomplished professional with strengths in applying knowledge of complex regulations to oversee financial operations. Areas of expertise:

- Cash Controls
- Financial & Operational Audits
- Contract Review & Payments
- Project Planning & Execution

- Financial Administration & Reporting
- Standard Operating Procedure Development
- Training & Development
- Legal & Regulatory Compliance

PROFESSIONAL EXPERIENCE

UNITED STATES ARMY, 1994–Present
Cash Control Officer and Disbursing Agent, Ft. Riley, KS

- Supervise a staff of four employees providing disbursing and funding support to the Combined Joint Civil Military Operations Task Force, as well as cashier support to the U.S. Embassy.
- Analyze all vendor contracts for legal and regulatory compliance, review invoices, approve payments, and issue public vouchers for payment.
- Train, supervise, and direct 90 sub-agents responsible for making local purchases. Advise on legal and regulatory issues, track spending, and prepare expenditure reports.
- Maintain all records, prepare daily reports of all transactions, and arrange for bank transfers to include requesting currencies (U.S. and foreign) and making deposits.

Accomplishments:

- Successfully maintained accountability for $35 million in disbursements in multiple currencies.
- Audited more than 10,000 commercial vendor contracts and paid more than 4,000 contracts.
- Led more than 25 Finance Support Team (FST) missions to three locations in the combat zone.
- Created standard operating procedures for disbursing operations, significantly reducing collection time.

Previous assignments included the following:

Chief Quality Assurance Officer

- Conducted audits to determine the adequacy of existing processes and procedures to preclude fraud, waste, and/or abuse of resources. Presented findings with recommendations to address issues.
- Advised senior managers on financial issues by identifying, interpreting, and presenting regulations relevant to their concerns. Delivered briefings to agents deploying worldwide.

Accomplishments:

- Earned "commendable" ratings on annual inspections.
- Achieved highest ratings for processing accuracy as compared to other finance offices.

Disbursing Agent

- Managed the disbursement and processing of documents worth more than $1.3 million to include approximately $99,000/week in payments, checks, and currency conversions, as well as $80,000/week in contract payments.
- Provided support for more than 6,500 employees. Planned, coordinated, and executed more than 100 pay-support projects.

Accomplishments:

- Maintained an average of 97% for timeliness and accuracy of reports, well above the standard of 90%.
- Designed spreadsheet and work processes to facilitate the exchange of country-specific currency following the introduction of the euro currency.

Disbursing Deputy

- Directed disbursing operations to support 428 employees and maintained accountability for more than $1 million in U.S. and foreign currencies as well as other negotiable instruments. Served as primary advisor to senior managers in regard to accounting policies and procedures. Oversaw the development of two employees.

Accomplishments:

- Initiated an audit of pay accounts and recovered more than $28,000 in overpayments. *(continued)*

Corporate rather than military terms are used throughout to show that this candidate "speaks the language" of his target employers.

Jordan Cravett
(785) 210-3822 ■ jcravett@hotmail.com   page 2

Team Leader
- Managed 20 employees to include planning and coordinating training, conducting performance evaluations, and administering personnel records. Directed the processing of finance documents for 10,000 divisional personnel.

Assistant Comptroller
- Assisted in the planning and execution of a $12 million budget designated for humanitarian relief and reconstruction projects following a natural disaster.
- Advised project managers on the proper and legal use of funds, allocated funds to projects, and provided managers with reports pertaining to their actual expenses as compared to budgeted amounts.
- Maintained fiscal controls by supervising the budget staff, directing the processing of more than 300 commitment documents, and tracking the charge-card program for all assigned personnel.
- Assisted in developing regional strategies and training other agencies regarding budgeting functions for the purpose of supporting interagency operations.

Accomplishments:
- Enhanced research capabilities by maintaining an efficient filing system.
- Instituted clear and concise guidelines to facilitate smooth transitions of staff members.
- Assumed the duties of the Director/Resource Manager in his absence.

Cash Control Officer
- Managed customer service, retirement/separations, and processing sections to ensure accurate, timely support for more than 4,000 personnel. Supervised 15 employees in daily work to include certifying disbursements of more than $120,000/month in multiple currencies.

Accomplishments:
- Reduced document turnaround for pay processing from 10 days to 3 days.
- Led department to reduce governmental debt from more than 13% to 4%.
- Coached two employees to win corporate "Employee of the Quarter" competitions.
- Planned and conducted training that resulted in qualifications of 100% of assigned staff.

EDUCATION

Bachelor of Science in Business Administration, KANSAS STATE UNIVERSITY, Manhattan, KS, 2009
- Major in Management

Associate of General Studies, BARTON COUNTY COMMUNITY COLLEGE, Great Bend, KS, 2004

Additional Training:
- Primary Leadership Development Course
- Equal Opportunity Leadership Course
- Finance/Accounting Advanced Management Course
- Finance/Accounting Midlevel Management Course
- Finance Specialist Course

CHAPTER 5

Resumes for Careers in Technology

- Avionics and Electronics Technicians

- Network Administrators

- Web Developers/Systems Administrators

- IT/Project Managers

- Communications Systems Controllers

- IT/Project Management Directors

In most technology resumes, it is important to spell out specific technology expertise—hardware, software, systems, programming languages, and so forth. In most of the resumes in this chapter, a separate Technology section is included to draw attention to this critical information and make it easy to read in a quick skim. You will see that the writers have used both chronological and functional formats.

NANCY MITCHELL

80 Anderson Drive • Parsippany, NJ 08859 • 732-204-5055 • mitchelln@yahoo.com

AVIONICS AND ELECTRONICS TECHNICIAN / TROUBLESHOOTER

Expert in Flight Deck & Engine Components

- Diagnose faults in signal encryption equipment and transceivers.
- Work well individually or as team member.
- Perform efficiently in fast-paced, high-pressure situations.
- Communicate well in technical and nontechnical environments.
- Supervise, train, and evaluate up to 10 employees.

SKILLS AND EXPERIENCE

AVIATION ELECTRONICS
Repair transmitters, receivers, transmission lines, antennae, and navigation and communication systems.

TECHNICAL REPAIR
Build and fix "cannon" plugs, wire bundles, and coaxial cables.
Solder and crimp connections.

DIAGNOSTICS AND TROUBLESHOOTING
Read and interpret schematics and wiring diagrams.
Detect breaks in wire using Time Domain Reflexometer (TDR).
Operate multimeters and oscilloscopes.

COMMUNICATIONS GEAR
Determine faults in radio equipment.
Encode "scrambling" for secure-voice broadcasting.

PERSONNEL MANAGEMENT
Maintain training records for up to 25 employees.
Oversee operations teams.
Perform human resources functions of first-line supervisor.

EXPERIENCE

U. S. NAVY, NAS Whidbey Island, WA   *2007–2010*
Aviation Electronics Technician, Second Class
- Worked outdoors in severe weather conditions on an airfield.
- Quickly diagnosed and repaired flight-deck problems prior to takeoff.
- Oversaw 10 personnel working in shifts.
- Secret security clearance.

EDUCATION AND TRAINING

KEAN UNIVERSITY OF NEW JERSEY, Union, NJ
B.A. in Psychology, GPA 3.6

NAVAL AIR TACTICAL TRAINING CENTER, Pensacola, FL
Certificate of Completion, Aviation Electronics Technician "A" School

NAVAL AIR STATION WHIDBEY ISLAND, Whidbey Island, WA
EA-6B Electronic Countermeasures Maintenance Technician School
Electrical Connector/Wire Bundle Repair Program • NALCOMIS Maintenance Repair Program
Second Class Petty Officer Leadership Course

COMPUTER SKILLS

Microsoft Word, Excel

Technical and professional skills are showcased at the center of the page to paint a broad picture of this electronics technician's capabilities.

RESUME 10: BY *CJ JOHNSON, JCTC, CHRM, FJST, CCC, MSVA*

John Boyd

135 Professional Drive
Chicago, IL 60605

jboyd@comcast.net
Home (630) 562-9283
Cell (630) 581-2528

PROFESSIONAL OBJECTIVE AND PROFILE

Network Administrator with more than 20 years of increasing responsibilities in technical leadership, computer technology, and business-critical management. Expertise in networking concepts, TCP/IP protocol family, and network security; knowledge of firewall setup and administration, NAT, VPN, bandwidth management, and quality of service. Proven diagnostic abilities with attention to detail and ability to work effectively in a fast-paced environment. Demonstrated abilities to set strategic direction while obtaining superior results.

Seeking a Network Administrator position that will provide a challenging opportunity for significantly contributing to a company's efficiency, organization, innovative product development, growth, and productivity.

TECHNICAL CERTIFICATIONS/SKILLS

A+; Network+; Linux+; LPI; MCSA; CNA
Web Design/Publishing Certification (Dreamweaver)
Hardware, Assembly, Set-up & Troubleshooting
Convergent Technologies Operating System (CTOS) Manager

Windows XP, NT, 2000 Pro, 2000 Server, Vista, 7
NetWare 4.11/5.0/6.0; Exchange Server 5.x; TCP/IP; MS DOS
LAN/WAN, firewall configuration/administration
Excel; Access; Outlook; PowerPoint; Word

SUMMARY OF QUALIFICATIONS

TRACK RECORD OF SUCCESS
Background exemplifies a successful track record of accomplishments throughout career, encompassing positions such as system manager, supervisor, and training and development leader. Professional progression to senior management positions utilizing natural leadership ability, effective interpersonal skills, organization, strategic planning, and project management.

NETWORK ADMINISTRATION
Provided workable and proven solutions to maintain various operating environments. Installed, configured, and maintained the network for military training school resulting in zero classroom downtime for more than 3 years. Proven diagnostic abilities with attention to detail and ability to work effectively and efficiently in a fast-paced environment. Competent and credible authority on establishing procedures, conducting tests to verify that equipment/systems operate correctly, designing and implementing fault-tolerant procedures in the event of hardware/software failure, and designing audit procedures to test the integrity and reliability of networked systems.

PROJECT MANAGEMENT
Successfully managed $3.5 million supply inventory and ship's combined annual budget of more than $600,000. Provided all logistics, including parts issues, contingency purchasing, and emergency field delivery with no measurable losses.

RISK ANALYSIS
Identified potential liabilities in computerized military accounting system training program. Analyzed accuracy, usage feasibility, and deficiencies while providing solutions for obstacles.

LEADERSHIP
Natural leader who received numerous awards for excellence. Motivated and inspired organizations ranging in size from 30 to 4,000 personnel. Effectively guided and directed associates to achieve their highest potential. Encouraged and supported a teamwork environment that resulted in increased efficiency and productivity.

INSTRUCTION
Major contributor to the design and implementation of self-paced curriculum at a military training facility, increasing throughput and retention of more than 150 students per year.

EDUCATION

B.S. Computer Science, Excelsior University   2010
Specialized Associate Degrees: Computer Technology, Cisco, and Linux: Empire College, Santa Rosa, CA   2007–2008

EXPERIENCE

United States Coast Guard   1985–2006
- Supply Officer/Department Head—USCGC BOUTWELL (WHEC-719), Alameda, CA, 2003–2006
- Office Supervisor/Asst. Branch Chief—Maintenance and Logistics Command Pacific, Alameda, CA, 2001–2003
- Instructor—USCG Training Center, Petaluma, CA, 1997–2001

PERSONAL   Currently hold a Secret security clearance; eligible for Top Secret security clearance

To pursue a career unrelated to his military experience as a supply officer, this candidate returned to school and completed a B.S. in computer science. His resume combines educational experiences with transferable skills from his military career.

RESUME 11: BY PETER S. MARX, JCTC

RAYMOND J. JOHNSON

3210 W. Leila Ave.
Tampa, FL 33611

http://www.WebMasterJ.net

818-835-1111
rayjohnson@earthlink.net

OBJECTIVE	Web Developer / System Administrator			

Operating Systems	Solaris, UNIX, Windows NT Server, Windows NT, Windows XP/Vista/7			
Software	Apache	MS Exchange	MS Office	MS IIS
	AltaVista Search	JavaScript	MS Outlook	Perl
	Adobe Photoshop	ColdFusion	MS Access	HTML

EXPERIENCE	U.S. Army, 1991–2010

Web Developer

➢ Supervise 9 Web programmers who administer, operate, and maintain a $4M intranet and database effort.
➢ Provide oversight of 300K documents (28 gigabytes of disk space) on the Web server. Directly maintain more than 25K files, including all ColdFusion files.

- *Consolidated multiple Web servers; cut systems maintenance and support costs by 66% and increased speed of service 38% while saving $55K per year.*
- *Planned and consolidated cutting-edge intranet environment during the first phase of a UNIX-to-Windows transition effort.*
- *Created search capability for more than 1,000 forms and publications on the Web server, saving time and effort in locating data. Awarded the Quality Leadership Team Award for this implementation.*

Systems Administrator

➢ Install new terminals, associated file servers, and application software.
➢ Serve as Systems Security Officer for a worldwide network.
➢ Supervise 7 computer programmers who maintain all automation requirements.
➢ Manage 11 computer technicians in Microcomputer Repair Department. Support a broad range of more than 800 microcomputer systems, LANs, and worldwide networks.
➢ Control and maintain more than $1M in computer parts and equipment and an annual budget above $300K.

- *Selected from many as a member of the Local Area Network install team, which implemented more than 400 LAN accounts during a 3-month period.*
- *Designed and developed programs to improve system security and efficiency. Rewrote the software utilized to grant and revalidate user access to the host computer system.*

EDUCATION / TRAINING

Bachelor of Science in Computer Science, Brown University, Providence, RI, 2006
Associate of Arts in Liberal Arts, Rhode Island College, Warwick, RI, 1990

Sexual Harassment	2010	MS Project	2006
EEO	2009	Internetworking with TCP/IP	2005
Web Site Fundamentals	2008	Supporting MS Windows NT Server	2005
Web Security and Administration	2008	Solaris	2004
JavaScript Fundamentals	2007	Advanced PC Troubleshooting	2004

The section at the top of the resume highlights this individual's tools in a quickly visible presentation. His accomplishments are set off to make them easy to spot. At the top of the page, notice the link to his online portfolio.

Jenna L. Raft

330 W. Mueller Street, Unit 3
Arlington Heights, Illinois 60004
(847) 399-7808 • jlraft@ameritech.net

INFORMATION TECHNOLOGY/PROJECT MANAGEMENT

Confident, dependable, versatile management professional with extensive diverse experiences enhanced by graduate-level studies. Global perspective based upon military assignments and travel abroad. Articulate, sagacious problem solver with superior analytical and communication skills. Organized, meticulous, and methodical: particularly adept at problem identification, research, analysis, and resolution. An innate ability to develop loyal and cohesive staffs dedicated to the task at hand. Well versed in information system implementation methodologies.

COMPETENCIES

- Communication Skills
- Computer Systems
- Human Resources
- Leadership & Supervision
- Operations & Planning
- Organizational Skills
- Project Management
- Staff Coordination
- Time Management

SPECIAL ACHIEVEMENT

Implemented the annual enrollment process for a Fortune 100 client.

COMPUTER SKILLS

- Mainframes, workstations, and personal computers
- Visual Basic, Fortran, and C
- SQL, DB2, JCL, SAS, QMF, UNIX, and Windows
- CASE tools
- Lotus Notes and Microsoft Office applications

PROFESSIONAL EXPERIENCE

Branch Chief, NATIONAL AIR INTELLIGENCE CENTER, Dayton, OH   2007–Present
Branch Chief, PACIFIC METEOROLOGICAL RECONNAISSANCE NETWORK, GUAM   2005–2007
  Successfully streamlined business processes to a manageable structure. Provided counseling, performance reviews, evaluations, process requirements, and follow-up. Responsible for all activities and subordinate personnel.

Project Manager/Officer in Charge, WEATHER SQUADRON (USAF), Shreveport, LA   2003–2005
  Focal point in management was to coordinate plans and simultaneously handle multiple projects, including customer communications and personnel services.

System Analyst, USAFETAC (USAF), Scott AFB, IL   2000–2003
  Originated systems applications from design to creation. Used structured programming language; designed simulation models; produced analytical work. Assisted customers if needed on their system program. Directed full cycle from design to debugging and verification.

Student, AIR FORCE INSTITUTE OF TECHNOLOGY (USAF), St. Louis, MO   1998–2000

EDUCATION

M.B.A. (Management Information Systems)   WRIGHT STATE UNIVERSITY, 1998
B.S. (Meteorology)   NORTHERN ILLINOIS UNIVERSITY, 1993

Technology-related skills and experience are concentrated in this concise resume.

MARK S. WILLIAMS

5204 Buckley Street, Aurora, CO 80013 ~ Home: (303) 555.5555 ~ Cell: (303) 555.5554
Williams29@yahoo.com

COMMUNICATIONS SYSTEMS CONTROLLER

Proven skill in installing, maintaining, and troubleshooting communications systems. Expertise with routers, modems, circuits, and cabling. Ability to manage and motivate cohesive teams and to organize, streamline, and attend to fine details. Talent for working efficiently under pressure and stress in busy atmosphere. Adept at handling confidential information and situations with discretion. Committed to creating atmosphere of exceptional employee morale and superior customer relations. Top Secret security clearance.

PROFESSIONAL EXPERIENCE

UNITED STATES AIR FORCE, Colorado Springs, CO   02/06–present
System Controller

Accountable for ensuring the integrity of communication lines vital to maintaining national defense. Provide expeditious response to troubleshoot and repair communications lines. Direct up to 5 communications personnel. Noted as a skillful and reliable technician with motivational management capabilities and strong ability to anticipate problems and implement timely solutions.

> ➤ Ensured 99% circuit-availability rating for Non-Secure Internet Protocol Router Network (NIPRNet), Secure Internet Protocol Router Network (SIPRNet), Joint Worldwide Intelligence Communications System (JWICS), Video Teleconferencing, and Defense Switched Network for 3,000 users.
> ➤ Completed more than 40 weekly and monthly re-keys, including a highly commended performance for re-keying of SIPRNet circuits and secure trunks with no downtime.
> ➤ Served as team member in installation of SIPRNet circuit for Intelligence Work Center. Created point-to-point circuit through utilization of current supplies, enabling 24-hour combat coverage.
> ➤ Selected as shift supervisor responsible for 5 recruits while deployed for 3 months in Kuwait. Oversaw and maintained communications infrastructure for 45th Air Expeditionary Wing at Kasim Air Base. Installed new NIPRNet circuits, including configuring modems and cables to expand communications capability.
> ➤ Achieved recognition as Airman of the Quarter.
> ➤ Awarded as Honor Graduate from basic training for exemplary physical and written performance.

TECHNICAL SKILLS

TimePlex, IDNX, PSU, SCIS.
Microsoft Windows XP, Vista, 7; Microsoft Office (Word, Excel, PowerPoint, Outlook).

PROFESSIONAL EDUCATION

COLUMBIA COLLEGE, Denver, CO
Bachelor of Arts Degree, Business Administration   G.P.A. 3.85

COMMUNITY COLLEGE OF THE AIR FORCE, Colorado Springs, CO
Associate of Applied Science Degree, Electronic Systems Technology

PROFESSIONAL DEVELOPMENT

Survivable Communications Integration System
Airman Leadership & Drill Course
Communications—Computer Systems Control, Apprentice Course (637 hours)
Multiplexer Operations, Provisions & Maintenance (35 hours)
Telecommunications T-1 Transmission Frame Signaling

This resume focuses on relevant experience and concludes with a strong section on education and professional development.

DAVID SCOTT

62 Beaufort Lane, Philadelphia, PA 19105
(215) 630-5629 • dmscott@google.com

• Career Objective

Director-level position with responsibility for project management in an electronics, telecommunications, or IT company.

• Summary

Twenty-eight years of increasing responsibility in the development, operation, and management of mission-critical technical systems. Consistent professional progression to senior management. Demonstrated success in setting strategic direction with superior results.

• Technical Systems Management

Director of an engineering and support facility serving the western United States, including Alaska and Hawaii; responsible for budget planning and execution, project planning and execution, and life-cycle support for ship- and shore-based communication systems, radio-navigation and sensor systems, and networks and computer systems. Analyzed requirements, set course of action, and prioritized assets to meet organizational goals. Directed workforce of more than 250 (50 office staff and 200 at 4 remote units) and administered an annual budget of more than $17.6 million.

Achievements include the following:
- Replaced aging radio and power systems for the Alaska VHF-FM radio distress system; improved reliability, system coverage, and fuel savings.
- Fielded innovative thin-client computing solution, significantly improving performance for remote access and nonstandard application users.
- Replaced private analog microwave network with $4+ million digital spread spectrum network, completed under budget; state-of-the-art network management tools significantly enhanced supportability, saving about 1 FTE.
- Installed Differential Global Positioning System (DGPS) network; provided significant value-added post-install engineering to stabilize or improve system performance (e.g., post-installation antenna replacements, analysis of antenna guy cable failure, improvement of ground planes).
- Under tight funding and time constraints, planned and executed major communications suite upgrades—e.g., commercial and military satellite communications and associated cryptographic equipment and HF (ham radio) e-mail (a huge morale builder for deployed personnel)—to prepare 2 of our largest vessels to deploy to the Middle East with a Navy battle group.

• Financial Management

Extensive experience in funds management, from project level to enterprise-wide financial management. Planned and executed $17.6 million budget to recapitalize existing communications systems, networks, and other electronic systems; provide customers with new capability; and provide follow-up support.

• Quality Management

Developed division performance plan based upon Baldrige Criteria, developed measurement metrics, set strategies, and directed action resulting in staff being recognized for quality actions in the second year of implementation. Considered a leader in quality planning and execution within my organization.

(continued)

This resume translates 28 years of military experience into corporate language and paints the picture of a candidate who is well qualified for the director-level position he is seeking.

DAVID SCOTT

(215) 630-5629 · dmscott@google.com

· Project Management

Planned and directed many large and small projects involving communications systems, radio-navigation and sensor systems, and network and computer systems.

Achievements include the following:
- Planned and coordinated replacement of obsolete computers and network with PC-based systems and high-speed, scalable network.
- Spearheaded highly visible streamlining initiative that realigned Coast Guard staff in the midwestern U.S., entailing reduction in force, relocation of staff, and realignment of staff (part of much larger reorganization of the entire Coast Guard).
- Planned and executed multiyear project valued at about $1 million/year to replace cabling and phone systems at many Coast Guard ship and shore units throughout the western U.S. and Pacific Rim.
- Developed statements of work for contracts, establishing priorities and level/quality of service for preventive and corrective maintenance of communications, electronic, and IT systems support throughout the western U.S. and Pacific Rim.

· Employment History

2003–Present **Director, Maintenance and Logistics,** Command Pacific, Electronic Systems Division

2002–2003 **Director (Commanding Officer),** Electronic Systems Support Unit, St. Louis, MO

2000–2002 **Director of Telecommunications,** Second Coast Guard District, St. Louis, MO

1997–2000 **Technical Director, Shore Radio Systems,** Electronic Systems Division, Maintenance and Logistics Command Pacific

1994–1997 **Director, Electronic Systems Support Unit,** Alameda, CA

1990–1994 **Technical Director, Electronics Repair and Module Repair Branch,** Coast Guard Supply Center, Brooklyn, NY

1982–1990 **Various assignments:** Basic Coast Guard electronics technician training; two shipboard tours; Coast Guard Officer candidate school; Coast Guard headquarters assignment, and undergraduate electronics training.

· Education and Professional Development

San Diego State University—Major in Electrical Engineering

Various commercial short courses: Microwave Concepts; Time Management; Personnel Procedures for Managers; HF Communications Technology; Antenna Engineering; Modern HF Techniques; High-Impact Public Speaking; Building Effective Teams

· Personal

Currently hold a Secret security clearance, eligible for Top Secret clearance. Completed a successful U.S. Coast Guard career with the rank of Commander.

CHAPTER 6

Resumes for Management and Executive Careers

- Hospitality Managers
- Airport Managers
- Senior Executives (General Management)
- Upper/Middle Management Professionals
- Directors/Vice Presidents
- Chief Operating Officers
- Senior Vice Presidents
- Process Analysts
- Operations Executives

For these individuals seeking a military-to-corporate transition at the senior manager or executive level, accomplishments that would be relevant in the business world form the centerpiece of the resume. The "right" language has been used to communicate measurable results such as cost savings, efficiency increases, and performance improvements. In several cases, job titles have been "translated" into titles that are meaningful to a corporate audience. Most of the resumes in this chapter lead off with a very strong summary that effectively positions the individual for his or her current goal.

MARIA J. KELLY, CHS

916 Patriot Drive
Newport News, Virginia 23602

Home: (757) 872-6054
E-mail: MJKelly@yahoo.com

HOSPITALITY MANAGER
CORPORATE HOUSING INDUSTRY

QUALIFICATIONS SUMMARY

CERTIFIED HOSPITALITY SUPERVISOR with 12-year military career highlighted by increasingly responsible positions in housing, food services, and management. **Strengths:**

- Food Services Operations Management
- Housing Operations Management
- Zumwalt Compliance Standards
- Extensive Travel to Europe and United Arab Emirates
- Staff Development & Training
- Customer Service & Client Relations
- Business-to-Business Marketing
- P & L and Occupancy Goals

PROFESSIONAL EXPERIENCE

Bachelor Housing Manager   2005–Present
CHEATHAM COLONIES, Williamsburg, Virginia, and DAM NECK (FCTC), Virginia Beach, Virginia

Direct the production and control of support services program, managing an operating budget more than $260K and more than 3,065 military and civilian personnel. Train staff on regional standard operating procedures. Negotiate contracts for vendor services. Prepare written reports and deliver oral presentations. Use various methods to conduct business-to-business marketing.

- Navy Achievement Medal for meritorious service as Food Services Department Petty Officer.
- Gold Pineapple Award from the Education Institute of America for Hotel/Motel Management.
- Admiral Zumwalt Award for contributions at Dam Neck Fleet Combat Training Center.

Bakeshop Supervisor   2003–2005
USS *DWIGHT D. EISENHOWER* and USS *THEODORE ROOSEVELT*, Norfolk, Virginia

Managed and trained 10 pastry chefs serving crew of 3,200. Directed bakery production, inventory, equipment, menus, and transactions aboard ship.

- Completed Private Mess Operations/Advanced Food Preparation School. Graduated number 1 of 54.
- Sailor of the Quarter for "outstanding" Physical Readiness Training and Military Bearing.
- Manager comments: "Outstanding Petty Officer who always achieves divisional and command goals."

Bakeshop Watch Captain   2000–2003
U.S. NAVY HOSPITAL, Camp Lejeune, North Carolina

Supervised 1 bakeshop supervisor and 9 support personnel. Trained culinary specialists on bakeshop techniques and procedures. Directed all orders, supplies, and issues of subsistence product from the nutrition management department. Conducted orientation for new facility residents.

- Navy Achievement Medal for revising inventory control measures resulting in cost savings of $35,000.
- Numerous Letters of Commendation and Good Conduct Awards for excellent teamwork.
- Recognized for successfully performing duties of every position reporting to Watch Captain.

EDUCATION

Certified Hospitality Supervisor (CHS) program, certificate awarded 2008
AMERICAN HOTEL AND LODGING ASSOCIATION, Educational Institute

Translating military experience to civilian language was the primary challenge in this resume for a hospitality manager. A traditional chronological format is enhanced by a strong summary.

JONATHAN R. MILES

265 Charlotte Street • Asheville, NC 28801 • (828) 254-7893 • jrmiles@aol.com

HOSPITALITY MANAGEMENT

Food Service Management • Financial Management • Facility Management • Personnel Training & Supervision
Budget Forecasting & Control • Purchasing & Inventory Management • Cost Control
Retail Sales • Food Preparation & Presentation • Menu Development
Customer Service & Guest Relations • Regulatory Compliance

Twenty years of management experience in food service and financial arenas of hospitality industry. Consistently meet budgets of up to $250,000 at or under forecast. Inventory control held to high standard of responsibility with 100% validity. Certified instructor in food production, cake decorating, baking, sanitation, sexual harassment, equal opportunity, Total Quality Management, and rodent and pest control. Skilled in cake decorating and ice carving. Stickler for details.

MAJOR ACCOMPLISHMENTS

- Nominated for Navy's highest award in food service.
- Named Sailor of the Year 2000 for outstanding performance as Kitchen and Officer Dining Manager.
- Awarded Navy Achievement Medal for reengineering dining facilities and achieving positive cash flow.
- Nominated as one of top 3 dining facilities of Atlantic Fleet in 2004 as result of outstanding customer satisfaction.
- Directly responsible for achieving first-time profit ($17,000) for "open-mess" (subsists on own profits) dining facility.
- Significantly upgraded an already high level of cleanliness, scoring 98% on Sanitation scores (norms are 70%–80%).
- Nominated for 2004 Ney Memorial Award for audit techniques and implementation of new procedures that improved grades on weekly sanitation inspection from 86% to 96%.
- Received Humanitarian Medal for assistance during Hurricane Katrina.

HIGHLIGHTS OF PROFESSIONAL EXPERIENCE

UNITED STATES NAVY • 1990–2010

Food Service Manager • *Resolute* AFDM-10 • 2009–2010
7 cooks, 10 food service workers serving crew of 600 on repair ship for submarines.
- Wrote 5-week-cycle menu; ensured regulatory compliance ("State Inspection Ready"); managed procurement and cost control with an average yearly budget of $200,000.
- Delivered training classes on food production, sanitation, sexual harassment, equal opportunity, and Total Quality Management.

Financial Records Accountant • USS *Asheville* submarine • 2005–2009
4 cooks and 5 food service workers serving 155 crew members.
- Maintained financial records on annual budget of $175,000 and cost control on all food items.
- Supervised and trained personnel on sanitation, food production, cake decorating, and baking.

Food Service Manager/Financial Manager • USS *Nevada* submarine • 2001–2004
11 food production workers serving 155 crew members.
- Directed inventory control of all food service products with 100% validity.
- Trained all incoming personnel (sanitation, food production).
- Managed annual budget of $180,000.

—Continued—

The success secret for this resume was using common language to describe highly relevant hospitality experience earned while in the Navy.

JONATHAN R. MILES
(828) 254-7893 • jrmiles@aol.com

Page 2

Kitchen Manager/Officer Dining Manager • USS *New York* submarine • 1999–2001
Full meals for 150-man crew 3 times a day on fast-attack submarine with meat cookery, vegetable preparation, baking, and cake decorating areas.
- Supervised 2 waiters in officers' dining facility with emphasis on proper table settings and serving techniques.
- Planned, prepared, and served dinner for commander of submarine force, U.S. Atlantic Fleet (highest-ranking officer in Navy).
- Dramatically increased effectiveness of junior personnel through individualized hands-on training.

Resident Manager • Naval Supply School • 1996–1998
200-unit complex, staff of 13 custodial personnel.
- Forecast and maintained yearly budget of $250,000, including linen service and furniture procurement (which was rotated regularly). Trained and supervised custodial staff.
- Maintained reservation desk for up to 1 year advance notice.

TRAINING & CERTIFICATION

Completed hundreds of hours of professional training, seminars, and workshops throughout career. A brief listing includes
- Nutrition & Menu Planning, 2005
- Hotel/Motel Management (3 months), 2006
- Financial Accounting, 2006, 2008
- Sanitation Instructor, 2008
- Organization Assessment Team/Organization Training Team, 2008
- Rodent & Pest Control Instructor, 2009
- Emergency Medical Technician, 2010

RESUME 17: BY PETER S. MARX, JCTC

Sandra McIntyre

813-595-1234	178 Westchase Lane, Tampa, FL 33569	sandymac@gmail.com

OBJECTIVE   Airport Manager for Lakeland County, Florida

EXPERIENCE   Airfield Manager, U.S. Air Force, 1990–2010

- Plan, direct, supervise, and perform airfield management functions and activities.
- Ensure compliance with Federal Aviation Administration policies and directives.
- Develop and coordinate operating instructions and letters of agreement.
- Conduct daily airfield inspections, impose airfield restrictions, disseminate information, and coordinate corrective actions with operations and maintenance departments.
- Manage and control facilities, state-of-the-art computer equipment, UHF and VHF radio communications, and BASH equipment.
- Coordinate with air traffic control, civil engineers, and operations personnel to ensure support of airfield management activities.
- Supervise 17 airfield management personnel.
- Responsible for maintaining a safe and efficient airfield capable of supporting the largest aircraft in the Air Force inventory.
- Bilingual English / Spanish.

PROFESSIONAL ACCOMPLISHMENTS

- Reduced airfield waivers by 40%, creating a much safer flying environment.
- Developed a comprehensive Flight Line Driver's Training Program.
- Received a Meritorious Service Medal for expediting a two-week runway repair project in four days.
- Earned an Air Force Commendation Medal for correcting airfield operating deficiencies.
- Received a Service Commendation Medal for recognizing and correcting airfield safety hazards.
- Corrected serious problems with airfield markings, lighting, and signs, improving overall safety.

ACADEMIC

Bachelor of Aeronautical Science, Embry-Riddle Aeronautical University, 2007

Associate of Applied Science in Airport Resource Management
Embry-Riddle Aeronautical University, 2001

Associate of Applied Science in Maintenance Production Management
Community College of the Air Force, 1996

PROFESSIONAL TRAINING

MAC C2 IPS Operator, Aircraft Tracking	2001	Supervisor Leadership and Management	1997
Maintenance Scheduling Technician	2000	Human Resources Management	1994
Supervisor Orientation	1999	Maintenance Scheduling Specialist	1993
Personnel Supervisor Course	1997	EEO and Sexual Harassment Briefings	Annual

This person's military position was the exact equivalent of her civilian target, so all that was needed was to "demilitarize" the language used in the resume.

JAMES BARNES

166 Ortley Road • Denver, NC 28037 • (704) 483-0500 Home • (704) 902-9501 Cell • jbarnes@charter.net

SENIOR EXECUTIVE

Results-oriented executive practiced in providing vision, strategy, and innovative ideas to complex operations. Skilled in coordinating the efforts of multiple cross-functional teams. Demonstrated ability to deliver under pressure and produce desired results. Former carrier pilot noted for exceptional communication and people skills, leadership, moral character, integrity, and grit.

**Strategic Vision – Logistics – Planning – Complex Scheduling
Air Transportation – Safety – Employee Development**

PROFESSIONAL EXPERIENCE

UNITED STATES MILITARY OFFICER   1993–2010
U.S. NAVY/ U.S. MARINE CORPS

Loyal, dedicated, and professional leader consistently recognized for superior performance. Notable positions include the following:

STRIKE OPERATIONS ✦ USS *NIMITZ* ✦ 2008–2010

- Composed and coordinated the carrier's daily schedule of operations during around-the-world deployment, including 4 months in the Persian Gulf in support of Operation Iraqi Freedom.
- Coordinated all operational missions with U.S. Air Force, Coalition Forces, and other Navy ships and commands in Iraqi theater of operations.
- Recognized for the successful completion of more than 17,000 accident-free flight hours and 8,000 carrier landings, with no loss of life or international/diplomatic incidents. Received Navy Commendation medal for contribution to missions.

AIRWING OPERATIONS DEPARTMENT HEAD ✦ 2006–2008

- Accountable for all airwing flight and training operations for 3,000+ base personnel in support of the production of carrier pilots for the U.S. Navy and Marine Corps.
- Managed multimillion-dollar budgets, schedules, planning, and production for 7 departments and 175 jet aircraft.
- Coordinated all civic and military operations with the local community, FAA, USAF, and multiple Navy commands, including the President of the United States and congressional delegations.
- Received Navy Commendation Medal from the Chief of Naval Training for exceptional managerial, leadership, and administrative contributions during tenure as operations officer.

TRAINING SQUADRON OPERATIONS MANAGEMENT ✦ 2001–2005

- Led 500+ personnel in all aspects of production and training of 180+ advanced jet Navy carrier pilots per year.
- Managed more than 28,000 accident- and incident-free flight hours, 22,200 sorties, and 1,780 carrier landings per year.
- Planned, managed, and executed several highly successful detachments throughout the U.S. and several aircraft carriers to meet Navy student pilot production crisis ahead of schedule.
- Received Navy Achievement Medal from Commander of Naval Air Training for leadership and management abilities.

EDUCATION

**MBA, Business ✦ Summa Cum Laude ✦ New Hampshire College
BBA, Business Management ✦ Morehead State University**

Military experience is recast into executive-level management abilities; just the highlights are included in this concise resume.

MATTHEW O'DOUL

260 South Finch Road
Glendale, WI 53217
414-228-7284
matthewodoul@worldnet.att.net

SUMMARY OF QUALIFICATIONS

Seasoned *upper/middle management professional* with 20+ years of experience. Recipient of many management and leadership awards through the United States Armed Forces. Skilled in long-term planning, multimillion-dollar budgeting, contract administration, public relations, international relations, special operations, and crisis management. Master of Science in Management.

SUMMARY OF ACHIEVEMENTS

- Productively initiated and monitored long-range planning and multimillion-dollar budgets for day-to-day and special operations, including purchasing, strategizing, relocating, and training.
- Efficiently administered internal controls for 40 facilities and personnel.
- Successfully directed the hiring, training, and management of 200+ civilian and military staff (including officers and recruiters).
- Effectively planned, coordinated, and implemented quarterly media campaigns for recruitment.
- Selected and authorized to perform staff studies for approval by the Secretary of Defense and Chairman of the Joint Chiefs of Staff.
- Chosen to provide independent support to multiple governmental interagencies for special projects in coordination with several departments within the Pentagon and Washington, DC, area.
- Achieved cultural awareness through multiple international tours of duty and life in Germany, Lebanon, and Haiti.
- Recipient of numerous management and leadership awards and the following: Joint Meritorious Service, Army Meritorious Service, and Army and Joint Service Commendation and Achievement medals.
- Attained Master of Science, Bachelor of Arts, and Associate of Arts while working full-time.
- Developed computer proficiency and a working knowledge of German language.

OPERATIONS/ADMINISTRATION

Human Resources: Provide final interviews and decision making for hiring civilians (one-third of staff annually) throughout the year. Establish training programs, ensure standards are met, determine training sites (in-house or off-site), and monitor same.

Budget Management: Establish and monitor $1.6M annual budget (excluding payroll) for training, equipment, supplies, transportation, and daily operations. Generate long-range planning two to three quarters in advance and execute same. Supervise executive officer in charge of purchasing. Administer all internal controls for 41 facilities and personnel.

Public Relations: Coordinate advertising and public relations with staff to include print, Internet, radio, and television. Plan and execute quarterly media campaign. Speak to business organizations, colleges, high schools, veterans' groups, Chambers of Commerce, etc.

Page 1 of 2

A strong introduction and summary of achievements precede functional headings that relate to different areas of executive management.

MATTHEW O'DOUL   Page 2 of 2

414-228-7284   matthewodoul@worldnet.att.net

INTERNATIONAL RELATIONS

Europe: Accountable for selected Secretary of Defense–approved special operations activities in locations throughout Europe, including NATO and former Warsaw Pact countries, as well as security operations for special events.

Iraq: Commanded units performing peacekeeping functions and helping to stabilize new government.

Africa: Integrated, synchronized, and developed staff of 50+ to support deployment of an isolated support group of 350 for crisis intervention and joint training with numerous African nations. Staff managed personnel, intelligence, training, maintenance, medical, and logistics within a $2M annual budget. Also commanded unit of 100, and prepared for contingencies, crisis intervention, and training for 15 African nations.

Kosovo: Commanded unit in this region during the crisis years.

CIVILIAN EDUCATION

Cramer University, St. Belling, MO   **MASTER OF SCIENCE—MANAGEMENT:** 1999
Franklin State College, Cherry Hill, NJ   **BACHELOR OF ARTS—HISTORY:** 1992

MILITARY EDUCATION

Armed Forces Staff College, Newton, VA   **COMPLETED:** 2003
Command and General Staff College, Fort Leavenworth, KS   **COMPLETED:** 1999
Numerous Military Schools   Pre-1995

MILITARY SERVICE

United States Army (1981–Present)
LIEUTENANT COLONEL—O/5
- **Recruiting Battalion Commander (Regional Manager)—Regular Army and Reserves— State of Wisconsin and Upper Peninsula of Michigan** (2004–Present)
- **Operations Officer for Chairman of Joint Chiefs of Staff—Pentagon** (2002–2004)
- **Commander—Special Forces Command—NC** (1999–2002)
- **Scenario Developer/Warfighter Exercise Controller—Battle Command Training Center— Fort Leavenworth, KS** (1997–1999)
- **Operations Officer/Observer Controller—Joint Readiness Training Center—Fort Chafee, AK** (1995–1997)
- **Pre-1995:** Enlisted in the Army in 1981, progressed to commissioned officer and received promotions regularly thereafter. Commanded special forces and infantry units, attended numerous military schools, and was stationed in Europe and various states.

RESUME 20: BY ABBY LOCKE, MRW, NCRW, ACRW

MICHAEL J. TRAVIS

2904 Glen Burnie Road, Baltimore, MD 21209 ▶ Phone: 410-295-0912 ▶ Email: michael.travis@comcast.net

SENIOR OPERATIONS MANAGEMENT
Director / Vice President

Forward-thinking operations executive with 15-year record of enhancing processes and driving internal improvements that ensure high quality and strong customer satisfaction. Consummate leader able to establish vision, strategy, and execution of long-term / short-term objectives for complex, evolving environments. Exceptional communicator and negotiator with success leading cross-functional teams through high-level, critical projects. Expert in business planning, resources maximization, financial / budget management, and staff development. Competencies include the following:

Strategic Planning, Vision & Direction ▶ Revenue & Profit Growth ▶ Tactical Planning & Operations
Cross-Functional Team Building & Leadership ▶ Contract Negotiations & Agreements
Financial Management & Budget Administration ▶ Productivity, Process & Efficiency Improvements
New Program Development & Execution ▶ Strategic Partnerships & Alliances

OPERATIONS MANAGEMENT & LEADERSHIP EXPERIENCE

INSTRUCTOR—U.S. Naval Academy, Annapolis, MD   2007 to 2010

Led project planning and management efforts for local governments, federal agencies, nonprofit entities, and private companies (engaging student input and expertise) in areas of oceanic engineering and research. Interfaced directly with government representatives and other key decision makers to conceptualize solutions that maximize students' capabilities and limited project budgets.

Strategic Impact & Performance:

- **Project Planning & Implementation:** Provided strategic guidance and direction in engineering and systems planning, decision making, and problem resolution for students assigned to 18 projects.

DIRECTOR, Civil-Military Operation—Combined Joint Task Force Eastern European Operations, Pristina, Kosovo   2007

Drove strategic direction, operational planning, and project management activities for 100+ human assistance projects—building schools, clinics, water supply sources, and medical services—in several Eastern European countries in a six-month special assignment. Collaborated with local government, embassy, and national government officials and managed cross-functional team on all projects. Administered $10 million budget.

Strategic Impact & Performance:

- **Financial Solutions:** Secured $750,000 in project funding for special operations facilities through delivery of well-articulated and documented statement of need—cementing significant success where others had failed in previous three years. Designed, engineered, and managed complete construction in five-month period.

- **Relationship Management:** Transformed the Project Review Board into a highly effective, efficient working group by consistently promoting team cooperation, consensus building, and collaboration.

OPERATIONS MANAGER—Navy Public Works Center, Norfolk, VA   2005 to 2007

Revamped and transformed organization plagued with heavy customer complaints, inefficient workflows, and poor financial tracking. Assumed leadership of Public Works Center delivering $250 million a year in facilities maintenance, repair, utilities, transportation, and construction services to 200+ clients in 10 military locations. Managed waterfront construction and renovation for local counties / municipalities and supervised 250 management and direct-labor production employees.

Strategic Impact & Performance:

- **Strategic Planning & Direction:** Executed cost-effective reorganization plan that included new staff training, revised job descriptions, ISO 9000 certifications, and union agreements during 18-month period.

- **Operations / Project Management:** Employed innovative strategies for $1 million renovation of the Norfolk air terminal through expert coordination and astute negotiations with contractors and government workers. Completed project within strict funding / statutory constraints and achieved / surpassed all customer requirements.

▶ continued ▶

Crisp and easily scannable despite being packed full of information, this resume positions Michael as a top-notch operations executive with a wealth of measurable accomplishments and is presented in high-impact corporate language.

MICHAEL J. TRAVIS ▶ PAGE TWO　　　　　　Phone: 410-295-0912 ▶ Email: michael.travis@comcast.net

Public Works Manager / Contracting Manager—Naval Station Pearl Harbor, Honolulu, HI　　　　2003 to 2005

Directed and managed the delivery of $25 million per year in facilities maintenance, repair, transportation, construction, and environmental services to more than 1,000 research engineers, military staff, and residents. Supervised and led 75 management and production employees.

Strategic Impact & Performance:

- **Technology Integration:** Improved problem resolution and decreased operating costs by introducing new state-of-the-art facilities and personnel software systems that automated manual, paper-driven processes.
- **Facilities Planning:** Enhanced the design and construction of four publicly funded construction projects by spearheading comprehensive, $70 million facilities recapitalization program.
- **Cost Containment:** Identified cost-saving solutions by advocating energy conservation methods, alternate environmental resources, and expanded project funding for facilities and installation issues.
- **High-Level Communications & Negotiations:** Achieved amicable relationships and met compliance with the Native Hawaiian Graves Protection Act by managing highly tense, sensitive meetings and negotiations with local groups. Overcame significant friction and animosity and subsequently forged positive working alliances.

Enrolled as full-time graduate student at University of Maryland, College Park, MD　　　　2001 to 2003

Assistant Public Works Manager—Naval War College, Newport, RI　　　　2000 to 2001

Directed program activities and related assignments for $35 million per year facilities maintenance and repair program that supported 2,200+ housing units. Managed entire housing operation, including supervision of 240 employees and implementation of critical housing renovation projects.

Strategic Impact & Performance:

- **Operational Planning:** Conceptualized and developed a five-year strategic plan for facilities management including long-term maintenance, recapitalization, space utilization, and minimization planning.
- **Public-Private Partnerships:** Developed a joint public/private venture program—including business plan and real estate transfer concepts—to outsource housing management for all units and improve operational efficiency.
- **Customer Relationship Management:** Generated unprecedented level of customer satisfaction, decreased customer complaints, and expedited customer requests by implementing improvements in housing management practices.
- **Engineering Solutions:** Garnered more than $800,000 to fund research and training facilities for special operations personnel in the wake of 9/11 attack. Expedited project life cycle and lowered project development costs through frequent contact and liaisons with congressional staff and local government contractors.

Held series of construction management positions in overseas locations leading construction and renovation projects with more than 130 employees and valued up to $47 million.

Construction Manager—Special Detail, Djibouti, Africa　　　　1998 to 2000
Construction Manager—Zaragoza, Spain　　　　1997 to 1998
Assistant Construction Manager—Sasebo, Japan　　　　1995 to 1997

EDUCATION & CERTIFICATIONS

MS—Civil Engineering, University of Maryland, College Park, MD (2003)
BS—Systems Engineering, U.S. Naval Academy, Annapolis, MD (1994)

Government Contracting Officer: Construction Contracting ACQ Level 2
Professional Engineer, State of Maryland (Civil License #12345)

RESUME 21: BY ARNOLD BOLDT, CPRW, JCTC

GEORGE E. WARREN
3613 Culver Road
Erie, Pennsylvania 16567
814-544-9769 • gwarren@earthlink.net

CHIEF OPERATING OFFICER / SENIOR MANAGER / OPERATIONS MANAGER

Demonstrated success directing operations, finance, purchasing, logistics, facilities, human resources/employee development, and public relations functions for organizations with up to 2,300 employees and multimillion-dollar operating budgets. Experience establishing vision and outlining strategies for achieving organizational mission and day-to-day objectives. Strong capacity to foster teamwork environments, motivate team members to achieve organizational goals, and manage cross-functional teams.

Extensive experience developing and administering training programs for federal, state, and local agencies and functioning as liaison between various government and military operating entities. Former officer, U.S. Army Reserves, with current Top Secret security clearance.

PROFESSIONAL EXPERIENCE

DEPARTMENT OF THE ARMY—PENNSYLVANIA ARMY RESERVES NATIONAL GUARD HQ
Chief of Staff / Intelligence Security Officer / Finance Officer / Training Officer   1980–2010
(Lt. Colonel, U.S. Army Reserves)

Fulfilled various senior management roles, reporting directly to the Adjutant General (chief executive) for Pennsylvania Army Reserves National Guard. Accountable for training and readiness of 2,300 personnel, as well as preparedness of facilities and equipment, for remote deployments and support of federal and state law-enforcement initiatives.

- Designed and managed training programs to meet the needs of multiple agencies, including FBI, DEA, U.S. Marshals, Pennsylvania State Police, Philadelphia Police Department, and County Sheriff's offices statewide. These programs prepared law-enforcement officers at all levels for joint operations targeting drug enforcement as part of national "War on Drugs" initiative.

- Briefed civilian authorities on operations and management issues.

- Coordinated the allocation and deployment of equipment to support federal, state, and local law-enforcement agencies.

- Made recommendations regarding allocation of more than $1 billion in assets seized from drug suspects.

- Coordinated support of civilian agencies in response to natural disasters, civil disturbances, and domestic security issues.

- Managed the preparation and deployment of units in support of NATO exercises in Europe. Coordinated movement of equipment and personnel and ensured quality of unit performance.

- Co-founded and served as Commandant of statewide Corps of Cadets Program for youth at risk. Served as Deputy Commandant of Keystone State Military Academy for training military officers.

- Planned and implemented safety and security programs for reserve, active-duty, and civilian personnel at U.S. Army facilities across Pennsylvania.

Continued

The summary section describes capabilities using terminology that resonates with a business audience, even though the experience was acquired in a military context.

George E. Warren

Resume—Page Two

814-544-9769 • gwarren@earthlink.net

ADDITIONAL EXPERIENCE

U.S. DEFENSE SECURITY SERVICE
Investigator (Contractor)   2008–2010

Conducted thorough background investigations of individuals who were required to have security clearances in order to perform their job functions. Checked criminal records and credit reports, interviewed acquaintances, and interviewed applicants to develop information relevant to the awarding of security clearances.

Independent consultant to various local and state law enforcement agencies in northwestern Pennsylvania. Provide technical advice to Erie County Sheriff's Office and City of Erie Police Department on drug interdiction, counterterrorism, and civil defense issues.

Conducted insurance fraud, arson, and accident investigations for private attorneys in conjunction with personal injury and liability cases.

Additional experience teaching and coaching in a public high school setting.

EDUCATION

U.S. Army Command & General Staff College (Honor Graduate)
Advanced management training comparable to Master of Science degree in a civilian setting

Niagara University / State University of New York at Buffalo
Graduate-level study in education

Bachelor of Science, Education
Mercyhurst College, Erie, Pennsylvania

Keystone State Military Academy
Officer Candidate School graduate

Extensive leadership and management training through U.S. Army, U.S. Air Force, FBI, State of Pennsylvania, and other state and local agencies.

RESUME 22: BY DON ORLANDO, MBA, CPRW, JCTC, CCM, CCMC

William C. Cross, Jr.

720 Inner Circle   wccross@aol.com   [334] 953-5555 (Office)
Maxwell Air Force Base, AL 36113   [334] 264-4444 (Home)

WHAT I CAN BRING TO THE **ORION COMPANY** AS YOUR **SENIOR VICE PRESIDENT**:

✧ **Skill** to meet your customers' toughest demands,

✧ **Intelligence** to translate ideas into tangible payoffs, and

✧ **Experience** to transform diverse people into capable teams.

RECENT WORK HISTORY WITH EXAMPLES OF SUCCESS:

✧ _Promoted to_ **Director of Staff,** Air University, Maxwell Air Force Base, AL (2007–Present). _Air University awards degrees from A.A. to Ph.D. in engineering, acquisition, and logistics. AU is the sole source for guiding how every employee is given key professional competencies and leadership tools they need for the Air Force to do its job. AU's 8,500 employees produce more than 400,000 students annually. Budget: $250 million._

  ✧ Inherited problem that kept staff from fully serving customers and added costs no one could afford. Redesigned training for many key managers. Distilled key facts from mountains of data. _Payoffs:_ **Customers happy.** The **$3.5 million saved** here **boosted productivity** in other programs.

  ✧ Found a better way to gather, transmit, and act on information that drives lead product. Optimized how organization manages expensive "consultants," educates and houses 30,000 students a year, and keeps schools at peak production—without losing quality. _Payoffs:_ In 90 days, **costs fell 25%** ($1.4 million) in contract housing alone. Benefits of new system being realized across the organization.

  ✧ Got machines working for people. Made—and kept—a dozen LANs compatible. This new, powerful computer capability gets better products to customers around the world faster. _Payoffs:_ **Nine executives freed** to solve the problems they were hired to solve. Replaced millions of pages of products with CDs that **cost 95% less.**

✧ _Promoted to_ **Chief Operating Officer,** Air Force ROTC, Maxwell Air Force Base, AL (2003–2007). _AFROTC recruits 2,000 new managers a year. Its 144 locations support 800 college campuses._

  ✧ Got needed ROI to continue a program that was not fulfilling its potential. Redefined program objectives, and then let employees meet them. _Payoffs:_ **ROI improved in 30 days.** Met targets fully for three years thereafter. **Market** outlets more than **doubled.** No increase in costs.

  ✧ Implemented ways to cut production costs, stay competitive, _and_ meet the customer's high quality standards. Guided teams that found how to measure ROI and redistribute costs. _Payoffs:_ **Saved $2.5 million** annually. **Production up 50%.**

More indicators of performance Orion can use →

This resume was designed to show the candidate's capability as a proven leader in terms that other senior executives—most with no experience in the military—would value.

William Cross   [334] 953-5555
Senior VP

✧ *Promoted to* **Special Assistant to the Senior Vice President for Plans and Programs,** *promoted to* **Senior Strategic and Policy Advisor to the CEO,** Headquarters, Air Combat Command, Langley Air Force Base, VA (2001–2003). *Air Combat Command is the largest operational organization in the Air Force with 180,000 employees worldwide.*

  ✧ Led potentially "hostile" takeover of another organization's division—from my first day on the job. Found the "hidden assets." Planned transition of 1,300 jobs. Assimilated corporate headquarters and 12 operating locations worldwide. *Payoffs:* Smooth, **on-budget transition** in 100 days. Dissatisfied customers became strong supporters.

  ✧ Chosen by CEO to answer this question: Which problems must we solve to meet our mission? Analysis experts with better tools searched for the answer for 18 months, but missed the mark. I found just the right people. Brought key issues into sharp focus. *Payoffs:* In three weeks, our efforts started **sharpening organizational focus, shaping funding and personnel issues** at very high levels.

✧ *Promoted to* Deputy Commander for Maintenance **(Vice President for Production),** *promoted to* Vice Commander **(Executive Vice President),** 379th Bomb Wing, Wurtsmith Air Force Base, MI (1999–2001). *Senior leader for 3,800 employees (800 civilians). Operating budget: $200 million.*

  ✧ Promised to meet customer's toughest demand: Increase production by 150% indefinitely—even though I was new in the job. Helped my people reengineer the old way of doing things. *Payoffs:* Met demand so well that we outstripped supplier's ability to deliver resources!

RELEVANT EDUCATION

✧ M.A., **Administration** (concentration in **Management**), Georgia College, Milledgeville, GA, **GPA 3.9.** *Earned while working 55 hours per week and carrying academic load at night (1990).*

RECENT TRAINING

✧ "Sensitivity and EEO," annually, latest course completed in 2009

✧ "Metrics and Data as Tools and Techniques for Senior Leaders," 2008

✧ "Senior Leaders' Management Course (TQM)," 2005

AWARDS AND HONORS

✧ Recognized for advanced project management support of Desert Storm (1991).

2

RESUME 23: BY DIANE BURNS, CPRW, CCM, IJCTC, FJST, CCMC, CEIP

JOHN M. SMYTHE

1234 Trout Pond Way
Elkridge, MD 21045

310.295.4681
johnms@hotmail.com

EXECUTIVE-LEVEL OPERATIONS MANAGER / PROCESS ANALYST
Project Management · Training · Business Development · IT Solutions

PROFESSIONAL & PERSONAL VALUE OFFERED

Optimize investments with effective business and operational solutions. Provide functional guidance on multifaceted projects through competencies as skilled business analyst, processes planner, and technical expert. Conduct advanced and complex systematic reviews to formulate and execute business strategies, reducing risk and enhancing customer satisfaction.

- Offer a broad range of technical proficiency; consistently successful at furnishing complete operational or organizational solutions through the definition of customer requirements and design of training programs. Consistently demonstrate strong interpersonal skills.

- Analyze operations, identify and report trends, determine solutions, make viable recommendations, and implement strategies to achieve organizational objectives, correct or streamline activities, and promote improvements in programs, policies, methods, procedures, systems, or techniques.

- Assemble and build talented teams, promote consensus, and establish a comfortable working environment conducive to optimum production. Determine manpower and resource needs.

PROFESSIONAL EXPERIENCE

U.S. Army Reserves, Active Duty, Senior Officer (Colonel) / SECRET Clearance
"His ability to synthesize complex training issues that have no clear solution is second to none." — Performance evaluation

Senior Liaison and Readiness Officer, Regional Support Command, Fort Meade, MD　　　2006–present
Equivalent to Executive 1st Vice President of a large company or medium-size city government

- The organization oversees a 6-state area with 6,500 employees and manages all budgetary, engineering, training, personnel management, risk assessment, safety, and logistical support for 4,500 military personnel deployed to Afghanistan. Strategic planner for complex logistical requirements.

- Upon reporting to this new position, quickly and resourcefully undertook the challenge of upgrading the organization from the lowest position in readiness for 11 similar organizations to the 4th position in 6 months, a significant accomplishment recognized by senior management. The future goal is to raise the organization to the 1st position in the next year.

- Devised and implemented a program providing "measurement indicators" of success for subordinate organizations, arming the CEO with a tool to measure the effectiveness of the organization.

Director, Plans and Operations, Area Support Group, Atlanta, GA　　　2001–2006
Equivalent to Operations Director/Comptroller of a large company or medium-size city government

- Directed and monitored all areas of operations, mobilization planning, and training. Developed and justified the organization-wide budget and designed an effective budget tracking system.

- Created an organization career specialty matrix that provided data for better management of personnel.

- Built computer-based digital videos and created spreadsheets for accounting and budgetary tabulations.

- Very successfully coordinated logistics and security requirements for the 2002 Winter Olympics. Conducted liaison with military organizations, community/city managers, and operations planners to coordinate large-scale mobilization of units, security, and support of 4,500 personnel.

Page 1 of 2

To connect with readers, equivalent corporate position titles are shown under military titles. A strong introduction precedes a traditional chronological format.

310.295.4681   **John M. Smythe,** Page 2   johnms@hotmail.com

Secretary to the General Staff, U.S. Army Reserve Command, Atlanta, GA   2000–2001
Equivalent to Executive Assistant to CEO of a large corporation

- Supervised a staff of 12 responsible for supporting the CEO and vice presidents. Provided administrative control, guidance, and tracking for correspondence and suspense actions. Advised staff on policy. Directed the Protocol Office. Rewrote the U.S. Army Reserves Staff Officers Writing Guide.

- Improved a number of processes: analyzed and streamlined flow of staff actions and reduced turnaround time by 50%; planned, determined space usage, and executed an 840-person organizational relocation.

- Organized and managed 4 military General Officer conferences with 450 participants from around the globe. Addressed a number of very large groups.

Chief, Training Management Branch, Hill AFB, Utah   1998–2000
Equivalent to Director of Training for a large corporation

- Directed installation and facility management on 6 military bases, inventory accountability and distribution, and training, including software design, assessments, and regulations.

- Reviewed policy and implemented training guidance, priorities, procedures, strategies, and a multimillion-dollar budget. Monitored assignments for 1,600 units in support of nationwide training programs.

- Moved the Reserves into the age of technology and orchestrated the formulation of a relevant vision statement and management strategy to guide the future development of world-class training facilities.

Operations Officer, 34th Logistics Support Center, Germany   1995–1998
Equivalent to Operations Manager in a medium-size business running the entire operation

- Supervised operational requirements for a 250-person unit supporting an operations center.

- Deployed to Southwest Asia during crisis response. Managed plans, operations, and policy. Supervised a staff responsible for tracking logistical requirements and inventory for 485 units with more than 400,000 personnel.

Training Officer, Headquarters Command, Fort Meade, MD   1992–1995
Equivalent to Training Specialist for a large company

- Monitored training cycle management and provided pertinent feedback to various processes.

- Created a program to "fix" the utilization of a software school training program for 1,600 units worldwide. Managed analysis, development, program education, and distribution of hardware and software resources. Developed, staffed, and implemented a major effort to "Train the Trainer."

Previous active-duty and USAR nonactive duty assignments:
Assistant Professor of Military Science, Jacksonville State University
Maintenance Officer, 592nd Ordnance Company, MT
Physical Security Officer, 125th Ordnance BN, MT

EDUCATION
MBA, University of Maryland, 2003 · BS in HPER, University of Maryland, 1991

Completed numerous executive-level courses in management, leadership, and administration. Earned prestigious awards and decorations for professionalism. Please inquire as to nature of specialized education and awards.

BAXTER SHELBY

5296 Appleville Pass, Elm Cove, TX 76522

(254) 984-5900 (C)   bshelby@yahoo.com   (254) 697-8829 (H)

EXECUTIVE MANAGEMENT PROFILE

Results-oriented leader with 22 years of experience providing strategic yet creative management in areas of operations, human resources, recruiting, training, projects and programs, process improvements, and facilities maintenance. Highly focused visionary with experiential knowledge necessary to oversee and direct multilevel, cross-functional initiatives through successful completion. Upper-level leadership trainer able to develop top performers. Career-oriented life learner with passion for continued learning and advancement. Multiple degrees and extensive leadership training. Multiculturally sensitive. Familiar with Arabic and Spanish.

Core Competencies:

Organizational Leadership	**Program Creation and Enhancement**	**Bilateral Negotiations and Mediation**
Strategic Planning	**Motivation and Team Building**	**Interagency Relations/Coordination**
Project Management	**Staff Development**	**Networking and Public Relations**
Change/Crisis Management	**Quality Assurance**	**Recruiting, Staffing, and Training**
Problem Identification and Resolution	**Instructing and Public Speaking**	**Conflict Resolution**

EDUCATION

Bachelor of Science in Psychology, 2007 (GPA 3.5), EXCELLENCE COLLEGE, Morgantown, NY

Master of Science in Industrial/Organizational Psychology, expected 2011, OXFORD UNIVERSITY, Trenton, MN

PROFESSIONAL HIGHLIGHTS

UNITED STATES ARMY   1988–Present

Operations Manager (Command Sergeant Major), Ft. Tarpton/Arabia, 2007–Present

Direct 900-person task force, simultaneously overseeing six staff sections and five subordinate organizations, each performing multilevel tasks. Provide training and create programs for noncommissioned officers. Write and revise policy and procedure. Supervise personnel functions such as rewards program, evaluations, and promotion selections.

o   Operations Management: Effectively monitor quality control for assignment readiness in both structured and nonstructured environments. Oversee all facilities, including housing, maintenance, office space, food services, and grounds.

   ▪   **Readied and dispersed 900-person task force without injury or equipment damage/loss.**

o   Staff Development: Provide training, discipline, morale building, and welfare to all assigned personnel.

   ▪   **Achieved 100% graduate rate from all leadership-training courses for entire task force as a result of implementing promotions selection process and criteria.**

   ▪   **Greatly enhanced team's capabilities and effectiveness in the Middle East by coordinating and executing an Arabic-language training program.**

   ▪   **Ensured critical thinking in crises by conceiving and applying five-step mental checklist using concepts of cognitive chunking and short-term memory.**

o   Program Management: Manage multiple programs addressing quality of life, wellness, and well-being.

o   Operating Procedures: Actively participate in writing improved procedures. Utilize innovative ideas to bring new life to stagnant concepts and processes.

   ▪   **Assisted in writing stellar tactical standard operating procedure adopted as standard by many other units.**

o   Communications: Utilize sensitivity, discretion, and good judgment in relating information to staff and their families, negotiating with foreign dignitaries, and reporting to upper echelon.

   ▪   **Enhanced the efficacy of U.S. strategic efforts through successfully conducting many bilateral negotiations with prominent Arabic leaders.**

   ▪   **Assisted families through the implementation of casualty/injury notification and support systems.**

o   Technology: Assured smooth transition from analog to digital command and control systems.

Page 1 of 3

Subheadings under each chronological section call attention to achievements in different areas of management. Good organization keeps this three-page resume inviting to the reader.

RESUME 24, CONTINUED

BAXTER SHELBY
bshelby@yahoo.com

Operations Manager (Sergeant Major), Montague Transformation Staff, Montague, AK, 2006–2007

Led organization involving more than 10,000 military and civilian personnel on two separate installations of structure update transformation. As force modernization advisor for procurement and usability, assisted in planning for fielding and integration of $5+ billion in equipment and monitored construction in excess of $1.2 billion.

o   Change Management: Led staff effort of force structure transformation.
  - **Mentored subordinate senior leaders and peers in process of organizational transformation.**
  - **Chosen as "Subject Matter Expert" for evolving training doctrine for Department of the Army.**

o   Staff Development: Provided organizational development training for transformation and installation staffs, tenant units, and surrounding communities.

o   Program Creation: Researched and explored new and innovative programs for employee fitness.

o   Communications: Acted as public relations ambassador for U.S. Army transformation activities.
  - **Increased awareness of military changes in Alaska by conducting television interviews and numerous public-speaking engagements.**

Attended United States Army Sergeants Major Academy, 2005–2006

Senior Instructor of Military Science, Central University, Coastal Way, TX, 2004–2005

Coordinated and executed training in areas of leadership, strategic problem solving, critical thinking, negotiation, crisis management, and multilevel functional skills to 200+ cadets. Oversaw consolidated efforts of 103 officer candidates and 8 senior trainers. Acted as safety officer for all training and activities.

o   Teaching Achievements: Integrated live, virtual, and constructive training methodologies both on- and off-campus. Incorporated risk assessment and mitigation into all initiatives.
  - **Attained 100% graduation rate for assigned students from advanced camp at Ft. Lewis, WA.**
  - **Selected to edit training doctrine for Cadet Command using interactive multimedia instruction modality.**
  - **Continuously requested as "Subject Matter Expert" for training and motivation by adjoining universities.**
  - **Personally trained highly praised Longhorn Battalion Color Guard who performed for U.S. dignitaries.**

o   Program Design: Used conceptualization to develop innovative performance-based training initiatives.
  - **Developed performance-oriented training program that earned praise of Commander, Training and Doctrine Command.**

Managed several golf courses in central Texas from 2004–2005 in addition to performing in primary occupation.

Training Administrator (First Sergeant), Fort McAvee, NC, 2001–2004

Administrated training program for 208-person organization with a global distribution endeavor. Acted as primary trainer of all individual and team-based training. Oversaw the maintenance, accountability, and distribution of equipment and supplies valued in excess of $2 million. Identified needs and assessed/improved programs.

o   Professional Achievements:
  - **Selected as "Hero of the Battlefield" by Observer/Controllers at Joint Readiness Training Center.**
  - **Supervised evacuation of 200+ personnel from forest fire encroachment without injury or equipment damage.**
  - **Repeatedly praised for tactical skill and initiative.**

o   Training Achievements: Developed 72 noncommissioned officers in all areas to include personal, professional, and educational endeavors.
  - **Coordinated and conducted numerous high-risk training events without injury to trainees.**

o   Procedure/Program Development: Used conceptualization to develop time- and money-saving procedures and programs.
  - **Wrote reception and integration policy that earned commendable ratings during inspections.**
  - **Fostered team climate and set personal example that enhanced food locker program.**
  - **Developed live-fire training, greatly increasing morale, proficiency, and discipline.**

BAXTER SHELBY   **Page 3 of 3**
bshelby@yahoo.com   (254) 697-8829 (H)

Recruiter (Recruiting Station Commander), Eagles Nest, TX, 1998–2001

Oversaw recruiting operations for 640,000-square-mile area in West Texas. Supervised recruiters in multiperson station, closely following recruiter station guidelines. Analyzed assigned area for market share and viability. Managed face-to-face and telephone prospecting/cold calling and directed community activities. Increased community awareness through effective advertising, promotional events, and public relations. Represented the Army at job fairs and career days. Raised educator confidence in the Army as a viable opportunity for all students. Reviewed all applications and waiver requests.

o   Professional Achievements:
   ▪   **Selected to act as Company Commander and First Sergeant over senior station commanders.**
   ▪   **Esteemed by upper-level management for creativity and originality.**
o   Recruiting Achievements:
   ▪   **Awarded ultimate gold recruiter badge for exceptional recruiting numbers.**
   ▪   **Accomplished 100% assigned annual sales goals throughout tenure as Commander.**
o   Training Achievements: Trained all recruiters to ensure comprehensive knowledge of all programs.
   ▪   **Chosen to provide training in novel techniques and conceptual thinking to all station commanders in Texas.**
o   Procedure/Program Development:
   ▪   **Consistently the lead in implementing new operational procedures.**

SELECTED LEADERSHIP DEVELOPMENT PROGRAMS

Distinguished honor graduate of every level leadership training course.

▪   **Executive-Level Leadership, Management, and Administration (for 750+ person, multilevel, multiple organizations) (U.S. Army Sergeants Major Academy),** *Graduated with Honors,* **September 2005–June 2006**
▪   Advanced Leadership and Special Operations (U.S. Army Ranger School)
▪   Equal Opportunity Representative Course (problem identification and conflict resolution)
▪   Instructor Training Course (certification as trainer in lecture, conference, and demonstrative training)
▪   Recruiting, Training, and Retaining Officers (School of Cadet Command)
▪   Lee Dubois Sales Training (specialized sales techniques)
▪   Recruiter School (sales and sales management)

COMMUNITY AND PERSONAL ACTIVITIES

▪   Volunteer, Heart of Texas German Shepherd Rescue
    —President, Director, and Training and Behavior Consultant
▪   Avid golfer with multiple tournament championships in amateur competition

– References Available upon Request –

CHAPTER 7

Resumes for Careers in Operations, Purchasing, Supply Chain, and Logistics

- Distribution Managers
- Quality Assurance Specialists
- Project Leaders
- Operations Managers
- Inventory Control Managers
- Business Managers
- Logistics Managers
- Maintenance and Materials Managers
- Vice Presidents for Construction
- Operations Executives

Transitioning to a career in operations and logistics is a natural move for many military members who have specialized in acquiring, distributing, and managing the flow of large quantities of material to globally deployed forces. Several of the resumes in this section use functional headings to showcase operations-related accomplishments; others use a more traditional chronological format. In every case, the focus is on relevant achievements presented in language that will appeal to profit-minded corporate executives.

Sally Murdock

smurdock@gmail.com • 617-440-1099
49 B Street, Apt. 4B • South Boston, MA 02127

Warehousing/Distribution Professional

Seven years of experience in high-volume, fast-paced distribution environments in the United States and around the world. Knowledgeable about hazardous materials handling; materials stocking and inventory control; and record-keeping, both manual and computerized.

Personal assets include the ability to mentally process information quickly, strong troubleshooting skills, an exceptional memory for details, and a strong work ethic developed during Army service. Recognized by superiors for accuracy, efficiency, and reliability.

Summary of Relevant Experience

Warehousing/Inventory Control
- Oversaw unloading and placement of retail merchandise in 1.3 million–square–foot warehouse.
- Scheduled delivery, assigned docks, and coordinated the unloading of 30–50 trucks each day. Verified and authorized freight bills.
- Served as Supply/Warehouse Manager for military centers ranging in size from 5,000 square feet with 1,000 parts to 10,000-square-foot, brigade-level depot stocking 10,000+ parts.
- Managed repair parts requirements for more than 2,500 work orders, averaging 300 per day.
- Maintained 93% accuracy of inventory.
- Conducted manual inventories; utilized Army-specific software packages for inventory control.
- Operated forklift trucks to 10,000 pounds.

Supervision/Communication
- Managed motor pool; instructed, tested, and issued licenses to drivers of motor pool vehicles.
- Supervised squads of 5–6 soldiers; trained new trainees and mail carriers.
- Provided support to and communicated with internal customers to ensure their satisfaction.
- Selected for periodic special assignment to research and track accumulated nondeliverable mail.
- Developed supervisory style that facilitated teamwork, dedication, and camaraderie.

Army Commendations
- Certificates of Achievement (4)
- Achievement Medals for Meritorious Service (2)
- Good Conduct Medals (2)
- Commendation Medal

Employment History

United States Army • Stationed at bases in the United States, Europe, and Asia **Rank E-4 Specialist**		2003–2010 Honorable Discharge
United States Postal Service • South Boston, MA **Mail Carrier**		2000–2003

Education & Training

Bunker Hill Community College • Charlestown, MA
Course work toward **Associate Degree**

Selected Training & Certifications
- Introduction to Defense Reutilization/ Marketing System (software)
- Unit Level Logistic System (software) Operator & Supervisor courses
- Defense Packaging of Hazardous Materials for Transportation
- Hazardous Materials Driver Training course
- Sling Load Inspector certification
- Equipment Preparation course
- NBC Officer/NCO Defense course
- Inprocessing Training & Headstart
- Combat Life Savers course

A concise one-page format uses a functional style to group relevant experience in one section—even though it was gained during a 10-year career in military and civilian positions.

DAVID M. STONE
23 Barrington Road
Seminole, FL 33776
Home (727) 899-2415   Cell (813) 915-0674
dmstone@yahoo.com

QUALITY ASSURANCE SPECIALIST

Detailed, dedicated professional with solid contractor, military, and federal government experience.
20+ years of service with the United States Air Force. Retired with numerous accolades.
IATA Certified in the Technical Transportation of Hazardous Materials.
Proven record of outstanding work performance across multiple environments.

PROFESSIONAL EXPERIENCE

Quality Assurance Evaluator   November 2006–February 2010
United States Federal Government   Maxwell, AL
Managed the receipt, storage, segregation, and inspection of all explosives entering and leaving this
2,500-personnel Air Force base. Reported directly to the Base Commanding Officer.

- Provided input for 14 quality assurance safety plans to remain current with changes to the
  base operating services contract and subsequent changes in fleet posture and commitments.
- Developed comprehensive training and testing program to certify personnel in the safe
  handling and transportation of ammunition and explosives.
- Handpicked to serve as a member of five-person Ordnance Certification Board.

Quality Assurance Inspector   April 2006–November 2006
Capital Factors Applications   Maxwell, AL
Secured the safe loading, receipt, segregation, issue, and grading of all ammunition and explosives
leaving the base. Reported directly to Company Project Manager.

- As Wharf Supervisor, personally responsible for the safe loading of more than 7,000 lifts of
  ammunition and explosives over a four-month period without incident.
- Noted by military command ships USNS *Flint* and USNS *Kiska* as having **exceptional
  foresight** that contributed to complete consumer satisfaction.

Quality Assurance Supervisor / Quality Assurance Representative   1994–2006
United States Air Force   Tampa, FL & Maxwell, AL
Supervised 13 senior personnel in quality assurance and reported directly to the manager of the
quality assurance management program for the entire base. The department managed seven of its
own programs and audited an additional 13 quality assurance programs throughout the base.

- Managed and monitored programs with an overall grade of **outstanding** in Commander
  Naval Air Forces Pacific inspection for three consecutive years.
- Developed and implemented quality assurance safety plans for aviation safety through field
  research and technical expertise.
- Promoted through superior knowledge, technical skill, and dedication to duty.

(continued)

*To position David as an experienced quality assurance professional, his resume pulls out all of his
relevant quality assurance experience from a 20-year military career and presents it in nonmilitary
language.*

DAVID M. STONE   Page 2
(727) 899-2415 • dmstone@yahoo.com

ADDITIONAL AIR FORCE EXPERIENCE

Search and Rescue (SAR) Instructor E-6   1990–1994
- Managed the training and flight schedules for more than 70 crewmen.
- Managed daily mandatory physical training sessions for 70 SAR crewmen in the squadron.
- Tracked and assured all qualifications were current to facilitate full-mission capability.
- Handpicked for instructor duty and independent duty requiring no supervision.

Air Crewman   1987–1990
- Graduated **number one** from Air Crew Candidate School—1987.
- As Operations Manager, supervised the maintenance and upkeep of 24 aircraft. Managed more than 270 maintenance personnel during high-tempo operations.

Aviation Electrician   1984–1987

QUALITY ASSURANCE TRAINING

- Quality Assurance Evaluator course (40 hours), U.S. Federal Government—March 2007
- Instructor Training course (120 hours), U.S. Air Force—November 1995
- Quality Assurance Supervisor course (40 hours), U.S. Air Force—June 1991

LICENSES AND CERTIFICATES

- Inspector, Technical Transportation of Hazardous Materials, International Air Transport Association (IATA)—March 2007; ranked **number one** in a graduating class of 35 (75% attrition rate)
- Naval Motor Vehicle and Railcar Inspector, U.S. Federal Government—March 2007
- Facilities Services Support Contract Evaluator, U.S. Federal Government—February 2007
- National Registered EMT—July 1998 (160 hrs)
- American Heart Association CPR Instructor—September 1996 (80 hrs)

SELECTED MILITARY HONORS

- Air Force Achievement Medal—1997, 2001, and 2004
- Rescue of the Year—2001
- Air Force Commendation Medal—1998 and 2001; rated **Outstanding Inspector for Search and Rescue**
- Humanitarian Service Medal—1999
- Air Force Unit Commendation—1989 and 1990
- Meritorious Unit Commendation—1985 and 1986

COMPUTER SKILLS

Proficient in Microsoft Word and Excel.

WILLIAM C. NICHOLSON

888 Woodside Lane ~ Denver, Colorado 80203

720-249-5985   wnicholson@net.net

Project and Operations Leader

Team Leadership... Project Coordination... Data Analysis

Progressive, dedicated analyst with verified success delivering worldwide, multimillion-dollar equipment distributions within tight deadlines. Superior problem-solving, time management, and communications skills. MCSE, A+, N+, CCNA, and CNE certifications candidate, knowledgeable in UNIX, DOS, networking, and file services. Expertise in motivating teams, developing operating procedures, and conducting training. Proficient in Microsoft Windows NT/XP/Vista/7, Excel, Word, Access, and PowerPoint, with knowledge of Oracle applications. Additional strengths include the following:

- ✓ Quality Standards
- ✓ Inventory Analysis
- ✓ Team Supervision
- ✓ Asset Management
- ✓ Disaster Analysis
- ✓ Performance Reviews

Selected Accomplishments

- ◆ **Medal winner recognized for outstanding leadership** in handling of worldwide engine-failure equipment crisis and management of crucial FA-18 equipment distribution process.

- ◆ Attained **Enhanced Comprehensive Asset Management System credential** to support time-critical engine and component removal, distribution, and reporting accuracy.

- ◆ **Raised more than $6,000 in two weeks, directing fund-raising program** during Operation Enduring Freedom deployment in Kyrgyzstan.

- ◆ Handled **highly sensitive flight recording data of strategic importance** in numerous operations.

- ◆ Awarded Achievement medal, **single-handedly performing duties of six people** and creating front-line reporting procedures using satellite communications in Operation Restore Hope.

Professional Experience

UNITED STATES MARINE CORPS   1990–2010

Critical Support Analyst, 2006–2010

Supervised and organized administrative functions to support equipment maintenance activities, handling wide range of duties within various Marine Corps positions. Created regular reporting and summaries, extracting, analyzing, and formatting data utilizing relational database tools.

Key Contributions

- Reduced loss of lives and equipment, furnishing crucial real-time technical data to engineering teams to aid in part-failure discovery.
- Supplied key analysis of equipment and part failures by evaluating plans, estimates, and exceptions to standards.

Continued...

A strong summary and Selected Accomplishments section bring key skills, awards, and experience to the forefront.

WILLIAM C. NICHOLSON

PAGE TWO

720-249-5985

wnicholson@net.net

UNITED STATES MARINE CORPS *(CONTINUED)*

- Enabled strategic logistical transfer process of RFI (Ready for Installation) engines, based on assessment of location and world situations.
- Managed effective training and conflict functions by establishing technical equipment change-tracking program.

System Administrator, 2000–2006

Ensured database integrity and accurate validation procedures, performing database updates. Implemented and supported local maintenance and inventory programs on UNIX-based systems.

Key Contributions

- Administered system and database backups, removal and restoration of historical data, and processing functions.
- Managed all aspects of data transfer between sites and Automated Information Systems.

Aircraft Maintenance & Inventory Administration, 1990–2000

Supported maintenance and repair facility operations, managing logbooks as well as naval equipment-related publications and files for more than 50 FA-18 aircraft. Handled administrative duties within different Marine Corps positions. Developed reports, logs, records, directives, and correspondence.

Key Contributions

- Facilitated fleet readiness, maintaining database of engine modules and components.
- Ensured proper distribution of cargo, calculating accurate loading figures and supervising loading operations.
- Created data analysis application to calculate scheduled maintenance relative to flight time.

Education & Professional Development

Bachelor of Business Management Degree Candidate, 2010
UNIVERSITY OF PHOENIX, Denver, Colorado

United States Marine Corps Training:

~ Tactical Communications

~ Personnel Administration

~ Fundamentals of Total Quality Leadership

~ Non-Commissioned Officer Career School

~ Basic Aerospace Physiology Indoctrination

~ Naval Aviation Water Survival Program

~ Aircraft Weight and Balance Schools

Thomas Jeffers

1404 Custer Avenue, Fort Hood, TX 76544
Home: 254-288-5102
Work: 254-288-1000
E-mail: Thomas.Jeffers@aol.com

SUMMARY OF QUALIFICATIONS	**Operations Manager** with diverse skill set; proven leader for both small and large organizations, able to motivate others to exceed normal expectations for individual and group performance. Started and completed multifaceted projects on time, for the least cost, in a safe manner. Blended a forte for balancing complex problems with strong leadership skills, impeccable integrity, and a solid work ethic.
RESOURCE MANAGEMENT	Effectively managed scarce personnel and financial resources as the U.S. Military Academy's Engineer and Director of Housing and Public Works with a staff of more than 650 people and an annual program budget exceeding $120 million. Supervised all planning, programming, designing, budgeting, construction, and maintenance operations.
PERSONNEL MANAGEMENT	Assessed the capabilities of my subordinates and developed, coached, and trained them to identify problems and create innovative, practical solutions to solve them. Forged cohesive, professional teams that included men and women from diverse backgrounds, races, and educational levels. Subordinate leaders and blue-collar workers were afforded far more education and training opportunities both on and off a military installation than in previous years.
MANAGERIAL LEADERSHIP	Remained focused, systematic, and aggressive when planning and executing infrastructure and improvements. Mentored 56 subordinate senior managers, made safety second nature for each supervisor and employee, adhered to EPA and OSHA environmental laws, and resolved labor issues. Emphasized the need to get parochial interests to share resources and work toward common goals.
PROGRAM MANAGEMENT	Effectively decentralized decision-making authority, significantly improving project planning and execution time while productivity and quality increased proportionately. Managed the training for more than 40,000 personnel. Renovated all housing, dining, and administrative facilities within the organization.
EXTERNAL RELATIONS	Served as the driving force in developing a politically sensitive Republic of Korea–U.S. cost-sharing agreement that captured the total support of the Korean Institute for Defense Analysis and Headquarters, U.S. Forces Korea. Obtained Department of the Army support for West Point's Operations and Maintenance buyout program and family housing master plan.

Continued

Functional headings for key skills highlight the first page of this resume; the employment history is of secondary importance.

Thomas Jeffers   **Page 2**
254-288-5102 ● Thomas.Jeffers@aol.com

**EMPLOYMENT
HISTORY**

- Assistant Division Commander, United States Army, Fort Hood, TX, August 2007–May 2010

- Director of Housing and Public Works, United States Military Academy, West Point, NY, July 2004–July 2007

- Brigade Commander, United States Army Engineer School, Fort McClellan, AL, July 2002–July 2004

- Chief, Engineer Plans Division, Combined Forces Command, Seoul, South Korea, July 2001–July 2002

- Battalion Commander, United States Army, Fort Carson, CO, June 1998–July 2001

- Director of Public Works, United States Army, Fort Campbell, KY, April 1996–June 1998

EDUCATION

- Master of Science, National Resource Strategy, National Defense University, Washington, DC, 2001

- Master of Science, Construction Management, Wichita State University, Wichita, KS, 1994

- Bachelor of Arts, Economics, University of Arkansas, Fayetteville, AR, 1992

Steve Ireland

3269 Rio de las Animas
Houston, TX 77010
Home: 832-215-6305, Mobile: 832-963-5252
sireland42@sonic.net

OBJECTIVE

Operations Management position with a major retail distribution center, involved in coordinating and directing logistics.

SUMMARY

More than 20 years of hands-on experience in all phases of inventory management. Skillful communicator with significant organizational abilities. Operational experience includes

- **Leadership**
- **Training**
- **Diversity**
- **Communications**
- **Operations**
- **Inventory Management**

ACCOMPLISHMENTS

Leadership Coordinated and directed inventory analysis enabling the reconfiguration of three warehouse spaces for maximum capability and personal safety. Resulted in overall savings of $683,000.

Training Instructed 84 supervisors from 13 branches in automated inventory management, including hardware and software application, increasing inventory accuracy levels 90%. Trained 13 branches in the use of inventory barcode system while providing critical data procedures to management, cultivating a working knowledge of proper implementation of a centralized supply center.

Diversity Effectively managed a diverse workforce. Through leadership and a strong personal commitment to fair and equal treatment of others, significantly enhanced morale through positive recognition and reinforcement. Improved employee self-esteem and retention by implementing a training program that resulted in more than 67% of workforce being promoted. Exemplified professional conduct by promoting and supporting respect for rules as evidenced by 0% disciplinary actions.

Communications Strong ability to identify and discuss key issues, and to express thoughts clearly, coherently, and extemporaneously with credibility. Possess effective presentation techniques that captivate and persuade audiences. Actively sought by management to make presentations on complex, sensitive, and unusually significant issues. Well-written material set example for brevity, clarity, logic, persuasion, and tact.

Operations Implemented a master-key security locking system for inventory storerooms that provided protection of assets and reduced high maintenance cost due to inventory shortages. Excelled at getting personnel to work together consistently, effectively, and productively to achieve goals of customer satisfaction, meeting deadlines, and working within budget. Consistently sought additional responsibilities while skillfully persuading others that all work, including unpleasant special projects, contributed to achieving team goals.

(continued)

The hybrid format of this resume focuses on key functional skills and accomplishments on page 1, while career history showing scope of responsibility appears on page 2.

Steve Ireland   **PAGE 2**
832-215-6305   sireland42@sonic.net

WORK HISTORY

LOGISTICS MANAGER   **2005–2010**

Coordinated and directed training for branches in automated inventory management systems. Identified, reviewed, and provided recommendations to management for improvements, resulting in a centralized supply center. Developed inspection checklist for inventory accuracy and management. Developed and implemented program activities while coordinating efforts of subcontractors and field service personnel. Active member of Human Relations Resource advisory board, resulting in proactive diversity awareness program.

AREA SUPERVISOR   **2004–2005**

Managed 17,000 line-item inventory valued at more than $7,000,000. Supervised three supply storerooms. Responsible for daily operations of centralized supply center. Developed and initiated preparation of handbooks, bulletins, and information systems to provide and supply logistics support. Planned and organized the training and scheduling of a labor force that enabled the supply center to comply with management objectives regarding production deadlines, cost, quality assurance, shrinkage, and safety guidelines.

FINANCE AND SUPPLY MANAGER   **2000–2004**

Managed eight budget accounts that exceeded $2,000,000. Developed and managed purchasing accounts for more than 40 branches. Provided 10 branches with training in supply concepts, inventory management, and purchasing procedures. Responsible for providing accurate monthly reports for energy consumption, vehicle usage, and budget updates.

LOGISTICS SPECIALIST   **1995–2000**

Managed all phases of warehouse operations. Coordinated all shipments and receipts. Resolved problems in the area of logistics to ensure accuracy and timeliness of contractual commitments. Conducted monthly meetings with workforce to communicate performance results and management objectives.

CERTIFIED TRAINING

- Total Quality Management
- Leadership and Management
- Management Concepts
- Systems Management Course
- Commercial Purchasing
- Supply Indoctrination
- Small Purchasing
- Large Branch Financial System
- Accounting
- Standardized Civil Rights

Roberta C. Jackson

42 Shadycreek Drive, Indianapolis, IN 46239
Residence: (317) 356-9205
rcjackson@aol.com

INVENTORY CONTROL / MANUFACTURING MANAGEMENT

Secret Security Clearance / Logistics / Warehousing / Leadership / OSHA
Production / Quality / Training

Versatile, proven leader with demonstrated abilities to achieve company goals in cost-effective manner. Procured, supervised, and managed multimillion-dollar inventory. Directed inspection, assembly, quality, and distribution of mission-critical assets worldwide. Skilled in training and developing cross-functional manufacturing teams.

SELECTED ACHIEVEMENTS

Inventory Control: Managed company's 615 line-item, $25 million stock inventory warehouse. Oversaw all inspection, maintenance, warehousing, and control and distribution functions. Attained 100% asset accountability and 99% warehouse location accuracy for September 2007 semiannual inventory.

Management: Directed manufacturing efforts of 85-person team as acting Department Manager. Devised and implemented operational controls to maximize process effectiveness. Ensured consistent on-time delivery and 100% customer satisfaction.

Organization: Authored initial department relocation plans to 4 separate locations involving 70 people and $4.6 million in equipment. Developed detailed operational procedures based on job requirements, staff expertise, coordination, and support plan information. Achieved full operational capability in half the time planned.

Training: Led department training program for staff of 85 from 6 work centers. Established master training standards based on job requirements and individual expertise. Implemented precise training guidelines to maintain peak proficiency.

Quality Assurance: Oversaw the material procurement, inspection, and manufacture of 500 special, computer-controlled, precision military devices. Designed sound mass-production assembly-line techniques focusing on worker safety and time / motion principles to ensure 100% product technical accuracy.

Safety: Organized and managed department safety program. Performed facility safety inspections and revised and implemented lockout / tag-out program. Increased overall hazard awareness, resulting in zero safety mishaps during 3-year tenure.

(continued on page 2)

Skills and achievements that relate to civilian jobs in manufacturing are prominently placed on page 1, while military employment is shown on page 2.

Roberta C. Jackson
Page 2   (317) 356-9205 • rcjackson@aol.com

PROFESSIONAL EXPERIENCE

United States Air Force, 1989–2010

Production Superintendent, Minot, North Dakota, 2008–2010

- Maintained high manufacturing standards through efficient procurement of materials and scheduling of workforce.
- Implemented mass-production assembly-line techniques focusing on worker safety and time / motion principles.

Acting Plant Manager, Minot, North Dakota, 2007

- Demonstrated exceptional ability to maintain manufacturing productivity while serving as Acting Plant Manager during absence of Plant Manager.

Inventory Control & Warehouse Manager, Minot, North Dakota, 2005–2007

- Procured and maintained $25 million inventory to support manufacturing efforts.
- Devised document flow plan for shipment of 3,500 short tons of cargo valued at $10 million in 297 ISO containers; achieved 100% asset accountability.

Operations Control Center Manager, Kadena, Japan, 2002–2005

- Supervised organization scheduling and work monitoring process.
- Coordinated staffing and material support requirements to develop effective work schedules.
- Tracked work-order status, identified constraints, and implemented changes to maintain scheduling effectiveness.

EDUCATION and TRAINING

Bachelor of Science (BS), *Business and Management*
UNIVERSITY OF MARYLAND, College Park, Maryland, 2002

Associate of Science (AS), *Management*
IUPUI, Indianapolis, Indiana, 1999

Associate of Science (AS), *Systems Technology*
AIR FORCE INSTITUTE OF TECHNOLOGY, Wright-Patterson AFB, Ohio, 1997

Organizational Management
USAF SENIOR NCO ACADEMY CORRESPONDENCE COURSE, Kadena AB, Japan, 2003

RESUME 31: BY LAURA SCHEIBLE, CCMC, CJST, JCTC

FRANK J. WILLS

1379 Slagle Road ▪ Houston, TX 77058
Phone: (281) 591-2836 ▪ E-mail: fjwills@bellsouth.net

SENIOR-LEVEL BUSINESS MANAGER

**Quality Control ▪ Program Analysis & Management ▪ International Business Operations ▪ Risk Management
Contract Administration ▪ Organizational Improvements ▪ Team Building & Leadership**

Highly motivated, goal-focused MBA exceptionally qualified to advance the goals of an organization through documented accomplishments in quality control, program analysis, and contract administration. Strong familiarity with federal acquisition regulations, international treaties and contracts, ISO 9000 quality requirements, quality assurance / control systems, contractor operations, program test and evaluation, and risk reduction. Expert communicator working across diverse groups and at all corporate levels. Innovative problem solver and solutions provider able to deliver bottom-line results. Consistent high achiever, positive team builder, and natural leader. Extensive international business experience. **Hold international visas for the countries of Bahrain, Qatar, Turkey, Kuwait, and Jordan.**

Secret Security Clearance

REPRESENTATIVE CONTRIBUTIONS

Program Analysis / Management

- Evaluated major system programs associated with planning, development, funding, and management of present and future organization development plans.
- Collaborated in development of organization-wide program plans, policies, and procedures.
- Adapted analytical, evaluative, qualitative, and quantitative techniques to measure success of programs.
- Evaluated effectiveness of programs and operations based on goal fulfillment; quality and quantity standards; procedural, policy, and regulatory compliance; and technical competence.
- Reviewed, researched, interpreted, and eliminated problems in operations techniques and procedures.
- Identified, forecasted, and resolved areas of risk. Evaluated deficiencies and recommended remedial action.

Quality Control / Assurance

- Provided quality assurance and program analysis from pre-award through completion of complex classified contracts supporting biological detection and weapon systems to include battlefield contractor support.
- Key member of management staff, serving as the International Quality Assurance coordinator for U.S. Army and Department of Defense contracts in Europe, Scandinavia, and North Africa.
- Coordinated quality assurance of programs with NATO and non-NATO governments with scope of contract authority on average exceeding $3.2 billion.
- System manager for planning and monitoring production quality assurance procedures and systems.
- Developed new and improved quality assurance and contract requirements for procuring multiple commodities.

Contract Administration / Acquisition

- Negotiated and simplified acquisition procedures in "cradle-to-grave" contracting for a variety of supplies, services, and construction supporting installation operations and military units.
- Active participant in preparation of $52 million in contract packages for international army requirements.
- Enforced contract administration in accordance with the Federal Acquisition Regulation. Analyzed contracts for compliance with project specifications.
- Evaluated, audited, and analyzed both the contract and the contractor operations for design, fabrication, processing, and personnel assembly for documentation and overall contractual compliance.

Team Building, Leadership & Support

- Branch manager for personnel programs supporting more than 1,800 personnel in 84 units worldwide.
- Directed 5 branches, as Chief of the Quality Assurance Division, in monitoring, inspecting, analyzing, and reviewing contractor operations and performance across the breadth of the acquisition, utilization, operations, and logistics of the base operations contract.
- Recruited, interviewed, hired, and trained personnel.
- Advised operating officials and maintenance, contracting, and logistics personnel in the planning of projects with regard to safety, inspection and operational problems, transportation, storage, risk, and efficiency.

▪ continued ▪

Functional headings highlight specific achievements in operations management. The Selected Career Highlights section on page 2 contains additional, detailed information that is relevant to this individual's career goal.

FRANK J. WILLS ▪ fjwills@bellsouth.net ▪ PAGE 2

SELECTED CAREER HIGHLIGHTS

Joint Readiness Center, Directorate of Resource Management, Houston, TX   2003–2010

QUALITY ASSURANCE SPECIALIST (2006–2010)

- Deployed to Southwest Asia with military units to provide onsite program analysis and further identification and mitigation of risks. Contributed to units' ability to operate at 100% of capacity with contractor support.
- Catalyst for engineering changes to contract requirements, contractor management plans, standard operating procedures (SOPs), safety, and quality control.
- Achieved 4 successive monetary awards for exceptional service performed.

CONTRACT ADMINISTRATION SPECIALIST (2003–2006)

- Contracted equivalent of 2 years of contractual requirements in 3 months to support emergency deployment of military units. Successfully delivered 100% of contracted hardware and supplies prior to deployment.
- Built environment of constant communication among vendors, units, and paying organizations to ensure units received needed resources ahead of schedule and prompt payment to vendors.
- Recognized for superior performance with several certificates of appreciation, commendations, and monetary awards.

Office of the Deputy Chief of Staff for Operations & Plans, The Pentagon   1997–2003

PROGRAM ANALYST (2001–2003)

- Instrumental in development of program plans, policies, and procedures supporting effective implementation of the U.S. Army's 5-year test plan, which included more than 600 operational tests.
- Coordinated actions across all staff levels to ensure 100% incorporation of future testing requirements into 5-year plan.
- Received awards and commendations for delivering performance "above and beyond."

MANAGEMENT ANALYST (1999–2001)

- Adapted analytical, evaluative, qualitative, and quantitative techniques to measure complex technical programs.
- Awarded Department of the Army Superior Civilian Service Medal.

PROGRAM SUPPORT SPECIALIST (1997–1999)

- Reorganized operations and modernized programs in support of 1,800 personnel worldwide.
- Designed and published complex technical and strategic documents to facilitate staffing plans.
- Innovated new concepts for data utilization to ensure 100% staffing of critical, classified operations.
- Awarded Army Commander's Award, Achievement Medal, Superior Civilian Service Award, and Army Staff Badge.

U.S. Army / Defense Contractors, Various National and International Locations   1989–1997

QUALITY ASSURANCE SPECIALIST

- Liaison with senior-level program and procurement contracting officials, senior military and political personnel, NATO, State Department, and military attachés.
- Organized quality assurance operating procedures and automated quality deficiency tracking data, resulting in 100% of requests for assistance from U.S. and foreign countries processed within suspense requirements.
- Authored quality assurance handbook for personnel engaged in international contracting programs.
- Recipient of several commendations, awards, and presentations from NATO allied governments for achievements.
- Reduced employee turnover by 75%; launched a career education program utilized by 100% of division personnel.

PROFESSIONAL SUMMARY

M.B.A., Business—University of Mississippi, Jackson
B.S., Mass Communications / Business—California State University, Northridge

Additional Training: Extensive management, quality assurance / control, acquisition, contract, logistics, technical, and general leadership training through numerous organizations and spanning entire career. Full listing available upon request.

Computer Skills: Strong technical skills with working knowledge of diverse applications including Microsoft Office (Word, Excel, PowerPoint, Access, Outlook), Microsoft Project, and SPSS / PASW.

Professional Affiliations: American Society for Quality, Association of the Industrial College of the Armed Forces.

Language Skills: Familiarity with Italian and German.

RESUME 32: BY ANNEMARIE CROSS, CPRW, CEIP, CCM, CRW, CECC

PHIL B. ARBOUR

415-295-0049 ◆ philbarbour@hotmail.com
109 Polk Street, #2 ◆ San Francisco, CA 94115

OPERATIONS MANAGER & LOGISTICS SPECIALIST

Business Management / Project Management / Quality Assurance Management

Performance-driven professional with extensive experience and impressive achievements in pivotal logistics, operational, and project management roles. Influencer, driver, and catalyst for operational change and advancements maximizing operational efficiency, reducing expenditures, and enhancing staff performance across multimillion-dollar operations. Proven skills at strategizing, executing, and driving tactical global logistics initiatives and propelling challenging projects to successful fruition.

OVERVIEW OF EXPERTISE

LOGISTICS MANAGEMENT:	- Planned, distributed, and managed resources and assets valued at more than $200M. - Performed repair and requirements analysis; developed specifications; facilitated design activities; modeled/reported life-cycle costing. - Performed manufacturing planning and modeling, including failure analysis; presented logistical components at design reviews; managed defense publications.
PROJECT MANAGEMENT:	- Spearheaded multimillion-dollar projects from concept through completion across diverse and challenging environments. - Performed project appraisals and defined project scope; strategized system requirements and specifications; developed and managed contracts; monitored progress; managed risk. - Skilled in using Gannt and PERT tools and CSCS cost management methods. - Proficient in coordinating, developing, and scheduling deliverables to clients; meeting time-critical deadlines; and managing acceptance of contractor deliverables.
OPERATIONAL MANAGEMENT:	- Built best-in-class operations through analysis, planning, and management of business demands; identified key management process accountabilities/information tools. - Change agent, continually enhancing organizational efficiency through reengineering and streamlining processes and systems. Quantitative and qualitative appraisals. - Revitalized staff performance by identifying tasks/subtasks within workgroups, determining skill sets, and providing ongoing training and support. - Integrated information into procedures, IT design, and position descriptions. - Convened and led meetings; compiled/distributed meeting agendas, minutes reports.
QUALITY MANAGEMENT:	- Developed strategies toward Quality Certification. - Formulated procedural documentation to support ISO-9000 accreditation. - Executed and coordinated continuous improvement and quality assurance programs. - Conducted quality audits; developed contractual quality requirements.

*Technologies: Microsoft Word, Excel, PowerPoint, Project, and Outlook; Lotus Notes;
DOORS (Traceability Tool); and Stock Control & Finance Management Systems including SDSS and MIMS*

PROFESSIONAL EXPERIENCE

Project Engineering Manager   2007–Present
Defense Material Organization
Appointed to oversee all engineering aspects to facilitate the procurement, introduction, and efficient operational performance of highly specialized equipment/system into the organization.
- Developed and documented functional and performance specifications, test and evaluation master plan, and project design acceptance strategy. Scheduled staff and resources.
- Developed logistics and maintenance systems, plans, and procedures to support full system operability.

Operations Manager—Workshops   2004–2006
3rd Combat Engineer Battalion
Planed and coordinated day-to-day material and maintenance requirements of $200M fleet; optimized productivity of 365 staff through strategic training, support, and performance management initiatives. Appointed President of Battalion Trust fund, a nonprofit with 367 members and $90K annual revenue.

The first page of this resume identifies strong career achievements that show a diversity of skills in operations, logistics, project management, and quality assurance.

Phil B. Arbour	philbarbour@hotmail.com	page 2

Continued…

- Spearheaded deployment and maintenance of equipment for a special operation in East Timor, while maintaining 95% availability during stay.
- Reengineered and streamlined administrative systems, allowing a greater emphasis on core activities and securing significant improvement in efficiency throughout the organization.
- Conducted difficult negotiation for the provision of logistic and military support for complex, demanding, resource-intensive activities.
- Designed equipment management and maintenance plan and prepared standard operating procedures for organization's support elements.

Operations Manager—Logistic Support Team   2003–2004

Operation AWS Peace Monitoring Group

Managed expansive logistical requirements in support of operation requiring coordination of personnel and equipment from all three services (Navy, Army, and Air Force) and five contributing nations (U.S., Australia, New Zealand, Vanuatu, and Fiji).

- Planned, organized, and coordinated all in-country distribution supporting 356 personnel through use of air, sea, and land covering an area of 10,500 sq. mi. across six site locations. Developed and executed inventory plans and policies for bulk fuels and oils, rations, water, and general stores.
- Sourced and established contracts with local vendors for supply of labor/engineering services, including waste management, road/airfield management, and maintenance.
- Formulated and implemented the security plan, working closely with group security personnel in coordinating and maintaining operational security.

Operations Manager—Combat Service Support Squadron   2002–2003

3rd/12th Battalion

Directed operational and staffing requirements, including planning, training, and ongoing support for 135 personnel, while managing provision of logistical support for all activities. Negotiated logistic/military support provision as required for challenging and resource-intensive activities, overseeing Army, general reserve, and contractor staff.

- Developed equipment management plan and standard operating procedures.
- Enhanced organizational efficiency through administrative streamlining.

Operations Assistant   2001–2002
Officer Commanding/Second in Command Administration Company   2000–2001

4th Brigade Administrative Support Battalion

Held operational oversight for staff training, planning, and management for 115 personnel. Negotiated and coordinated logistical, administrative, and military support for demanding and resource-exhaustive actions.

- Achieved an average of better than 90% availability for the vehicle fleet.
- Slashed catering and accommodation expenditures from $1.9 million per year to $0.8 million without compromise to quality or efficiency.

Assistant—Logistics/Operations/Personnel Management   1996–2000

EDUCATION & PROFESSIONAL DEVELOPMENT

Master of Management—2002 ♦ University of California at Berkeley

Technical Staff Officer—2002 ♦ Army Technical Staff Officers' Course

Advanced Diploma in Engineering Maintenance Management (Civil Accreditation) – 2000
♦ Army Logistic Training Center

Associate Diploma in Personnel Administration (Civil Accreditation)—1992
Certificate in Vocational Training (Civil Accreditation)—1992
♦ Military College

Countless hours in Logistics, Project, and Operational Management training courses:
Certificate IV – Simply Procurement ♦ *PRINCE 2–PPM* ♦ *Microsoft Project* ♦ *Conflict Resolution* ♦ *Intermediate Operations Course* ♦ *Logistic Officers Advanced Course* ♦ *Logistic Officers Intermediate Course* ♦ *Intermediate Staff Course* ♦ *Regiment Officer Basic Course – EME* ♦ *Non-Public Moneys Accounting Course* ♦ *Total Quality Management Course* ♦ *OH&S for Managers* ♦ *Continuous Improvement Leader's Course* ♦ *Unit Emplaning Officers Course* ♦ *Sexual Harassment Contact Officers' Workshop*

DAVID A. JONES

85 Ellington Street • Groton, CT 06098 • (203) 437-6779 • dajones@snet.net

MAINTENANCE / MATERIALS / OPERATIONS MANAGEMENT
Transportation ~ Shipping Industry

"David is an exceptional planner, organizer, and innovative problem solver who has succeeded where others have failed ... he has exceptional operations expertise, strong leadership skills, and sound judgment."

—Bertrand Fisher
Commanding Officer

Management Professional offering 15 years of experience in electronics equipment maintenance, materials, operations, and security.

- Promoted through increasingly responsible technical and supervisory positions based on expertise, demonstrated initiative, and contributions to operational efficiency.

- Effective trainer who develops and leads staff to peak performance.

- Expert in navigation and ship-handling operations and systems.

- Recipient of 15 achievement, commendation, and distinguished service awards throughout naval career.

RELEVANT EXPERIENCE & ACCOMPLISHMENTS

Maintenance & Materials Management

- Improved operations through aggressive materials improvement and equipment refurbishment programs that were subsequently instituted throughout the organization.
- Supervised electronics technicians in maintenance / repair of various communications, radar, and other electronics systems, ensuring peak efficiency and reliability.
- Led implementation of efficient purchasing and JIT inventory-management system.
- Oversaw hazardous-cargo certification requirements, equipment maintenance, and safety deadlines.

Operations Management

- Managed the daily planning, coordination, and supervision of 45 staff members, effectively ensuring stringent compliance with vessel safety standards.
- Developed and executed detailed operational review plans for command administrative inspection, resulting in timely problem identification and corrective actions.
- Recognized for instrumental role in achieving excellent ratings in all areas during plant inspections.

Staff Training & Management

- Trained more than 500 military and civilian personnel in maintenance procedures, navigation, firefighting, damage control, security, and other areas.
- Turned around an underperforming division to rank #1 in productivity by improving the training curriculum.

CAREER HISTORY

United States Navy • 1994 to Present
Patrol Boat Captain • 2004 to 2010
Legal & Administrative Officer • 1998 to 2004
Assistant Operations & Electronics Material Officer • 1994 to 1998

EDUCATION

B.S., Electrical Engineering, Connecticut College • New London, CT
Additional Training: Electronics Material Management Training Program,
Boat Group Management Training Program, Military Justice Legal Training Program

A highlight of this resume is the powerful endorsement from a commanding officer. The resume includes expertise that is specific to the transportation/shipping industry because that is the intended target.

RESUME 34: BY DON ORLANDO, MBA, CPRW, JCTC, CCM, CCMC

Harold Wilson
1112 Norton Road ♦ Scott Air Force Base, Illinois 62225
hw1000@go.com ♦ [618] 249-1265

Value to Carlton Engineering: As your **Vice President for Construction,** bring in profit-building ventures on time and within budget.

Capabilities You Can Use:

♦ Translating plans into projects that satisfy demanding customers	♦ Negotiating contracts to increase profits and keep top subcontractors	♦ Keeping capability high and life-cycle costs low

Work History

More than 20 years as an Air Force **civil engineer (1989–Present)** accountable for all project management functions. This partial list of my current responsibilities typifies the kind of work I have done for the last five years:

- ♦ Build, defend, and administer annual budget of $60 million.
- ♦ Lead teams drawn from 450 engineers, craftsmen, administrators, and service providers.
- ♦ Guide maintenance of 511 buildings covering 5,000,000 square feet of office space, restaurants, meeting rooms, shopping malls, a supermarket, 884 homes and apartments, industrial plants, an airport, and academic facilities.
- ♦ Maintain plants used by a communications center, a fire department, a police force, and a full-service medical center.
- ♦ Keep water and sanitary distribution systems within tight standards.
- ♦ Keep electrical and steam generation plants fully operational.
- ♦ Build, pave, and repair nearly 50 miles of road.

Selected Examples of Success

SATISFYING THE CUSTOMERS

Asked to **turn** 50-year-old **derelict building into major corporate headquarters**—in six weeks! Contract I inherited allowed overextended contractor to "bail out" without penalty. Customers were on site every day.

Payoffs: Done **on time, on budget.** Customers *very* satisfied.

When customer asked me to repair underground utilities fast, I found ways to **save him lots of future dollars.** Made inevitable upgrades **faster** and **cheaper** and **improved** the road surface above the junctions at the same time.

Payoffs: Senior decision-maker spent scarce extra money and coped with road detours because he liked the **long–term savings** I gave him.

More indicators of performance…

This resume targets a specific position and leads off with capabilities that are valuable in the world of construction.

| Harold Wilson | Vice President for Construction | [618] 249-1265 |

Selected Examples of Success (continued)

MATCHING THE RIGHT CONTRACTOR TO THE RIGHT JOB AT THE RIGHT COST

The challenge: overhaul ceiling of 700-seat lecture hall between courses. Offered an alternative to the contractor's very costly method of reaching the 30-foot ceiling.

Payoffs: Innovative, untried method worked beautifully. **Saved 20%,** including proration for material that contractor could use on other jobs. Done **on time.** Customer pleased.

GETTING THE MOST FROM EVERY DOLLAR

Just as I took over a project to build a child development center planned at $2.6 million, **funds** were **cut by $1.0 million** even as **cost factors rose 14%.** Met with customer to find new ways to fill the need.

Payoffs: **Project on track,** even though I have 10% fewer people and 5% smaller operating budget.

Education and Training

✢ "Executive Leadership Course on Environmental Protection," 2008

✢ Master of **Public Administration,** Central Michigan University, 2005
   Attended nights and weekends despite very pressing professional schedule.

✢ B.S. **Electrical Engineering,** Virginia Military Institute, 1989

Professional Associations

✢ Society of American Military Engineers: Past President and Secretary of local chapter

2

RESUME 35: BY LAURA SCHEIBLE, CCMC, CJST, JCTC

Justine Harding

17 Marina Drive
San Diego, CA 92101
(619) 881-8925 ▪ harding12@hotmail.com

> *"Finely honed leadership and management attributes. Organized personnel and assets into a highly cohesive team.... Has on countless occasions demonstrated the unique ability to think and act independently from the status quo. Exemplary results from any task are the norm..."*
> —*Performance evaluation*

Executive Profile

High-energy, results-driven professional offering 18+ years of experience reflecting continuous contribution and achievement. Superior leadership and management experience. Dynamic problem solver able to innovate compelling, win-win solutions to complex situations. Exceptional relationship-building skills, fostering unified teams and cohesion across all levels of staff, management, and customers. Technically fluent, rapidly assimilating cutting-edge technologies, ideas, and processes.

Areas of Expertise

- Vision & Mission Planning
- Training & Development
- Project Life Cycle Management
- Budget Control

- Operations Management
- Change Management
- High-Impact Presentations
- Process Development

- Strategic Problem Solving
- Team Building & Leadership
- Public Relations
- Logistics Planning

Value Offered

- **Trailblaze New Processes / Operations Management:** Change agent for continuous process and operations improvements, achieving management success with multimillion-dollar inventories and budgets in multiple locations. Introduced innovative training initiatives and procedures, reducing instruction period from 32 weeks to 26 weeks per course.

- **Results-Focused Project Management:** Life-cycle leadership in Toys for Tots campaign spanning public relations, warehousing operations, acquisition, and distribution. Culminated in an exceptionally successful campaign with more than 95,000 toys collected and distributed.

- **Bridging Gaps Through Communication and Relationship Building:** Primary liaison across diverse community, corporate, and military groups through such activities as public affairs events, drug-free program in local schools, Sea Cadets, Boy Scouts, and Adopt-a-School program.

- **Motivational Team Builder and Leader:** Developed and managed top-performing, high-capability teams. Built top levels of consensus and team cooperation toward achievement of common goals.

Professional Highlights

U.S. Marine Corps   1993–2010

Series of progressive leadership positions for diverse areas—strategic planning, training and development, operations management, and personnel administration. Consistently recognized for energetic leadership and relentless drive for exceeding performance objectives.

SENIOR INSTRUCTOR / OPERATIONS CHIEF—San Diego, CA (2003–2010)

Lead strategist for training support to all military branches, enabling unprecedented levels of quality training through exceptional administration, innovative management, and astute insight. Role model, mentor, and professional developer. Supervised, evaluated, and counseled 21 instructors and 87 students. Developed and presented training programs; enforced training policies and procedures.

Interfaced closely with executive officers as a key member of the management staff. Facilitated public relations for several detachment social and family functions. Coordinated such programs as Adopt-a-Highway. Certified substance abuse counselor.

Page 1 of 2

Narrowing a broad career focus down to operations management was the critical factor in creating this resume. The quote at the top captures attention and provides an exceptional endorsement.

Justine Harding

Page 2

(619) 881-8925 ▪ harding12@hotmail.com

Professional Highlights—continued

OPERATIONS MANAGER—El Toro, CA (2000–2003)

Piloted logistics, operations, and security for 13 armory locations with million-dollar inventories and budgets. Managed and motivated personnel in each location to maximum potential and performance. Troubleshot potential problems and innovated solutions. Provided training and operations support to the FBI and DEA. Led public relations and community outreach programs.

STATE DEPARTMENT INSTRUCTOR / TRAINER—Saudi Arabia (1999–2000)

Coordinated resources to build up Saudi Royal Marines and provide guidance to develop and implement training course in small arms. Formulated innovative periods of instruction and resolved numerous maintenance issues to maximize training opportunities and ensure mission success. Introduced new, cutting-edge equipment. Strengthened relationships with allies.

INSTRUCTOR / INSPECTOR—Aberdeen, MD (1996–1999)

Operations and security authority for 23 locations, personnel, inventories, and budgets. Transformed reserve armory section into an effective, cohesive, and independent group. Team leader and liaison in multiple community programs including drug-free campaign and Toys for Tots drive. Communications manager with Secret security clearance.

GROUND ORDNANCE CHIEF—Quantico, VA (1993–1996)

Led resource allocation and operations management for 19 armory locations, expansive inventories, and budgets. Developed and implemented Wing Armed Awareness safety program and standard operating procedures. Fully accountable for personnel and ordnance materials valued at more than $9 million. Streamlined arrival/departure processes of 200 aircraft and interactions among several units.

Education & Awards

Bachelor of Science Coursework in Computer Science—2002
University of California, San Diego

Professional Development

Advanced training in Leadership, Communications, Public Speaking, Administration, Operations, Technical Issues, Applied Management, Physical Education, and Military Science.

Formal Recognition

Extensive awards, service and achievement medals, and letters of commendation testifying to performance "above and beyond" in every situation.

CHAPTER **8**

Resumes for Careers in Sales, Communications, Human Resources, Training, and Teaching

- Sales/Recruiting Professionals
- Writers/Broadcasters/Public Affairs Specialists
- Corporate Trainers
- Human Resources Managers
- Training and Administrative Managers
- Performance Process Advisors
- Academic Chairs/Professors/Academic Administrators

Representing diverse professions, the resumes in this chapter use chronological, functional, and hybrid formats to present relevant skills and accomplishments acquired in the military. The desired transition is not always a direct match with military experience, but the resumes clearly show how qualifications are transferable to a new field.

Bernard R. Lawton

(305) 443-7365 ♦ 1034 SW Fourth Court, Miami, FL 33150 ♦ brl86@aol.com

QUICK PROFILE:

Solid experience in staffing and recruitment within a "selling" environment. Excellent organization and time-management skills, with a history of earning trust and rapport with all levels of management, peers, subordinates, and recruits. Outstanding communication, interpersonal, and public relations skills. Results-oriented and capable of taking on added responsibility. Energetic and assertive, adept at coordinating and implementing multifaceted operational procedures, and proud of personal performance. Proficient with Microsoft Word, PowerPoint, and Excel.

CORE COMPETENCIES:

- Sales / Marketing
- Public Relations

- Training / Development
- Staffing / Recruitment

RELEVANT EXPERIENCE:

United States Air Force, 1992–2010
Recruiting Manager (2007–2010)
Senior Recruiter (2004–2007)

- Planned and directed activities of nine recruiters supporting Air Force recruiting effort in Houston, Texas.
- Set recruiting goals and timetables and led staff in executing plans to meet goals.
- Analyzed and validated lead-generating activities, including surveys, statistics, market trends, demographics, and short and long-term programs, determining what worked and adjusting operational strategies in response.
- Defined strategies and created PR programs to influence positive support from diverse audiences. Created advertising campaigns, promotions, special events, and presentations to increase public awareness.
- Ensured quality control of all policies/procedures and compliance with organizational regulations and practices.
- Compiled and administered statistical reports concerning recruitments, interviews, hires, transfers, promotions, discharges, and performance appraisals.

Significant Achievements:
- **Achieved 115% of established recruitment goal as manager, 123% of goal as recruiter.**

Recruiter (2001–2004)
- Responsible to meet stringent goals for recruiting from the civilian sector.
- Developed a productive sourcing system and interviewing style that resulted in "top-drawer" candidates.
- Planned and coordinated a series of successful media recruitment campaigns, including radio, television, and print advertising as well as public relations programs with colleges, junior colleges, high schools, service organizations, social service agencies, job fairs, and other forms of community outreach, all designed to increase organization (Air Force) awareness.
- Delivered presentations to civic and social groups, school officials, and religious leaders concerning military career opportunities; organized and conducted base tours.

Previous Employment
1998–2001	Inspection/Repair Crew Leader, Incirlik Air Base, Turkey
1995–1998	Quality Assurance Inspector, Offutt Air Force Base, Nebraska
1992–1995	Aerospace Ground Equipment Mechanic, Offutt and MacDill Air Force Bases, Nebraska / Florida

EDUCATION & PROFESSIONAL DEVELOPMENT:

- Associate of Applied Science Degree, AGE Community College, Alabama, 1996
- Professional Sales Skills Core Course Training
- Professional Sales Skills Applications Training
- Professional Sales Skills Coaching

Designed to facilitate a transition from military recruiting to sales, this resume emphasizes sales-related activities and achievements.

TERRELL R. DANIELS

1301 Diamond Road, Charlotte, NC 28218
Home: (704) 825-0110, Cell: (704) 825-3012, E-mail: trdaniels@isp.com

QUALIFICATIONS SUMMARY

- Sixteen years of experience as a writer, communicator, and public affairs specialist.
- Extensive international travel experience and familiarity with multiple cultural protocols.
- Accustomed to performing effectively in deadline-oriented and crisis situations.
- Top-notch research/analysis and information-dissemination skills.
- Fluent in Spanish.

PROFESSIONAL EXPERIENCE

UNITED STATES MARINE CORPS (USMC)   1994–2010
Public Affairs Officer, Bellagio, Italy (2007–2010)

- Wrote, edited, and photographed for a weekly electronic news publication.
- Authored 400+ articles and edited hundreds more during tenure.
- Facilitated direct communication between senior officers and constituents.
- Provided timely information to members of the local military community.
- Served as the senior officer's direct advisor on all public affairs matters.
- Briefed the senior officer weekly and prepared talking points for all public appearances.
- Facilitated media coverage of events by internal military and global news outlets.

Public Affairs Specialist/Office Supervisor, Bellagio, Italy (2005–2007)

- Monitored and selected relevant news events for daily briefings of the senior officers.
- Correlated media coverage with intelligence reports to provide key decision makers with both classified and unclassified perspectives.
- Worked among military intelligence professionals in top-secret/classified environments.
- Trained, supervised, and evaluated the performance of 6 public affairs staff members.
- Spearheaded a comprehensive training program addressing all aspects of public affairs.
- Created and maintained an extensive digital archive of images, raw video, and press releases.
- Facilitated news coverage and significant exposure to major U.S. and foreign news outlets, including CNN International, Associated Press (AP), and Reuters.
- Briefed military and civilian leadership prior to internal and external news media interviews.

Writer/Photojournalist, Mahón, Spain (2002–2005)

- Researched and wrote high-impact feature stories and provided supporting imagery for the USMC's official magazine (worldwide distribution).
- Covered high-priority issues such as personnel retention and development.
- Supervised the writing and delivery of press releases and reports for the public and military.

- Continued -

Extensive international experience in broadcasting and journalism (as a military public affairs officer and writer/editor) is highlighted to position this individual for roles in the private sector.

Terrell R. Daniels   Cell: (704) 825-3012

Editor, USMC Official News Wire Service, Washington, DC (2000–2002)

- Edited articles for electronic dissemination for subsequent use by base newspapers, radio, television, and other internal print and broadcast media outlets.

Producer/Broadcast Journalist, Washington, DC (1997–2000)

- Produced radio and television spots using raw video footage.

Public Affairs Specialist, Tel Aviv, Israel (1994–1997)

- Selected to create a radio station providing informative and entertaining programming for 5,000+ personnel deployed in Asia and the Middle East.
- Collaborated with engineers to implement 24/7 operations for 3 radio channels.

EDUCATION

Bachelor of Science, Economics/Political Science (GPA: 3.65 on a 4.0 scale)   2003
University of Phoenix, Phoenix, AZ

PROFESSIONAL DEVELOPMENT

- **Advanced Writing/Interviewing,** 16 classroom hours, 2003
- **Intermediate Photojournalism Course,** 8-week curriculum, 2000
- **Video Post-Production,** 40 classroom hours, 2000
- **Television News,** 40 classroom hours, 2000
- **Shipboard Information, Training, and Entertainment (SITE) System,** 1997
- **Basic Journalist Course,** 16-week curriculum, 1996

HONORS & AWARDS

1st Place, Print/Broadcast Journalism Competitions, 1995, 1996, 1998, 2000, 2002
Joint Service Achievement Medal, 2004
Letters of Commendation, 1997–2002, 2005–2009
Humanitarian Service Award, 2005

PC SKILLS

Proficient in Adobe Photoshop and Microsoft Office (including PowerPoint).

- Page 2 -

Trenetta Johnson

717 Cattail Circle, Harker Heights, Texas 76548
Home 254-768-0379 ● trenetta.johnson@us.army.mil

HUMAN RESOURCES/CORPORATE TRAINING
Supervision ~ Coaching ~ Mentoring ~ Management

Energetic and adaptable professional with more than 13 years of experience in personnel management and supervisory leadership. Results-oriented with exceptional communication, interpersonal, multitasking, administrative, organizational, and problem solving leadership skills. Accurately perform challenging tasks with precision and attention to detail. Excel at organizing and setting up new procedures, troubleshooting and taking adverse situations and making them positive. Demonstrated ability to manage, motivate, and build cohesive teams that achieve results.

Summary of Qualifications:

- Human Resource Management
- Operations Management
- Team Building/Leadership
- Training & Development
- Organizational & Project Management
- Problem Resolution

- Staffing Requirements
- Employee Scheduling
- Security Clearance
- Proficient in Microsoft Word, PowerPoint, Excel, Outlook, and Internet Explorer

Professional Experience

United States Army   1997–2010
Supervisor, Distribution Supply 2007–2010
- Managed and accounted for $3 million worth of organizational equipment with 0% defects to maximize productivity and customer service.
- Directed diverse work groups of technical and professional employees.
- Trained and experienced in contract management, purchasing, and procurement.
- Conducted data analysis, program evaluation, and risk management.
- Interviewed and placed new employees. Wrote job descriptions and employee evaluations.
- Created and presented training on leadership and management.
- Interpreted federal regulations. Wrote company policies to comply with current regulations.
- Mediated disputes and disciplinary actions.

Manager, Senior Administrator 2002–2007
- Trained and supervised more than 80 subordinates.
- Managed over 30 junior leaders.
- Provided guidance in the areas of training, conduct, leadership, professional development, assignments, and safety.
- Served as principal advisor to the commanding officer by providing statistical graphs and briefings related to logistical distribution.

continued

Because all of Trenetta's military experience related to her goal of a corporate training position, her resume follows a traditional chronological format. For each position, bullet points showcase relevant and distinguishing accomplishments.

RESUME 38, CONTINUED

- Exercised executive-level management for establishing, maintaining, and administering an integrated human resource management program for assigned organization.
- Wrote standard operating procedures and worked closely with senior-level management from diverse organizations to achieve goals.
- Selected over several employees to serve in sensitive position providing assistance to families who have been affected by tragedy. Utilized compassion and counseling skills to provide the highest level of customer service to assigned families.

Corporate Trainer 1999–2001
- Served 2 years as a trainer, instructing new personnel in the basic fundamentals of becoming a logistics specialist.
- Provided formal classroom instruction, teaching more than 500 learners for 9 weeks at a time.
- Utilized PowerPoint displays, projectors, handouts, CDs, DVDs, and videos.
- Prepared training manuals, student guides, and academic examinations. Tested and evaluated learners.
- Resolved complaints and grievances regarding employee relations and management.
- Served as human resource liaison between 200 employees and finance and personnel management office; reviewed and consolidated reports; statistics, and applications and prepared recommendations for personnel actions.

Instructor/Writer 1997–1999
- Planned and designed curriculum and instructional materials and conducted classes for more than 1,000 personnel on basic petroleum operations.
- Mentored hundreds of new personnel, facilitating their skill development, advancement, and success.
- Reviewed and rewrote technical material relating to petroleum science; administered written and hands-on exams.
- Supervised, counseled, and performed diverse tasks pertaining to student training.
- Planned, coordinated, and conducted graduation and recognition of training ceremonies.

Education and Training
M.A., Human Resources Administration (Cum Laude)   2006
     Hawaii Pacific University, Hawaii
B.A., Justice Administration   2004
     Hawaii Pacific University, Hawaii
A.A., Supervisory Leadership   2002
     Hawaii Pacific University, Hawaii
Equal Opportunity Leaders Course   1999
Instructor Development Course   1998
Primary Leadership Development Course   1992

RUSSELL ALBANO

5120 Shore Drive, Palm Harbor, FL 34685   Home: (727) 787-6464, Cell: (727) 846-6333

HUMAN RESOURCES PROFESSIONAL
Extensive background in all HR Generalist functions. Significant experience in recruiting, hiring, training, and development. Proven ability to plan and implement programs for all levels of diverse staff.

RELEVANT EXPERIENCE
U.S. Navy, Tampa, FL (MacDill Air Force Base)   1985–Present
Sr. Enlisted Advisor / Command Master Chief (Top Secret Security Clearance)
Human Resources:
> - Plan and carry out policies relating to all phases of staffing activity, including identifying, recruiting, and attracting top-notch candidates.
> - Develop sources of qualified applicants.
> - Manage job requisitions, define jobs and skill sets, place ads, review resumes, schedule and conduct interviews, and extend offers.
> - Oversee logistics of transfer, schooling/job indoctrination, housing, and advanced training.
> - Utilize PeopleSoft program to administer and compile records and reports concerning staffing, interviews, hires, transfers, promotions, mission timelines, schooling, performance appraisals, and emergency data.
> - Supervise the activities of 175 senior Intelligence Analysts; oversee their mission by working in tandem with local commanders while assisting in developing their requirements.

Training & Development:
> - Served 3½ years as a trainer. Instructed new recruits from the Navy, Army, Air Force, and Marines in the basic fundamentals of becoming an Intelligence Analyst.
> - Provided formal classroom instruction, teaching 18–33 learners for 14 weeks at a time; utilized PowerPoint displays, overhead projectors, handouts, CDs, and videos. Tested and evaluated learners.
> - Other aspects of training included cryptology, intelligence gathering, and counterterrorism; required knowledge of other nations' civil infrastructures.

At Sea:
> - Served 5 years at sea as a Section Supervisor responsible for 60+ sailors.
> - Responsible for general military training, generating watch schedules, and organizing various kinds of skill sets while on board submarines or surface ships.
> - Provided instruction and training demonstrations on cryptography, firefighting, first aid including CPR, and safety issues.
> - Achieved ongoing compliance with EPA regulatory standards, especially with respect to the development of a waste-disposal discharge system.
> - Functioned as a Cryptologic Specialist, analyzing and reporting intelligence data.

COMPUTER SKILLS
PeopleSoft; Microsoft Word, Excel, Access, and PowerPoint; ACT!

EDUCATION
> - Bachelor of Science, Business Management, University of Phoenix, St. Petersburg, FL, 2009
> - Special government-sponsored courses covering contemporary gender and racial issues, including sexual harassment training
> - Certified Adjunct Faculty

Subheadings divide military experience into relevant categories for corporate human resources focus.

Tom Summerview
9213 Sunny Dale Drive • Riverview, Florida 33569
(813) 989-0621 (home) • (813) 484-9611 (cell) • tsummerview@earthlink.net

---

HUMAN RESOURCES MANAGER

Experienced HR generalist with successful track record for assuming leadership of projects, programs, and initiatives that promoted efficiency, organizational effectiveness, and job satisfaction. Skilled in facilitating groups to achieve resolution to complex issues. Enthusiastic and personable; expert in resource management, strategic planning, leadership, team building, and mentoring.

EXPERIENCE

U.S. ARMY, Tampa, FL   1998–2010
Training & Human Resources Advisor (2006–2010)
Principal advisor to chief executive officer, making recommendations on staffing, training, readiness, and morale.

- Established employee recognition awards program designed to recognize the "best of the best"; currently being copied by other military organizations.
- Increased unit effectiveness and productivity by implementing professional development and training programs.
- Reduced turnover and costs while improving employee participation.

Operations Manager, Headquarters, 3rd Army, Atlanta (2005–2006)
Oversaw the well-being of all enlisted soldiers and advised on matters concerning the organization, functions, operational structure, capabilities, and employment of headquarters for joint, combined, or coalition operations.

- Developed training modules and methodologies for supervisors.
- Served as principal advisor to the commanding officer in formulating plans, orders, force requirements, and procedural guidance.
- Developed an operations manual that enhanced staff safety and security in Southwest Asia.
- Mentored new fraud-detection analysts.

Training and Human Resources Advisor, 1st Armed Division (2003–2005)
Provided guidance in the areas of training, conduct, leadership, professional development, assignments, and safety for geographically dispersed division with 17,000 soldiers and 45,000 family members living in 7 different communities.

- Resolved complaints and grievances regarding employee relations and management.
- Developed and implemented employment policies to ensure compliance.

Senior Personnel Manager, 10th Mountain Division (1998–2003)
Advised commander on all matters affecting the quality of life for 6,300 soldiers and 900 civilians. Formulated policies and procedures involving recruitment and placement of enlisted personnel to enhance organizational effectiveness.

- Developed a fitness/readiness program that increased the overall readiness of the organization.
- Created a standards manual and a self-paced testing program to enhance professional development.
- Brought my unit from below standard to 98% exceeding standards in less than 6 months.

EDUCATION

Pursuing B.S. in Human Resources: University of Florida
Anticipate graduation by December 2011

Leadership and Management Academy: Ft. Bliss, Texas

To position this individual for management-level positions in human resources, his resume emphasizes activities and achievements in the areas of policies, programs, and supervision.

Alan Hillman

234 Rolling Road, Princeton, NJ 02134
(609) 254-7393
ahillman@snowcrest.net

HUMAN RESOURCES / TRAINING / ADMINISTRATION

PROFESSIONAL ACCOMPLISHMENTS

HR Management:
- Member of senior leadership team working in conjunction with operations managers, training and counseling staff, and administrative personnel to meet all organizational goals.
- Recruited, interviewed, and hired new employees. Wrote job descriptions and classifications.
- Managed corporate benefits and compensation program.
- Conducted financial and administrative audits and salary surveys. Completed required reports.
- Presented training on leadership and management, hiring, termination, and other corporate practices.
- Interpreted state and federal laws. Wrote company policies to comply with current regulations.
- Communicated and negotiated effectively with two government employee labor unions. Investigated and arbitrated labor union grievances. Mediated disputes and disciplinary actions. Completed training in labor law and contract management.

Financial and Operational Management:
- Planned and managed $1 million budget to maximize productivity and customer service.
- Directed diverse work groups of up to 75 technical and professional employees.
- Conducted data analysis, program evaluation, and risk management.
- Directed purchasing and procurement activities.

Training:
- Trained and supervised more than 30 newly qualified instructors.
- Wrote training manuals, instructor and student guides, and academic examinations.
- Administered more than 3,000 academic examinations without loss or discrepancy.
- Developed curriculum and presented classes and seminars in workplace safety, prevention of workplace violence, equal opportunity, diversity, prevention of harassment, and computer software.

Additional Skills and Experience:
- Proficient in Windows, MS Word and Excel, WordPerfect.
- President of local Toastmasters. Won numerous awards at area and statewide speech contests.
- Trained and experienced in prevention of sexual harassment, government contracting and procurement, OSHA regulations, environmental law, Total Quality Management, leadership, and team building.

WORK HISTORY

Director	Family Service Center, Naval Air Station, Atlanta, GA
Executive Officer	Naval Air Reserve Center, Olathe, KS
Flight Programs Manager	Training Department, Naval Air Station, Meridian, MS
Instructor	Naval Air Training Unit, Pensacola, FL

EDUCATION

Master of Business Administration	National University, Sacramento, CA
Bachelor of Science	California State University, Sacramento, CA

A functional format was chosen to present a broad range of accomplishments and experience that would be relevant in a human resources management position. Dates and specific job details have been omitted.

RESUME 42: BY BONNIE KURKA, CPRW, JCTC, FJST

JOHNNA L. EDMOND

15783 Rotamer Road   jledmond@cox.net
Centennial, Colorado 80015   920.723.1841   johnna.edmond@us.army.mil

Enhancing Training Through Leadership and Program Development

SENIOR-LEVEL INSTRUCTOR AND ADMINISTRATIVE MANAGER

- More than 20 years of experience in training and administrative management. Extensive background in planning and implementing projects and classes. Team leader with a talent for developing young leaders.

- Persuasive communicator and negotiator. Successfully developed productive relationships with executives and colleagues. Continually selected to serve in positions of higher responsibility. Positive and willing to take on new challenges.

- Flexible, dependable, knowledgeable; learn new tasks quickly. Organized and detail oriented. Excellent communication skills. Expertise in most computer programs. Very thorough; ensure everything is right the first time.

- Top Secret security clearance.

PROFESSIONAL ACHIEVEMENTS

Training Coordinator
U.S. Army, Camp Zama, Japan
2007–Present

Planned and coordinated Department of Army schools for 13 organizations in Korea and Japan. Manage the schedule and ensure soldiers receive required training. Coordinate travel for instructional teams coming from U.S. Obtain funds and schedule hotel and transportation for instructors. Requisition supplies to facilitate training. Use *Army Training Requirements and Resources System* (ATRRS) to schedule training and process student records. Review all data for accuracy and quality assurance. Develop and conduct briefings for senior management.

- Work closely with senior-level executives from diverse organizations to achieve goals.

Administrative Manager
U.S. Army, Vilseck, Germany
2006–2007

Planned and organized office operations. Supervised a staff of 12 in performing general clerical and administrative duties. Prepared special and routine correspondence. Reviewed and edited correspondence for proper format and accuracy. Processed and distributed incoming mail. Screened incoming calls. Prepared daily, weekly, and monthly reports.

Instructor/Supervisor
U.S. Army, Vilseck, Germany
2004–2006

Handpicked senior soldiers to develop and implement Driver's Training Instruction Program curriculum—a 4-week class with 12 students per class. Planned training schedule, processed student slating, and checked to ensure qualifications were met. Briefed soldiers first day of course on administrative guidelines and expectations. Handled all administrative issues during course. Substituted for instructors in their absence. Served as liaison between soldiers and home units. Coordinated graduation ceremonies.

(continued)

Training and administrative skills were highlighted to help this individual transition to a senior-level corporate position. Corporate job titles are used rather than military titles.

Johnna L. Edmond   page 2
920.723.1841 • jledmond@cox.net

- Wrote standard operating procedures for licensing in company.
- Increased licensing of soldiers from 25% to 98%.
- Selected to be wellness/fitness instructor for female soldiers. Taught aerobics, basic care, etc. Attended one-day training course at hospital.
- Increased team training statistics from 40% to 90%.
- Served as mentor in elementary school. Worked with program Achievable Dreams.
- Received award for outstanding service to community.

Operations Manager
U.S. Army, Sinai, Egypt
2003–2004

Managed daily operations; planned and supervised transportation of food, water, and parts to 15 remote locations. Maintained 21-vehicle fleet worth more than $600,000. Processed requests for motor transport support; assigned tasks based on customers' needs and requirements.

Trainer/Instructor
U.S. Army, Fort Jackson, South Carolina
2000–2003

Taught groups of 35–80 students using experiential learning styles, group development, and small-group instructional methods. Developed various evaluation methods to ensure soldiers understood training.

- Nominated by students and voted by peers as Drill Sergeant of the Cycle.
- Commended by senior supervisor for superior teaching methods.
- Team won 1st or 2nd best for 6 months straight.

EDUCATION AND TRAINING

- Bachelor of Science, Criminal Justice, University of Maryland, Asian Division, 2009
- HAZMAT Certification, Defense Packaging of Hazardous Materials for Transfer, 80 hours, Camp Zama, Japan, 2008
- Diploma, Leader's Drug and Alcohol Prevention Course, 40 hours, Vilseck, Germany, 2006
- Diploma, Equal Opportunity Leadership Course, 40 hours, Vilseck, Germany, 2005
- Diploma, Drill Sergeant School, 40 hours, Fort Jackson, South Carolina, 2000
- Certificate, Small Group Leader Course, 4 weeks, Fort Hood, Texas, 1998

RESUME 43: BY GEORGE DUTCH, CFP, CCM, JCTC

LYLE BURKHOLDER

Home: (250) 275-1201   330 Davidson Rd., Vancouver, BC V1L 3C9   Email: lyleb@westnet.ca

PERFORMANCE PROCESS ADVISOR
Optimizing Performance Through Organizational Change and Proactive Leadership

Twenty+ years of experience in HR-related services. Proven experience in capturing cost reductions through process redesign and optimization. Problem-solving, performance-based analysis, and planning skills in performance revitalization. Leadership skills as a proactive change agent in motivating small groups. Expertise in conflict resolution and mediation in technologically sophisticated organizations. Top-flight background in military recruitment processes. Experience with the following:

Training & Development	Retention Solutions	ROI Analysis
Management Development	Employee Benefits	Quality Assurance / Control
Productivity Improvement	Recruitment	Strategy / Goal Implementation
Reward Systems	Labor Relations	Customer Service

HR Specialist in improving business practices and processes

KEY AREAS OF HR PROCESS DESIGN AND PERFORMANCE IMPROVEMENT

- Developing a corporate HR vision and leadership / management style.
- Designing and aligning organizational and management structures to meet targets.
- Defining an effective performance measurement framework based on a balanced set of nonfinancial and financial indicators.
- Integrating core competencies into management practices.
- Defining and implementing core values in behavioral principles and guidelines.

PROFESSIONAL EXPERIENCE

HR Specialist, DND, various postings, 1986 to 2010:
- File Manager Supervisor and File Manager @ Canadian Forces Recruiting Center Toronto, 2006 to 2010.
- Administrative Human Resources—Military, Group Training Coordinator & Group Tasking Coordinator @ National Defense Headquarters Toronto, 2004 to 2006.
- Air Navigation School—Assistant School Administrative Coordinator & Administrative Office Supervisor @ 17 Wing Winnipeg, 2001 to 2004.
- Relocations Specialist, Pension and Benefits Specialist, and Personnel Administration Specialist @ 17 Wing Winnipeg, 1997 to 2001.
- Human Resources Specialist positions covering all aspects of the human resource field, including overseas positions in Germany and across Canada, 1986 to 1997.

See **ADDENDUM** for sample achievements

EDUCATION

- M.A., Human Systems Intervention, May 2010: Concordia University, Montreal
- B.A., Management & Ethics, April 2007: University of Winnipeg

PROFESSIONAL ASSOCIATIONS

- Ethics Practitioners' Association of Canada (EPAC)
- Human Resources Professional Association of Ontario (HRPAO), "Practitioner"
- International Society for Performance Improvement (ISPI)

This resume was written to help a retiring service member transition to the relatively new niche of performance improvement. A crisp one-page resume is enhanced by a one-page addendum of achievements in a Challenge-Action-Results format.

ADDENDUM—LYLE BURKHOLDER
SAMPLE ACHIEVEMENTS

1. Problem-Solving Skills

- CHALLENGE: While I was a supervisor in a newly formed HR section, my section was downsized in anticipation of an HRIS solution that would efficiently redistribute the incoming paper and electronic correspondence. Suddenly, this solution was cancelled, creating a staffing shortfall. Plus, we reverted to a much slower, less efficient method.

- ACTION: Although my job did not require me to be directly involved in the slow distribution work, I did some. It then occurred to me that, as everyone had access to the network shared drive, we could place all of the multidistribution correspondence there and just inform everyone through a section-, department-, or group-wide e-mail, and they could view the document at this certain location on the network.

- RESULT: Internal clients did not have a large document taking up space on personal e-mail systems, and they received these documents in a more expeditious manner. Workload of the office staff was reduced by approximately 10%, resulting in lower stress levels.

- IMPACT: I rise to the occasion when no conventional solution appears likely to resolve a seemingly impossible process problem.

2. Planning Expertise

- CHALLENGE: The Air Navigation School required a completely new ergonomic solution for its 21st century student learning environment, as the old environment was creating overcrowded conditions and was not technically flexible to the various teaching requirements.

- ACTION: Along with the school administrator, I assisted in coming up with a cost-efficient but well-planned and ergonomically laid-out classroom. I encouraged a consultative process, getting all the stakeholders involved in the project. Implementation of a well-thought-out plan is always my goal. This was achieved by using standard, off-the-shelf, L-leg-style tables and standard two-drawer cabinets.

- RESULT: Saved the school 40% off the cost and gave 10% more space per student than other new ergonomically designed individual desks and pedestal storage cabinets. The end product was well received by both students and teachers.

- IMPACT: I come alive in situations where I am asked to research or investigate new or innovative ideas that would improve the efficiency and effectiveness of a work environment.

3. Leadership Skills

- CHALLENGE: Due to the numerous tasks and the voluntary workforce available to help organize for a one-day cross-gender counseling seminar, it was necessary to delegate several jobs to many people with different skill sets to accomplish the goal of a successful seminar.

- ACTION: I have a knack for correctly assessing people's character and skills to determine where they would best fit into a team. I organized people around an assigned task and then administered the day-to-day activities of the team, coordinating tasks while serving clients in an efficient and effective manner.

- RESULT: Commended by supervisors and participants for my choices and leadership.

- IMPACT: I am very much a team player, and I prefer to implement change through a team approach.

4. Financial Skills

- CHALLENGE: While chair of the entertainment committee for one of the clubs at a Canadian Forces Base, I was asked to bring the entertainment budget out of a significant deficit situation.

- ACTION: First, I gained a thorough understanding of what the club clientele wanted their club to be. Then I focused on procuring high-quality, cost-effective entertainment and completely updating the club interior.

- RESULT: For the first time in many years, we had an entertainment budget that consistently produced positive cash flow, giving us the flexibility to bring in more and sometimes expensive entertainment.

- IMPACT: I prefer analytical work, understanding what the numbers mean and doing a cost/benefit analysis of options. I am fascinated by the elements of ROI as a balanced set of financial measures and targets designed to effect continuous improvement and quality management in a change-oriented organization.

RESUME 44: BY ARNOLD BOLDT, CPRW, JCTC

THOMAS DEVLIN

16 Orange Street
Williamsville, New York 14221

716-863-1294
thomd@earthlink.net

ACADEMIC CHAIR / PROFESSOR / ADMINISTRATOR

Seasoned professional with experience chairing an academic department of a leading private university combined with success managing finance, strategic planning, and operations for large, international organizations. Offering strong capabilities in these key areas:

- **Setting mission and vision, establishing strategic direction, and motivating students and faculty.**
- **Developing and administering multimillion-dollar budgets and analyzing financial operations.**
- **Recruiting students and promoting program benefits to prospective students.**
- **Developing syllabi and providing undergraduate instruction in management and leadership courses.**
- **Identifying and pursuing cost savings and process improvements that enhance operations.**
- **Engendering cooperation and collaboration among diverse constituencies in a variety of settings.**
- **Advanced degrees in business, international relations, and strategic planning.**

RELEVANT EXPERIENCE

NIAGARA UNIVERSITY; Niagara Falls, New York   1998–2007
Department Chair, Naval Science Department, and Professor of Naval Science

- Directed Navy ROTC program serving students at three Buffalo-area institutions.
- Established curriculum, supervised faculty, and managed $3.5 million operating budget.
- Functioned as liaison among U.S. Navy, university administration, and admissions/financial aid departments.
- Taught undergraduate courses in organizational behavior, leadership and management in organizations, and ethics and moral reasoning.
- Served on National NROTC Scholarship Selection Board.

Key Accomplishments:

Conducted process analyses and spearheaded organizational restructuring to improve operational efficiency. Achieved $289,000 in annual cost savings.

Created three-course concentration in leadership that met both university and U.S. Navy requirements and provided students with enhanced course elective opportunities.

Negotiated with financial aid department to establish room and board waiver for ROTC scholarship students. This arrangement created an incentive for prospective students to join the program and was revenue positive for the university in the amount of $557,000 over a two-year period.

Reduced dropout rate and increased enrollment, resulting in a 375% increase in students participating in the program over a three-year period.

Implemented new computer systems for the department, which improved instructional capabilities. Funding for this capital project was realized through cost savings in other areas and required no additional budget requests.

EDUCATION

Master of Business Administration	Boston College, Boston, Massachusetts
Master of Arts—International Relations	Holy Cross University, Springfield, Massachusetts
Master of Arts—Strategic Studies	Senior Naval War College, Newport, Rhode Island
Bachelor of Science—Mathematics	University of Oklahoma, Norman, Oklahoma

(continued)

This individual hopes to parlay his experience leading an ROTC program at a university into a civilian job as a professor or possibly a department chair. His academic experience is highlighted on page 1, with less-relevant employment shown on page 2.

THOMAS DEVLIN   **Page Two**
716-863-1294   thomd@earthlink.net

ADDITIONAL PROFESSIONAL EXPERIENCE

SALOMON SMITH BARNEY, Batavia, New York   2007–Present
Financial Advisor, Planner, and Team Leader
- Ranked among top 10% of Salomon Smith Barney Financial Advisors for 2008 Net New Money.
- Provide comprehensive financial services to high-net-worth individuals and not-for-profits.
- Advise business owners on retirement plans, employee benefits, and liability management.
- ➢ **Doubled team production, attained highest client satisfaction rating, and achieved 98% client retention in first two years.**

NATO HEADQUARTERS, Brussels, Belgium   1994–1998
Senior Staff Analyst and Briefer
- Analyzed and monitored world situations, wrote intelligence reports, and conducted weekly briefings to NATO Ambassadors and NATO Military Committee.
- Promoted collaboration and cooperation among 19 very senior officers from 13 diverse NATO countries.
- Served on multinational committees to define U.S. objectives and desired NATO policy.

MARITIME PATROL FORCES, PACIFIC, Subic Bay, Philippines   1990–1994
Chief of Staff for Aviation Operations, Training, Intelligence, and Communications/Computers
- Directed aviation operations throughout the Pacific for six subordinate organizations.
- Conceptualized and designed new $6.7 million IT operations center serving eight organizations.
- ➢ **Reduced maintenance costs by $75,000 per year and labor costs by 35%.**
- Served as Project Manager for design of new multimillion-dollar headquarters building.
- ➢ **Interfaced with executives and government officials to negotiate two international agreements.**

PATROL SQUADRON SEVEN, Norfolk, Virginia   1988–1990
Commanding Officer and Executive Officer
- Directed 325-member organization with nine aircraft and $280 million in capital assets.
- Developed innovative tactical procedures that produced unprecedented operational successes.
- ➢ **Maintained "Mission Capable" rate of 92% and amassed 59,000 flight hours without incident.**
- ➢ **Received "Operations" award; nominated for John Paul Jones Inspirational Leadership Award.**

Identified by U.S. Navy for fast-track career development and promotion through operations, human resources, and shipboard positions. Rapidly progressed to leadership positions and command rank based on exceptional performance in these varied roles.

CHAPTER 9

Resumes for Careers in Federal, State, and Local Government

- Special Agents

- Government and Military Stores and Warehousing Managers

- Nuclear, Biological, and Chemical Operations and Training Managers

- Government Contract Administrators

- Program Managers

Because of the complexity of government-military contracts, the government sector often seeks to hire departing military members who can serve as a liaison between the two organizations. In these cases, military language and military-specific achievements become highly relevant, and there is less need to "demilitarize" the language in the resume. Additionally, reflecting the standards for federal resumes, government contractor resumes are often lengthier and more detailed than corporate resumes. Security clearances (such as Secret and Top Secret) are also important qualifications and are frequently highlighted in the summaries of the resumes in this chapter.

Brendan Moore

112 Penny Lane ★ Providence, RI 02911
Home: 401-998-8788 ★ Mobile: 401-320-4390 ★ E-mail: bmoore@email.net

Expertise and Qualifications
for position of United States Government Special Agent

★ Four years of service with the U.S. Marine Corps, attaining rank of master sergeant
★ Team leadership proven in multiple challenging situations
★ Surveillance, sniper operations, reconnaissance, and related reporting procedures
★ Expert marksmanship with a variety of firearms and grenade/anti-armor weapons
★ Instruction of others in weapons and tactical maneuvers
★ All forms of communications systems, including use of field-expedient antennae
★ Day/night all-terrain land and maritime navigation
★ Information collection/undercover intelligence activities
★ Operating and survival techniques in combat and extreme environmental conditions
★ Observation, identification, and deterrence of threatening circumstances
★ Top physical condition/endurance in severely rigorous situations
★ U.S. Top Secret clearance

Highlights of Leadership and Operations Experience

U.S. MARINE CORPS   2005–2009

★ **Observer NCO** (Camp Lejeune, NC):
Participated in Marine Corps urban warfare experiment. Advised a noninfantry
squad on how to conduct operations in an urban setting using lethal and nonlethal
experimental weapons.

★ **Chief Instructor** at battalion-level scout school (Parris Island, SC):
Led staff of 4 in training 30 recruits in basic scouting techniques, enabling them to
operate effectively in the absence of sniper and reconnaissance teams. Recommended
eligible candidates to join the Scout Sniper community.

★ **Squad Leader** for an infantry platoon (Fort Story, VA):
Participated in 5 weeks of cross-training with 15 non-NATO Eastern European
countries. Explored operations and overall cultural differences among these nations.

★ **Radio Communications Operator** (Africa):
Kept a detailed intelligence daily logbook during the evacuation of embassies in
western Africa. Briefed the battalion intelligence officer on all operations being
conducted in the platoon's vicinity. Took charge of the platoon headquarters in the
absence of the commander.

★ **Sniper Team Detachment Leader** (Afghanistan):
Reported to company commander. Participated in providing 24-hour surveillance
on the camp's perimeter. Conducted recon patrols and pattern analysis around camp
to identify/deter terrorist activities directed toward U.S. Marines and construction
workers as well as Afghani refugees.

★ **Scout Sniper Team Leader** (Iraq):
Conducted sniper/counter-sniper defense overtly and clandestinely in desert and
urban terrain. Watched over ground infantry operations to reduce the threat of
violence and looting. Routinely briefed officers ranging in rank from brigadier
general to captain on all operations.

continued

*This resume highlights training and leadership abilities under a variety of perilous conditions similar to
those that would be encountered in a position with the FBI, CIA, or ATF (Bureau of Alcohol, Tobacco,
and Firearms).*

Brendan Moore	bmoore@email.net	Page 2

Military Training

- ★ Camp Lejeune, NC:
  Basic training
  Marine Corps Scout Sniper course

- ★ Quantico, VA:
  Graduated School of Infantry
  Basic Recon course and indoctrination to platoon camp

- ★ Camp Butler, Okinawa, Japan:
  Group Coxswain course
  Special Operations training
  Jungle Warfare training

- ★ MCCDC, Bridgeport, CA:
  Mountain Warfare course in cold weather

- ★ MCAGCC, Twentynine Palms, CA:
  Sniper and recon operations in a desert environment

Nonmilitary Service

- ★ Participated in humanitarian relief, providing food, water, medical supplies, and shelter for earthquake survivors.

Decorations

- ★ National Defense Medal
- ★ Humanitarian Service Medal
- ★ NATO Medal
- ★ Navy Achievement Medal
- ★ Good Conduct Medal
- ★ Armed Forces Service Medal
- ★ Combat Action Ribbon
- ★ Navy Unit Commander Ribbon
- ★ Joint Meritorious Unit Commander Ribbon
- ★ Sea Service Deployment Ribbon
- ★ Meritorious Unit Citation Ribbon
- ★ 2 Meritorious MASTS

Current Status

Honorably discharged; inactive reserve

Brian Shedding

Home: (02) 2828 5931   1 Smith Road
Work: (02) 2825 6328   bshedding@amail.net.au   Richmond NSW 2755

EXPERTISE

Stores and Warehousing: Government/Military

QUALIFIED BY

Twenty years of service with the Australia Air Force with the last 10 years in stores and warehousing as a Line Manager responsible for 80,000 items of equipment and the supervision and training of 20 personnel. Extensive knowledge of contemporary warehousing and supply principles with a comprehensive understanding of complex organisational computerised supply systems. Planned the relocation of major warehouse facilities involving negotiations with contractors, builders, and planning authorities. Developed and implemented procedures to reach national quality assurance standards; prepared and transitioned a dangerous goods store from the military to a civilian operator.

CORE COMPETENCIES

■ Supervising ■ Communicating ■ Managing Time
■ Organising ■ Ordering ■ Auditing

APPLIED COMPETENCIES

- Extensive knowledge of contemporary warehousing and supply principles.

- Comprehensive understanding of computerised supply systems used by large government organisation.

- Provision of on-the-job training to individuals and groups in the principles of warehousing.

- Effective communication skills with the ability to work autonomously or within team-based environments as an active participant or team leader.

- Committed to occupational health and safety practices to ensure safe working environments.

- Building cohesive teams in a culturally diverse workforce.

- Meeting deadlines while maintaining a high level of accuracy and attention to detail.

- Excellent interpersonal and relationship-building skills, fully utilising negotiation techniques to achieve stated objectives.

RELATED ACHIEVEMENTS

- Planned and executed the relocation of a major warehouse facility containing 80,000 line items, as the Stores Officer with the Logistic Unit, Royal Australian Air Force, Richmond, requiring regular meetings with contractors and builders to address building concerns.

- Undertook a major stock purification involving the identification and return or disposal of approximately 10,000 inactive items prior to relocating a major storage facility for the Air Force; successfully addressed concerns over available space and long-term item redundancy.

—Continued—

This resume translates military stores experience to the government sector by downplaying the nature of the stored items. The ability to handle hazardous materials is stressed because it is common to both military and government sectors.

Brian Shedding _____ Page 2
(02) 2828 5931

RELATED ACHIEVEMENTS, continued

- Assessed, identified, and recommended improvements to warehouse procedures as the responsible Stores Officer with Logistic Unit, Royal Australian Air Force, Richmond, writing and implementing bench level instructions and performance measurements and achieving National Quality certification.

- Received a commendation from the Commander Logistic Unit, Royal Australian Air Force, Richmond, for performance as Stores Officer in managing the warehouse and satisfying customer needs during a critical manpower shortage resulting from the overseas deployment of troops on active service.

- Assisted in the preparation and transition of an explosive ordnance store from the military to a civilian operator in 2007, as the Non-Commissioned Officer in Charge of Explosive Storage; received letter of appreciation from Joint Ammunition Logistics Operation.

- Worked in an operational environment in Butterworth, Malaysia, for a two-year period as Stores Supervisor, often involving regular correspondence with Malaysian Customs and freight forwarders to ensure the timely delivery of aircraft spares from Australia to ensure the maintenance of operations.

RELEVANT EXPERIENCE

Stores Officer   2007–2010
Joint Logistic Unit
RAAF Richmond

Non-Commissioned Officer in Charge of Explosive Storage   2006–2007
Explosive Storage
RAAF Richmond

Non-Commissioned Officer in Charge of Equipment   2004–2006
92WG Detachment A
RMAF Base, Butterworth, Malaysia

Non-Commissioned Officer in Charge of Hazardous Store   2002–2004
Hazardous Goods Store
RAAF Richmond

Non-Commissioned Officer in Charge of General Warehouse   2001–2002
Number 6 Store
RAAF Richmond

Non-Commissioned Officer in Charge of Clothing Store   1999–2000
Clothing Store
RAAF Richmond

QUALIFICATIONS AND TRAINING

Certificate IV Transport and Distribution (Warehousing)	2008
Certificate in Simple Procurement	2007
Certificate III Information Technology	2007
Certificate III Transport and Distribution (Warehousing)	2006
Certificate III in Frontline Management	2006
Dangerous Goods Packaging	2005
Explosive Ordnance	2003
Shelf Life Management	2003
Basic Supplier Course	1990

RESUME 47: BY DIANE BURNS, CPRW, CCM, IJCTC, FJST, CCMC, CEIP

GEORGE K. JOHNSON, JR.

CMR 258 Box 408 * APO AE 09356
011-49-634-56902 * gkjjr@hotmail.com

CAREER FOCUS

Operations Management · Instruction · Training Program Development
Nuclear, Biological & Chemical (NBC) / Environmental Requirements

PERSONAL & PROFESSIONAL VALUE OFFERED

Currently hold a military SECRET security clearance.

Seventeen-plus years of combined experience in NBC operations and training as a program developer, advisor, maintenance manager, logistics specialist, and instructor. Establish, administer, and apply environmental defense measures and programs. Proficient in the following:

· NBC Detection & Decontamination	· Emergency Response	· Hazardous Materials
· NBC Equipment & Maintenance	· Training Course Development	· Problem Solving/Analysis
· NBC Defense Programs & Policies	· Communications Skills	· Liaison
· Weapons of Mass Destruction	· Computer Plotting	· NBC Intelligence
· Public Speaking/Briefings/Classes	· Team Leadership/Supervision	· Coaching/Mentoring

- ❑ Consistently plan and execute successful and effective environmental (NBC) training for organizations with more than 1,800 personnel. Envision, design, and execute projects and programs without start points.

- ❑ Possess strong oral and written communication skills and ability to interpret and explain, in lay terms, complex environmental requirements and contingency plans. Poised in public speaking and briefing delivery. Write SOPs, policies, technical reports, classroom curriculum, and emergency plans. Bilingual; speak fluent German.

Certifications
· Instructor
· Radiation Protection/Medical Effects of Nuclear Weapons
· Radiological Safety Officer

PROFESSIONAL EXPERIENCE

United States Army, 1989 to Present:
Nuclear, Biological & Chemical Operations Manager/Course Director   2005–Present
12th Chemical Detachment, Germany

- Technical Nuclear, Biological, and Chemical (NBC) expert and advisor—direct NBC operations. Manage the professional development, administration, HR, and training of more than 50 personnel.
- Course Director and Senior Instructor for the NBC Defense Course—train 1,500 senior managers in chemical detection and emergency management. Plan, organize, and coordinate all logistical and administrative functions for 12 environmental courses conducted annually in various locations. Manage and supervise the computerized worldwide address listing for the NBC Defense Course. Calculate all administrative student testing requirements and select honor and distinguished honor graduates.

(continued)

This resume sets up a smooth transition to the government sector by emphasizing expertise in nuclear, biological, and chemical safety instruction.

George K. Johnson, Jr., Page 2   011-49-634-56902 * gkjjr@hotmail.com

Achievements Continued...

- Advisor to the European Chemical Officer—provide information on matters pertaining to training and readiness of NBC defense, reconnaissance, decontamination, smoke and flame operations, and force protection. Guide senior management and staff in continuous appraisal of chemical operations and training situations. Establish priorities and inspect smoke production for compliance with operational procedures.
- Computer plotter—supervise the collection, interpretation, analysis, and dissemination of environmental information (NBC Warning and Reporting System) in support of NATO and other regional contingency operations to increase force protection. Plot and predict nuclear, biological, and chemical downwind hazards.
- Reviewed and improved the NBC Force Protection for the region by revising the NBC program of instruction for the senior-level courses. Served as subject-matter expert in updating and implementing new equipment and lessons into the 80-hour NBC Defense Course.
- Supervised automation upgrades resulting in accessible resource improvements from 65%–95%.
- Created and implemented a calibration program that increased equipment serviceability 100%.
- Completed a major biological operation by liquidating staff equipment worth $100,000.

Training Manager/Operations Manager/Intelligence Officer   2000–2005
17th Medical Brigade, Grafenwoehr, Germany

- Directed the coordination of all Department of Army, NATO, and V Corps NBC schools in a medical organization with six subordinate organizations and more than 1,860 personnel. Advised senior management regarding all aspects of NBC readiness.
- Planned all aspects of training and school functions. Consolidated and published the outline for the Primary Leadership Development Course. Maintained extensive training calendars.
- Planned, coordinated, and conducted mask confidence courses and exercises.
- Designed senior-level NBC training. Trained major subordinate units on NBC readiness. Conducted NBC site assistance visits for subordinate units.
- Created a well-received NBC inspection checklist. Established and wrote an NBC SOP—the first ever for the organization. Developed the NBC portion of a status report.
- Devised, established, and implemented a calibration program.
- Managed the accountability and requisitions of NBC supplies and equipment.
- Directed intelligence operations for a special task force. Supervised the collection and dissemination of security information with emphasis on medical and chemical intelligence to 10 subordinate units. Prepared daily security and intelligence briefings. Operated the medical intelligence computer system. Monitored the status of subordinate unit chemical operations and readiness programs.

NBC/Environmental Protection Manager, various worldwide locations, 1993–2000
Light Vehicle Wheel and Power Generation Mechanic/Supervisor, 1989–1993

PROFESSIONAL DEVELOPMENT

- Toxic Agent Training, Live Agent Chemical Training Facility, 2009
- Advanced Noncommissioned Officer Course/NATO NBC Defense Operations and Exercise Planning (Leadership, Briefings), 2004
- Instructor Course (Public Speaking), *exceeded standards*, 2003
- Quality Management Training, 2003
- Joint Warning and Reporting Network Phase 1A, 2003
- NATO NBC Defense Operations, 2002
- Medical Effects of Nuclear Weapons, 2001
- Local Radiation Protection Officer's Training Course, 2000
- Chemical Operations Specialist, *honor graduate*, 1991
- Member, Chemical Corps Regimental Association, 2003 to present

FRANCIS S. GREGORY
195 McCurdy Circle, Buffalo, NY 14288
716-387-1175 / 716-908-1959
gregfran@adelphia.net

Top Secret, Secret Compartmented Information (TS / SCI) Clearance

---

GOVERNMENT SALES / CONTRACT ADMINISTRATION / OPERATIONS MANAGEMENT
Competitive Bidding ● E-Procurement ● Corporate Security ● HR Management

Dynamic self-starter with demonstrated track record of exceptional results in both civilian and military settings. Excellent capacity to analyze operational needs and develop processes/procedures to meet organizational objectives. Proven ability to build consultative relationships with key decision-makers and to interact productively with team members at all levels of the organization. Areas of knowledge and expertise include

➤ **Researching government bidding processes, developing competitive bids, and securing preferred vendor status on procurement contracts for state, municipal, and institutional contracts.**

➤ **Negotiating with manufacturers and suppliers to develop joint agreements that facilitate successful bidding in competitive contracts.**

➤ **Managing customer relationships to ensure needs are met and customer satisfaction is maintained.**

➤ **Collaborating with IT professionals to develop in-house systems that capitalize on e-procurement opportunities with state and local governments.**

➤ **Establishing and monitoring protocols for controlling access to sensitive information and maintaining security within a large organization.**

➤ **Compiling and analyzing critical intelligence information in a fast-paced, demanding environment to make both tactical and strategic recommendations to senior military decision-makers.**

➤ **Addressing a broad range of HR management issues for organizations with up to 3,500 employees, including direct supervision of up to 80 people.**

➤ **Managing day-to-day operations of a military unit in the field with full accountability for $10 million in capital equipment.**

PROFESSIONAL EXPERIENCE

Executive Officer / Assistant to Director of Intelligence (Major)   Oct. 2001–Aug. 2009
United States Marine Corps—Assigned to Joint Intelligence Center, Central Command
Recalled to active duty following 9/11 attacks. Managed day-to-day operations of Joint Intelligence Center, including supervising a team of 40 people accountable for analyzing military intelligence data. Assigned to headquarters facility in Tampa, Florida, as well as deployments to Saudi Arabia, Qatar, Afghanistan, and Iraq, as part of **Operation Enduring Freedom** *and* **Operation Iraqi Freedom.**

- Coordinated the compilation of intelligence data from 30 countries and 10 U.S. federal agencies.
- Analyzed reliability and accuracy of compiled information and developed proposed action plans.
- Advised senior command staff on tactical and strategic options for engaging high-level targets.

Accomplishments:
Played a key role in locating and planning for the capture of numerous members of the so-called "Deck of Cards," 55 top members of the Saddam Hussein regime targeted by coalition forces. Assessed intelligence reports, developed rapid response action plans, and made recommendations to command officers and civilian officials at the highest levels. Awarded **Joint Commendation Medal** *by* **Secretary of Defense Donald H. Rumsfeld** *in recognition of these efforts.*

Selected to serve as Executive Officer during rapid ramp-up of operations following 9/11 attacks. Managed assessment and assignment of personnel; directed the setup of housing and food service for 1,200 military personnel; and addressed IT infrastructure issues to facilitate efficient operations.

Successfully served in assignments typically reserved for Lieutenant Colonels while still a Captain and was promoted to Major based on exemplary job performance.

(continued)

Called back to active duty following 9/11, this individual spent an additional eight years in the Marines after four years in the civilian workforce and a prior nine years in the military. Now returning to private life, he is targeting the government sector.

Francis S. Gregory   Resume—Page Two
716-387-1175   gregfran@adelphia.net

PROFESSIONAL EXPERIENCE (continued)

Fleet Manager, Niagara Commercial Sales; Tonawanda, NY   **Jan. 1999–Sept. 2001**
Accountable for sales, leasing, and service contracts for trucks provided to state and municipal governments and large public utilities.

- Managed bidding process to secure selection as a preferred vendor on state procurement contracts.
- Analyzed contracts and developed bid proposals based on past performance; forecasted future sales.
- Negotiated with OEMs, subcontractors, and other suppliers to achieve favorable agreements for the purchase and delivery of customized equipment.
- Consulted with individual purchasers statewide to assess needs, review technical specifications, and oversee custom building of equipment to meet customer requirements.
- Served as primary point of contact to address customer satisfaction issues, resolve problems, and manage account relationships, conforming to accepted government contract administration standards.
- Managed billing and accounts receivable functions related to government and commercial contracts.

Key Accomplishments:

Initiated firm's entry into government contract and large commercial contract segments of the business. Developed this sector into a lucrative profit center, growing bottom-line profits by more than 300% in a three-year period and increasing units sold by 150%.

Collaborated with IT staff to implement systems that capitalized on government e-procurement and electronic data interchange (EDI) procedures to secure increased business.

Received Ford Motor Company recognition as an advocate for alternative fueled vehicles.

Sales Associate, MONY Life Insurance; Buffalo, NY   **Oct. 1997–Dec. 1998**
Marketed insurance, annuity, and investment products to individuals as a licensed agent (NASD Series 6 & 63; NYS Life & Health). **Received Top Sales Associate Award for Fourth Quarter 1998.**

- Consulted with clients to assess needs, understand objectives, and recommend appropriate solutions.

Personnel Manager / Security Officer (2nd Lt. / 1st Lt. / Captain)   **May 1989–Oct. 1997**
United States Marine Corps—Domestic and Foreign Assignments
Completed advanced leadership and technical training, received TS / SCI clearance, and rotated to various field assignments. Deployed to Haiti, Guantanamo, and aboard ship, as well as serving stateside. Provided direct supervision and leadership to up to 80 Marines.

- Served as Security Officer for regiment with 3,500 Marines. Monitored access to Top Secret information, took action to control potential leaks, and advised commander on security issues.
- Managed the effective mobilization and utilization of up to $10 million in military assets in the field, including weapons systems and military communication systems, as well as other assets.

EDUCATION

Bachelor of Arts, Political Science—St. John Fisher College; Rochester, NY   **May 1989**

PROFESSIONAL DEVELOPMENT

Antenna Construction & Radio Wave Propagation	1993
Certificate in Information Management / Military Intelligence—USMC _(Honor Graduate)_	1995
Certificate in Military Specialty—Field Artillery—USMC	1992
Certificate in Leadership—The Basic School—USMC	1992

COMPUTER LITERACY / SPECIAL SKILLS

Windows; Microsoft Office; proprietary military applications; e-procurement applications.
Fundamental knowledge of Spanish and French.

Scott J. Mitchell, CPCM

818 Lodge Lane, Colorado Springs, Colorado 80901

Residence: (719) 969-3909
sjm1@hotmail.com

ACQUISITIONS MANAGEMENT / CONTRACTS ADMINISTRATION

Leadership / Proposals / DoD Purchasing / Senior Negotiator / Start-up Operations
Process Improvement / HR Management / Subject Matter Expert

Experienced and proven leader with exemplary, verifiable record of achievement in program management, acquisitions, and human resources. Successful in establishing new business operations and building high-performance teams. Skilled in proposal and solicitation preparation; detailed cost and price analyses; contract writing; and senior-level negotiations, awards, administration, closeouts, audits, reviews, policies, procedures, methods, and performance standards.

SELECTED ACHIEVEMENTS

Negotiations: Led negotiations of $760 million Korean F-16 Fighter Purchase Program. Saved $66 million from original proposal and additional $30 million by discovering vendor's misapplication of cost overrun. Project leadership set record for finalizing an airframe contract in only 45 days. Innovations included first fixed-price airframe contract in more than 6 years and first use of business base clause to limit liability. Assisted contractor with risk management and freed up additional $16 million for program use.

Organizational Leadership: Directed 20-person multiagency interdisciplinary team in $16 million missile program restructure in response to budget cuts and contractor delinquency. Restructured performance incentives and bought needed software ahead of schedule that enabled on-time fielding of systems improvements. Beat contract deadline by 6 weeks, cut price by a third (saved $8 million), and eliminated significant cost and performance risk.

Process Improvement & Cost Reductions: Created process for closeout and funds resolution for the F-16 Program's 195 contracts. Broke down barriers between Defense Contract Management Command, Defense Contract Audit Agency, Defense Finance and Accounting Service, and the contractor. Saved more than $8 million in first week and more than $120 million in first year, prevented Anti-Deficiency Act violations, saved current-year funding, and established new closeout branch and all supporting policies.

Training & Development: Identified and established interim training and certification procedures for agency out of compliance with congressional mandate. Authored training plans, calculated workforce requirements, and implemented process to achieve desired training quotas. Facilitated new agency to achieve customer-service requirements through excellence in training.

HR Management: Implemented plan to replace rapidly retiring civilian employees with experienced military retirees. Established relationships with transition offices to recruit trained military employees while instituting an intern program to meet long-range needs. Provided fully qualified staff ready to contribute from day one and internship program that exceeded expectations.

Subject Matter Expert: Eliminated 5-year backlog of contract changes. Completed more than $20 million in Engineering and Contract Change proposals in 6 months. Negotiated all at or below team's objectives, saving more than $3.2 million.

(continued)

Military executive experience was condensed into easily understood language for a government and possibly civilian audience. Bold functional headings call attention to skills and accomplishments.

Scott J. Mitchell, CPCM
Page 2   (719) 969-3909 • sjm1@hotmail.com

PROFESSIONAL EXPERIENCE

Professor, **Defense Acquisition University, Midwest Region**
Wright-Patterson AFB, Ohio, 2006–Present

- Teach acquisition workforce certification courses at introductory, intermediate, and advanced levels via lecture, case study, and computer-based training.
- Provide expert acquisition consultation to Defense Acquisition University customers.

General Manager, **Defense Contract Management Agency**
Fairfax, Virginia, 2004–2006

- Supervised civilian and military staff in direct support of active and reserve military for assignments, workforce training, and quality-of-life initiatives.
- Implemented agency-wide training reforms.

Senior Contracting Manager, **Joint Systems Program Office**
Homestead AFB, Florida, 2000–2004

- Directed contracting professionals in all phases of procurement, including support equipment, production contracts, and next-generation missiles.
- Led interdisciplinary teams of up to 30 in implementation of engineering change proposals.

Contract Manager, **F-16 Program Office**
Elgin AFB, Florida, 1997–2000

- Negotiated contract changes, support equipment, and foreign and domestic airframes.
- Negotiated $760 million Korean F-16 Fighter Purchase Program.

EDUCATION

Master of Science (MS), *Contract Management*
AIR FORCE INSTITUTE OF TECHNOLOGY, WPAFB, Ohio, 1997

Master of Public Administration (MPA), *Human Resources*
UCLA, Los Angeles, California, 1995

Senior Military Leadership School, *Human Resources*
AIR COMMAND AND STAFF COLLEGE, Montgomery, Alabama, 1994

Bachelor of Science (BS), *Industrial Labor Relations*
WRIGHT STATE UNIVERSITY, Dayton, Ohio, 1991

CERTIFICATIONS & MEMBERSHIPS

Certified Professional Contract Manager (CPCM)
National Contract Management Association, 2004

Certified Practitioner, Myers-Briggs Type Indicator (MBTI), 2007

Sigma Iota Epsilon National Honorary Fraternity, Academy of Management, 1997

Member, National Contract Management Association, 1997

BOYD J. ANDERSON

89 Trinity Place, Cherry Point, NC 28533
Cell: 252-710-1234 • bjanderson@verizon.com • Home: 252-349-1610

SENIOR-LEVEL PROGRAM MANAGER

Delivering cost savings, material gains, and innovative solutions
through strategic planning and decisive leadership

Performance-driven professional with extensive experience in fast-paced, high-intensity environments. Comprehensive understanding of relationships between programmatics, operations, training, and finance. Exemplary planning and organizational skills with demonstrated ability to manage myriad issues and merge competing priorities of separate organizations. Active Secret security clearance.

• Multisite Operations	• Cross-Functional Leadership	• Contract Administration
• Fiscal Management & Budgeting	• Productivity & Performance	• Program Design
• Workflow Planning/Prioritization	• Matrix Management	• Process Improvement

CAREER HIGHLIGHTS

Program Management

- Spearheaded performance measurement, methodology selection, and guideline development for the multibillion-dollar X-29 Program. Improved areas of program management including cost, scheduling, operations, logistics, and matrix management.
  —Identified a projected $3 billion in savings, equating to a 10% reduction in acquisition cost.
  —Pinpointed $10 million in parts savings.

- Implemented Airfield Improvement program and significantly improved Marine Corps' expeditionary air capabilities through strategic long-range planning, increased accountability, and stringent inventory control.
  —Reduced material requirement by 30%.
  —Established new material repair criteria that saved $1.5+ million of repair funds.
  —Reclaimed 145,000 sq. ft. of material that resulted in increased inventory and a reallocation of funds.

Management

- Directed and was responsible for 500+ personnel, $250 million in aircraft and other aviation assets, 60+ vehicles, and plant facilities. Managed multimillion-dollar annual budget. Directed planning, operations, training, maintenance, logistics, safety, and quality assurance. Conducted performance evaluations, promotions, and disciplinary actions.

- Managed the day-to-day operation of the academic program at NATO's key educational training facility. Supervised 15+ multiservice military and multinational civilian personnel. Planned and coordinated the administration of 70 classes to nearly 5,000 students annually. Oversaw all academic support branches, including Registrar, Student Administration, Visual Services, Interpretation, and Classroom Registry.

Operations

- Designed, planned, and directed training and operational commitments for CH-53 helicopter squadron that resulted in 93% combat readiness percentage (CRP), the highest for its type of aircraft in the Marine Corps at that time.

- Planned and executed detachment's physical relocation while fulfilling closure requirements and seamlessly integrating multiple squadrons into detachment.

PROFESSIONAL EXPERIENCE

MARINE CORPS OFFICER, NAVAL AVIATOR, United States Marine Corps   1991–2010
Successful and distinguished military career progressing to the rank of Lieutenant Colonel with increasingly responsible positions requiring direct leadership, project planning and execution, and fiscal responsibility.

COMMANDING OFFICER, Cherry Pt., NC, 2008–2010
Commanded a mission-capable military unit comprising 3 helicopter squadrons and administrative support.

- Melded separate organizations into a cohesive and effective unit. Achieved/surpassed all training and operational requirements in spite of scarce funding, fast operational tempo, and turbulence of 2 major relocations.

- Accomplished an exemplary Certified Safe for Flight record for 18 aircraft; in less than 10 months, elevated division from 17 unsatisfactory grades to all satisfactory and excellent grades.

- Coordinated successful Toys for Tots campaign with 205 civilian organizations; collected 175,000+ toys.

continued

In this resume, an extensive Career Highlights section uses functional headings to call attention to relevant experience and accomplishments.

BOYD J. ANDERSON Cell: 252-710-1234 • bjanderson@verizon.com • Home: 252-349-1610

DEPUTY ASSISTANT CHIEF OF STAFF, ACADEMICS, NATO School, Oberammergau, Germany, 2006–2008
The NATO School is NATO's leading training facility offering courses, training, and seminars to educate officers, noncommissioned officers, and civilians from the Alliance and Partner nations.

- Analyzed the workflow processes of 5 academic branches. Implemented improvements that afforded a cost-effective use of funds, expanded use of classroom capacity, and increased student confirmation capability.

- Revised course offerings and restructured scheduling to create a varied and challenging academic program while increasing course calendar availability by 14%.

- Conducted analysis for school expansion. Submitted solution-based, multimillion-dollar proposal that recommended the use of adjacent German government-owned unused buildings. Government and NATO both accepted proposal.

- Contributed and edited new *Cooperation Partners Procedures, Instructor Course Guidelines,* and *Conference Package Information;* oversaw complete rewrite of *Academics Operations Manual.*

MARINE DEPUTY PROGRAM MANAGER, Naval Air Systems Command, 2004–2006
Department of the Navy program responsible for fielding tilt-rotor aircraft, produced by Bell Helicopter Textron and Boeing Rotorcraft Systems, to fill critical multiservice missions.

- Developed and implemented initiatives that improved program's operational effectiveness, reduced program risk, and significantly decreased cost. Wrote *Concept of Operations* that incrementally introduced government personnel into the team. Resolved 20 operational issues.

- Conceived, planned, and chaired 4 critical teams:
  Medium Lift Requirements Team—Verified requirements and emerging needs; issued recommendations for inclusions, denials, or improvement.
  Affordability Trade Studies Team—Established methodology for analysis of 60 trade studies for cost/benefit analysis.
  Effectiveness Analysis Team—Constructed methodology to ensure projected changes to aircraft improved its ability to meet services' and program requirements. Evaluated cost against measures of effectiveness.
  Aircraft Parts Distribution Committee—Recommended time, quantity, and priority of initial stocking, and the distribution of parts and equipment for each service, based on projected contractor outputs.

- Served as point of contact for mishap activity. Orchestrated the coordination of salvage operations, movement of equipment, and involvement with national news media.

PROGRAM MANAGER/MARINE LIAISON OFFICER, Naval Air Systems Command, 2002–2004
Expeditionary Airfield Program (EAF) is a $20 million annual worldwide aviation program that deploys and constructs temporary/transportable airports to meet air support requirements established by the Marine Corps.

- Provided leadership and direction to ensure program delivery met aviation requirements. Organized and directed all program management functions, including strategic planning, financial management, logistical support, and military and civilian team coordination.
  —Increased budget by $9 million per year due to planning and the articulation of emerging requirements with ability to execute pre-placed contract options.

- Executed the reassignment and movement of EAF equipment to war zones by air and sea. Commended by Commander, Naval Air Systems Command, for major cost avoidance in shipping of materials supporting Marine Corps Harrier Hover-Pad installation at Lambert Field.

ADDITIONAL EXPERIENCE: Helicopter Pilot, Advanced Tactics Instructor, Functional Test Pilot, Mission Commander

EDUCATION

Program Management, Defense Systems Management College, Alexandria, VA
Marine Corps Command and Staff College, Marine Corps Base, Quantico, VA
Administration/Systems Acquisition graduate coursework, University of Rhode Island, Kingston, RI
Bachelor of Arts in History, University of Virginia, Charlottesville, VA

JOHN D. PERSHING

1610 Wellington Drive
San Francisco, CA 94129

jdp@cox.net

Residence: 415.627.9351
Mobile: 650.805.0098

Proven Leader / Innovative Planner / Effective Program Manager

"Give me your vision and mission, and I can turn it into reality. I motivate people, maximize resources, and devise successful action plans. I have the self-discipline, mental agility, flexibility, and determination to drive to the goal while maintaining a team with great morale and genuine job satisfaction."

- Renowned expertise in team building and leadership—able to quickly recognize and cultivate employees' strengths; earn respect from peers and superiors; work well with people from other nations and cultures.
- Ability to establish and maintain objective and quantifiable standards that superiors can measure.
- Strong analytical skills—systematically evaluate, identify the essential parameters, and devise solutions to complex, multidimensional problems.
- Level-headed, common-sense approach to problems—recognized for thoroughness, simplicity, and innovation.
- Confidence, commanding physical presence, and strong interpersonal skills—operate comfortably with individuals at the highest levels of government, private sector, Congress, and the media.

EDUCATION AND CERTIFICATION

Master of Science in National Resource Strategy,
Industrial College of the Armed Forces, Ft. McNair, Washington, D.C.

Master of Military Art and Sciences, School of Advanced Military Studies, Fort Leavenworth, Kansas

Master of Science, Engineer Management, University of Missouri at Rolla

Bachelor of Science, United States Military Academy, West Point, New York

Command and General Staff College, Fort Leavenworth, Kansas

Registered Professional Engineer, State of California, since 1990

PROFESSIONAL EXPERIENCE

Executive Officer to Assistant Secretary of the Army, Washington, D.C., 2009–Present

Principal staff coordinator, advisor, and personal administrative assistant to the Assistant Secretary of the Army. Participate in the formulation of policy, procedures, and programs. Liaison with the Office of the Secretary of the Army; Office of the Secretary of Defense; the Joint Staff; and counterparts in the Air Force, Navy, and other federal departments and agencies. Interact with the military's most senior leadership, congressional staffs and committees, the media, and private-sector business leaders on a daily basis.

- Established and implemented flawless plan to integrate this organization under the new functional reorganization of the Headquarters Department of the Army.
- Developed strategic overview of the organization and established four major areas of focus. Established short-term and long-range goals. Designed and implemented reporting systems.
- Developed plan, set parameters, and coordinated with HQDA Senior Executive Service to establish position of Deputy Assistant Secretary for Infrastructure Analysis in preparation for upcoming Congressionally mandated base realignment and closure.
- Programmed and managed the internal budget. Provided oversight of $13 billion in Army operation funds.

Page 1 of 2

Because this senior officer is applying for government contracting positions, some military jargon is included in the resume, but overall the language is easily understood by nonmilitary readers.

JOHN D. PERSHING
415.627.9351

PAGE 2
jdp@cox.net

Brigade Commander, 1st Combat Engineer Brigade, 1ID, Wuerzburg, Germany, 2007–2009

Senior Executive of an Engineer Brigade consisting of two Combat Engineer Battalions, an Assault Float Bridge (AFB) Company, and a Combat Support Equipment (CSE) Company—approximately 1,200 people. Managed a budget of $6 million. Served as the Division Engineer for planning and execution of all engineer operations within the division.

- Totally revamped training and maintenance program. Implemented certifications programs for operators and maintainers. Developed innovative rebuild program. Exceeded the Army average for operational readiness.
- Established solid relations with local elected officials, local business organizations, and local senior German Army commanders. Success was evident by the relationship that continues today.

Human Resource Branch Manager, PERSCOM, Alexandria, Virginia, 2005–2007

Planned and directed the leader development and career management of more than 3,500 engineer officers. Managed implementation of Officer Personnel Management System (OPMS) XXI for all engineer officers. Conducted professional development briefings, provided career guidance, and advised the engineer proponent, general officers, commanders at all levels, and engineer officers in the field on personnel matters.

- Demonstrated great professional judgment, integrity, and common sense when dealing with the issues associated with assignments and professional development.
- Showed thorough understanding of the "big picture."
- Implemented monthly branch notes that led to a better informed population of engineer officers. Received high volume of positive feedback from these monthly updates.
- Highly respected for ability to coach, teach, and mentor subordinates. Earned the trust of senior leadership as well as peers and subordinates.

Battalion Commander, 94th Engineer Battalion, Bamberg, Germany, 2002–2004

Senior Manager of a Combat Engineer Battalion located on two separate installations—approximately 600 soldiers. Ensured soldiers were trained and ready. Provided engineer analysis and planning for preparations of war plans in support of all units in Germany. Directed engineer support for range and road upgrade and maintenance.

- Brought unit's training, maintenance, and quality of life into balance, resulting in highly motivated and trained soldiers.
- Created a command climate that encouraged initiative from subordinates while tolerating honest mistakes, bringing junior leader confidence and initiative to an all-time high. No officers resigned from active duty while under my command.
- Unit won U.S. Army, Germany, "Army Community of Excellence Award."

Deputy Engineer Support Trainer, Fort Irwin, California, 1999–2002

Served as the Deputy to the Senior Engineer Trainer for operation and maintenance of the Combat Engineer Battalion Training Team (Sidewinder Team) of 35 selectively chosen officers, senior noncommissioned officers, and civilians. Trained rotational engineer battalion staff on doctrinal requirements and duties in support of a brigade combat team. Developed engineer-specific rules of engagement. Supervised preparation and execution of all-engineer, battalion-level after action reviews (AARs) conducted during a rotation as well as a take-home package to enhance home station training.

- Pioneered the establishment of critical link from NTC training battlefield to the Engineer Center, resulting in up-to-date engineer doctrine and better-trained engineer officers and soldiers.
- Developed standard operating procedures, logistical systems, and reception program for the team.

• • • • •

CHAPTER 10

Resumes for Careers in Health Care and Social Services

- Environmental or Occupational Health Technicians

- Medical Records Managers/Health Care Administrators

- Medical Laboratory Managers

- Occupational Health Nurses

- Disaster Response/Critical Care Nurses

- Social Service Managers

- Medical Facilities Construction and Site Managers

Most health care–related skills are readily transferable to any setting. In fact, military personnel often have an edge because they have proven themselves in fast-paced, intensive environments. The resumes in this chapter highlight both knowledge and job duties as well as specific achievements in a variety of formats.

MYLES KRISTOPHERSON

850 Bay Blvd.
Tampa, FL 33680

mylesk@tampabay.rr.com
(813) 828-3333

OBJECTIVE: Environmental or Occupational Health Technician

EXPERIENCE: Bioenvironmental Technician, U.S. Air Force 3/05–5/10

Maintain OSHA, federal, and state standards for environmental monitoring.
Identify asbestos hazards according to ACM conditions.
Determine collection methods for environmental surveys on a case-by-case basis.
Recommend pollution control methods.
Ensure occupational exposure levels are not being exceeded.
Identify and analyze sources of pollution.
Identify lead-based paint by swipe sample.
Monitor waste streams.
Test personnel for quantitative fit of specialized respiratory protection.
Conduct thermal stress index monitoring.
Sample air for toxic gases and particulates.
Sample and analyze water for pH and bacterial content.
Recommend methods for improving operations efficiency.
Conduct lighting surveys for worker safety.
Conduct surveys to evaluate noise-producing equipment.
Administer, monitor, and analyze noise dosimetry and results for hearing-conservation program.
Monitor organic and inorganic gases for potentially hazardous levels.
Conduct monitoring of radio-frequency radiation.
Perform preventative maintenance on vehicles to reduce carbon monoxide emissions.
Developed vehicle-management techniques that saved the department thousands of dollars.

EDUCATION/TRAINING:

Bachelor of Science in Medical Technology

Kennesaw State University, Kennesaw, GA; expected completion Fall 2010

Career Development Coursework included

Properties of Matter	Cells and Tissues
Introduction to Chemistry	Major Organ Systems
Bioenvironmental Publications	Dose-Response Relationships
Anatomy and Physiology	Exposure Routes

Bioenvironmental Engineering Training, 2004. Studies included

Lead and Asbestos Hazards	Toxicology	Ionizing and Nonionizing Radiation
Environmental/Industrial Hazards	Ventilation Systems	Ergonomics
Respiratory Protection		Octave Band Analysis

Extensive training and directly related work experience are highlighted in this concise resume.

ERNEST G. THOMAS

931 Devonshire Circle
Rochester, New York 14624
(585) 442-0078
E-mail: ernestt@frontiernet.net

EXPERTISE: MEDICAL RECORDS MANAGEMENT & HEALTH CARE ADMINISTRATION

Extensive experience supervising office staff, maintaining records, and coordinating billing/claims activities in the health care field. Additional experience delivering training on emergency medical topics to nonmedical audiences, advocating for patients with brain injuries, and serving as a pharmacy technician.

PROFESSIONAL EXPERIENCE:

UNITED STATES NAVY (1990–2010)
Medical Administration Technician (Shipboard)   2004–2010

Managed operations for shipboard medical department serving 1,250 people. Accountable for maintaining medical records and corresponding with medical facilities providing consultations, as well as supervising up to 28 corpsmen with administrative and operational duties.
- Ensured that medical records for each sailor on board were updated and accurate.
- Processed claims from civilian providers on behalf of Navy personnel and dependents.
- Tracked all official correspondence in and out of medical department.
- Documented vaccinations for 8,200 people with 100% accuracy.
- Prepared performance evaluations for subordinates.
- Provided administrative support to five physicians and six nurses aboard ship.
- Instructed approximately 900 Navy personnel in CPR.

Educational Resource Center (Norfolk, Virginia)   2003–2004

Developed training materials and other graphic presentation aids for internal Navy use.

Medical Administrator Training   2002–2003

Completed year-long training program to prepare for assignment as Medical Administration Technician.

Instructor—Afloat Training (San Diego, California)   2000–2002

Provided shipboard instruction to non-medical personnel on various medical procedures.
- Delivered programs on 33 ships deployed in the Pacific.
- Taught programs in First Aid and Mass Casualty Training.
- Provided instruction to Coast Guard personnel.
- Instructed more than 375 people in CPR.
- Rewrote medical inspection criteria for Coast Guard use.
- **Recognized as Master Training Specialist.**
- **Received Navy Achievement Medal for exceptional leadership and organizational skills.**

Medical Billing Processor (Pearl Harbor, Hawaii)   1998–2000

Served as part of seven-member team accountable for processing more than $28 million in medical bills from civilian providers.

(continued)

Every position this candidate held in the Navy related to his career goal. His community involvement is relevant as well.

Ernest G. Thomas
Resume–Page Two
(585) 442-0078 ☐ earnestt@frontiernet.net

Medical Records Technician (Okinawa, Japan)   **1995–1998**
Maintained medical records and coordinated sick call for Naval personnel.

Pharmacy Technician (various land-based assignments)   **1993–1995**
Managed pharmacy supplies and inventory and processed prescriptions for oral and IV medications
in hospital and shipboard environments.

Medical Corpsman / Pharmacy Training   **1990–1993**
Received extensive training in medical procedures and attended pharmacy technician school in
preparation for Pharmacy Technician assignments.

TRAINING / EDUCATION:

Certified CPR Instructor

United States Navy
- Medical Administrator School
- Instructor School
- Medical Corpsman Training

Massachusetts College of Pharmacy
Completed 45 credit hours as part of Naval training program.

Rochester Institute of Technology (Rochester, New York)
Extensive coursework in computer programming (Java) and graphics.

COMPUTER LITERACY:

PC: Windows XP, Vista, and 7; Microsoft Office (Excel, Word, PowerPoint, and Access)
Macintosh: Adobe Photoshop and Illustrator

COMMUNITY INVOLVEMENT:

San Diego Youth & Community Services   **2000–2002**
- Volunteer Training Coordinator
- Counselor to troubled teens
- Named **Volunteer of the Month,** June and July 2001

Helping Hands Hawaii   **1998–2000**
- Suicide and Crisis Hotline Counselor

References Available upon Request

Stephanie A. Johnson

203 Marler Boulevard • San Diego, CA 92100 • (619) 514-5569 • sajohnson@net.com

Medical Laboratory Management

Certified Medical Laboratory professional with more than 10 years of progressive team leadership, policy development, and management experience in major medical center, clinic, and field environments. Solid background in staffing, training, developing, and supervising emergency and lab personnel. Budget planning and administrative expertise includes successes in cost reductions while maintaining highest quality standards. Proven analytical, problem solving, and organizational abilities resulting in effective approaches to operations and administration.

Career Milestones

- **Selected to establish, staff, and manage medical lab operations at an overseas clinic. Developed policies/procedures and led operations to attain licensure and certification in only 14 months.**
- **Chosen to lead the start-up of medical laboratory functions at Naval hospitals in 2 states; coordinated staffing and procurement of state-of-the-art equipment.**
- **Achieved and maintained 100% safety record in laboratory operations through effective staff training, team building, and supervision in all clinical areas.**
- **Initiated the first blood DNA collection program for the Naval Academy and Department of the Navy to be launched organization-wide. Credited by senior management for "phenomenal planning, meticulous attention to detail, and flawless program execution."**
- **Achieved 5 promotions and annual awards for superior performance record and initiative in the development of staff educational and other programs.**

Experience & Accomplishments

UNITED STATES NAVY (1993–present)
Assistant Medical Laboratory Supervisor, Naval Hospital, San Diego, CA (2004–present)
Sr. Medical Laboratory Technician, Clinic & Naval Hospital, Albuquerque, NM (1998–2004)

Lab Operations & Management

- Supervise medical laboratory operations and staff of 24 technicians in performing more than 2,000 procedures weekly, utilizing state-of-the-art equipment.
- Plan and administer $150,000 annual budget for laboratory operations, successfully reducing costs and maintaining budget well under 20% through training and accountability.
- Involved in administrative functions, including medical billing, patient medical records, purchasing, and inventory/stock control.
- Coordinate and prepare all documentation required by JCAHO and OSHA regulatory agencies.
- Develop, implement, and monitor adherence to laboratory department policies and procedures.
- Ensure stringent compliance to standards on quality control, infection control, safety, and disposal of hazardous materials.

Staff Training, Development & Supervision

- Supervise and develop teams of up to 45 personnel, motivating and evaluating performance to maximize efficiency and productivity.
- Train staff on laboratory equipment procedures and protocols to improve productivity while maximizing safety.
- Develop and conduct training programs for new recruits on infectious diseases and preventive medicine.
- Implement training curriculum for health science students on nursing, laboratory policies, procedures, and operations.

continued...

An impressive Career Milestones section highlights key leadership and managerial accomplishments supporting this individual's career objective. Achievements in the chronological section are grouped under functional headings for emphasis and easy reading.

Stephanie A. Johnson

Page 2

(619) 514-5569 • sajohnson@net.com

Experience & Accomplishments continued...

Patient Technician, Naval Medical Center, Germany (1996–1998)
Emergency Medical Technician, Naval Hospital, Persian Gulf (1993–1996)

Lab Procedures & Emergency Medicine

- Performed hematology, blood banking, chemistry, microbiology, urinalysis, phlebotomy, serology, specimen collection, and other lab procedures.
- Diagnosed and provided routine/emergency medical care to broad range of patients (ICU, CCU, neuro ICU, geriatric, and pediatric) in emergency/trauma, home care, and acute care environments.
- Prescribed medications and performed thorough patient assessments and medical procedures: taking vital signs, audiograms, IV and oxygen therapy, suturing, casting, venipuncture, starting arterial lines, EKGs, and tracheotomies.
- Advocated and represented patients, effectively resolving issues to ensure quality care and excellent patient relations.

Education & Certifications

Bachelor of Science, Laboratory Science, 2005
University of California, San Diego, CA

Additional Training

UNITED STATES NAVY: **Advanced Laboratory School,** 1999; **Basic Laboratory School,** 1997; **Emergency Medical Technician School,** 1995; **Hospital Corpsman School,** 1993

Seminars

Leadership Development, Critical Care, Field Emergency Medicine, Bacteriology

Certifications

Laboratory Technician, Emergency Medical Technician, Phlebotomy, CPR/First Aid, Health Educator

JOANNA VIERA, RN

9434 Lake Drive, Apt. 29-B
Cleveland, OH 44108

Residence: (216) 349-1212
Cell: (216) 650-7243

Occupational Health Nurse

—Areas of Effectiveness—

- ☐ Evaluation of medical condition for job fitness
- ☐ Information and referral sources
- ☐ Patient records management
- ☐ Pre-employment physicals
- ☐ Employee health counseling

- ☐ Treatment planning
- ☐ Risk factor screening
- ☐ Pain control
- ☐ Major trauma/triage
- ☐ Regulatory agency compliance

—Personal Strengths—

- ☐ Strong medical knowledge base with the critical-thinking skills to act decisively within scope of authority
- ☐ Recognized for consistent dependability and resourcefulness in problem-solving situations
- ☐ Thorough and well organized in attending to administrative functions
- ☐ Willing team participant, equally adaptable to working independently
- ☐ Communicate effectively at all levels; trilingual in Spanish, Portuguese, and English

—Education—

Erie Community College—AAS, 2008
Passed RN Boards in August 2008

USAF School of Aerospace Medicine and
School of Hearing Conservation, 2004-2006

Certifications: CPR (current); Basic Arrhythmia; IV Administration; Angioplasty; Bedside Computer; Air Force EMT.

—Related Experience—

UNITED STATES AIR FORCE, Armed Forces Medical Center, Cleveland, OH
Telemetry Nurse, Open Heart Surgery Step Down Unit   2008-2010
- Provided support to surgeons, residents, attending physicians, other nurses, and technicians involved in caring for up to 9 post-surgery patients.
- Used bedside computer to enter patient data, such as medications, diets, and diagnostic testing results.
- Specialized in stents, angioplasties, and cardiac monitoring. Attached pacemakers in emergencies.

Aerospace Medical Service Technician, Reese AFB, TX   2005-2007
- Received initial medical training in a busy sick-call area, which treated up to 300 patients a day.
- Scheduled and conducted physical exams for new recruits, evaluating vision, hearing, pulmonary, and cardiac functions required for FAA licensing.
- During tenure responded to 4 in-flight emergencies, gathering information on aircraft accidents. Participated in triage and transport of the severely injured for immediate care and/or surgery.
- Counseled and referred accordingly any conditions limiting effective performance of pilot or flight crew duties. These conditions included pregnancy; STDs; and drug, alcohol, or psychological problems.
- Kept all records of physical exams/treatments administered. Requisitioned medications and supplies.
- Addressed groups of up to 100 recruits, providing tips on decreasing coronary risk factors.

This resume effectively positions an Air Force nurse as someone an insurance company can rely on to assess the fitness of workers' compensation claimants.

STANLEY MITCHELL, RN, BSN
125 Sunrise Lane Syosset, New York 11782
631-313-0665
mitchell@attmil.ne.jp

DISASTER RESPONSE • ACUTE & CRITICAL PATIENT CARE • MEDICAL / SURGICAL CARE
Pediatrics / Geriatrics / Postsurgical / Nuclear & Biological Hazards

---

Health care professional with more than eight years of intensive experience in fast-paced military hospital environments. Demonstrated capacity to provide direct patient care and effectively supervise support staff in a variety of clinical settings. Specialized training in dealing with nuclear and biological exposure, as well as experience treating patients with infectious diseases including typhoid, meningitis, AIDS, and other contagions. Proven capacity to function well in crisis situations, plus excellent ability to relate to patients from diverse cultural backgrounds and various age groups.

PRIMARY CLINICAL EXPERIENCE:

LIEUTENANT, UNITED STATES NAVY (2001–Present)
U.S. NAVAL HOSPITAL; Osaka, Japan
Patients encompass infants through geriatrics, with conditions including a broad range of infectious diseases and physical injuries.

Staff Nurse / Charge Nurse—Adult & Pediatric Care   2005–Present
- Provide bedside care to patients, administer medications, and implement physician orders.
- Confer with physicians and other care team members on treatment plans for various patients.
- Address the needs of patients in isolation with typhoid, meningitis, and other contagious diseases.
- Train and provide leadership for staff of seven RNs and LPNs in Charge Nurse role.
- Participate in field exercises to maintain readiness for combat deployment in support of Marine units.

Key accomplishment: Restructured medical supplies inventory and wrote new Standard Operating Procedures (SOPs) to improve departmental efficiencies.

Staff Nurse / Division Officer—Postanesthesia Care Unit   2004–2005
- Served needs of postoperative patients, addressing special concerns of postanesthesia recovery.
- Otherwise supported surgical teams in treating patients with a broad range of medical conditions.

U.S. NAVAL HOSPITAL; San Francisco, California
Patient base included military dependents and retirees, as well as active military personnel, including several "VIP" patients.

Staff Nurse—Medical / Telemetry Acute Care Unit   2001–2004
- Addressed acute-care needs of medical patients, including oncology and infectious disease patients.
- Cared for patients in isolation wards with tuberculosis, AIDS, and other contagious diseases.
- Monitored cardiac activity of patients using state-of-the-art telemetry technology.

Key accomplishment: Selected to serve as part of Humanitarian Relief Response Team.

CENTRAL SUFFOLK HOSPITAL; Riverhead, New York
Suburban/rural facility (eastern Long Island, New York) providing full range of medical services.

Staff Nurse / Charge Nurse—Medical / Surgical Unit   1999–2001
- Provided direct patient care including telemetry monitoring.
- Served needs of incarcerated individuals in conjunction with Suffolk County (NY) Sheriff's Office.

(continued)

The theme running through this resume is extensive and diverse clinical experience that will be valuable in any medical setting—military, government, or civilian.

Stanley Mitchell   631-313-0665
Resume–Page Two   mitchell@attmil.ne.jp

ADDITIONAL CLINICAL EXPERIENCE:

INTERIM MEDICAL SERVICES; San Francisco, California
 Per Diem Registered Nurse—Polinski's Children's Center   **2001–2004**
 • Served the needs of pediatric patients in a clinical outpatient setting.

ALLCARE NURSING SERVICES; Plainview, New York
 Per Diem Registered Nurse   **2000–2001**
 • Cared for burn victims, cardiac patients, postsurgical patients, ICU patients, and the terminally ill.

EDUCATION:

 WESTERN MICHIGAN UNIVERSITY; Grand Rapids, Michigan
 Master of Science, Community Service   *In Process*

 STATE UNIVERSITY OF NEW YORK AT ONEONTA; Oneonta, New York
 Bachelor of Science, Nursing   **1999**
 Sigma Theta Tau Honorary / Gold Key Award / Silver Key Award

 CULINARY INSTITUTE OF AMERICA; Hyde Park, Rhode Island
 Associate of Science, Hotel & Restaurant Management   **1991**

CERTIFICATIONS / SPECIALIZED TRAINING:

 Registered Nurse
 Advanced Cardiac Life Support (ACLS); Basic Life Support (BLS)
 Pediatric Advanced Life Support (PALS I)
 Intravenous Conscious Sedation (IVCS)

 Nuclear & Biological Hazard Medical Training
 Mass Casualty Training; Field Hospital Training; Shipboard Hospital Training
 Suturing; Chest Tube Insertion

References Provided on Request

Michael W. Barker

852 East Prospect Court, Kansas City, Kansas 66101
Residence: (913) 837-2487
mwb123@earthlink.net

SOCIAL SERVICE MANAGEMENT & ADMINISTRATION

Delivering operational improvements that contribute to success.

- Developing standardized policies and metrics to control and measure key areas.
- Creatively solving operational problems with innovative solutions.
- Leading teams and projects to successful conclusion; training staff for excellence.
- Delivering superior customer service on a continuous basis.

SELECTED ACHIEVEMENTS

Instituted new food-safety programs for overseas military base with population of 6,000. Enforced strict quality-assurance provisions and improved warehousing practices to improve food quality and protect staff. Reduced lost work-hours due to food-borne illnesses by 50% and saved more than $250,000 in storage losses.

Developed and implemented comprehensive management plan for major department in outpatient clinic. Identified and monitored 58 distinct performance metrics and tracked more than 500 recurring tasks from inception to completion. Improved delivery of cost-effective, quality-focused service to 15,000 members.

Organized and implemented merger of two specialty health care departments. Reengineered more than 200 individual processes and procedures, cross-trained and reassigned 11 staff members, and designed new office space. Created new organization devoted to delivering quality health care services to 4,000 patients per year.

Led multidisciplinary team investigating potentially serious measles outbreak. Quickly identified the agent, source, and exposed patients, and then interviewed and tracked susceptible individuals and immunized more than 3,600 potential contacts. Decisive response prevented potential epidemic of highly contagious disease.

Created new process to collect federally mandated hazard-communication training documentation for 4,000 employees. Decentralized collection process to reduce individual processing time and eliminate overhead. Saved more than 2,000 man-hours per year.

Revised anthrax vaccination program to deliver vital protection more effectively. Improved data collection and processing methods; rotated locations and times for vaccinations to encourage maximum participation. Raised vaccination rate from 49% to 94% in less than one month for 2,000 personnel in high-threat area.

Led process action team tasked to improve the disease-reporting process for large outpatient clinic. Utilized proven process improvement methods to study, benchmark, and revise disease-reporting and data-collection methods. Expected benefits are reduced health care costs and improved disease prevention for 36,000 beneficiaries.

(continued)

Military jargon has been eliminated, and job titles have been altered to fit the civilian social service environment. Achievements related to career goals are emphasized on page 1, whereas details of military experience appear on page 2.

Michael W. Barker

(913) 837-2487 • mwb123@earthlink.net   **Page 2**

PROFESSIONAL EXPERIENCE

United States Air Force

Supervisor of Public Health
Hickam AFB, Hawaii, 2008–2010
- Developed new tool to provide protection against eight recognized bioterrorism threats.
- Supervised public health initiatives for community of 15,000.
- Authored, controlled, and administered budget using generally accepted accounting principles (GAAP).

State of Florida

Sanitation and Safety Inspector
Tampa, Florida, 2006–2008
- Conducted health inspections of more than 350 public food-service and lodging facilities covering more than 100 square miles. Performed approximately 1,000 inspections annually, ensuring compliance with food/fire safety standards.

United States Air Force

Superintendent of Medical Operations
Hickam AFB, Hawaii, 2003–2005
- Senior administrative supervisor at outpatient clinic providing clinical, ancillary, preventative, and surgery services for 15,000 patients.
- Managed 80 paraprofessional and administrative personnel, providing mentorship on technical and professional matters.

Supervisor of Public Health
Peterson AFB, Colorado, 2000–2003
Elgin AFB, Florida, 1999–2000
MacDill AFB, Florida, 1996–1999
- Supervised public-health programs at air bases serving populations up to 35,000.
- Provided individual and group counseling on personal and professional issues.

Course Supervisor
USAF School of Aerospace Medicine, Brooks AFB, Texas, 1995–1996
- Taught basic to advanced instruction in technical school environment, planning schedules and administering all aspects of coursework.
- Counseled students on academic pathways.

EDUCATION and TRAINING

Bachelor of Science (BS), *Management—Human Resources*
PARK UNIVERSITY, Parkville, Missouri, 2008

Associate of Applied Science (AAS), *Environmental Medicine Technology*
COMMUNITY COLLEGE OF THE AIR FORCE, Montgomery, Alabama, 1998

EDWARD JAMES

12013 Beachcomber Drive, Apt. 311, Destin, FL 32540
Cell: (850) 650-2150, E-mail: captedjames@usa.com

PROFILE

Proven leader with six years of progressively responsible military experience specializing in medical facilities construction and management. Selected for supervisory assignments critical to the operation of the Navy's Global Defense Health Program with responsibility for multimillion-dollar budgets and resources. Experienced in collaborating closely with top-ranking military officials and adapting to a variety of environments. Familiar with various international and political protocols. Adept at coordinating project management, providing staff training, and preparing proprietary documentation.

Areas of Strength

Proactive Leadership ● Strategic Planning ● Feasibility Analysis ● Project Management
Regulatory Compliance ● Executive Liaison ● Decision-making

PROFESSIONAL EXPERIENCE

UNITED STATES NAVY 2003–Present
Medical Facility Planning Center, Ft. Myers, FL (2007–Present)
Chief, Program Analysis & Evaluation Branch

Serve as the Global Defense Health Program manager and advisor to the Navy's Surgeon General.

- Monitor Congressional appropriations and activities to identify prospective impact on military funding.
- Respond to Congressional inquiries within tight deadlines and draft responses to House Reports.
- Develop correspondence for distribution to Congress and top-level military officials.
- Administer the Navy's hospital construction program, evaluating needs of international facilities and establishing priorities in the allocation of $50 million in annual funds.

> Key Achievements:
> - Nominated as a Navy candidate for the White House Social Aide Program.
> - Managed the acquisition of seven bio-safety level-three laboratory modules, valued at $10 million, and facilitated the rapid design, engineering, and deployment of the labs in response to bioterrorism threats.

European Medical Center, Hamburg, Germany (2005–2006)
Company Commander (Site Manager)

Supervised 150+ people in Europe's only American medical center, a 200-bed facility with contingency expansion to 450 beds.

- Maintained responsibility for the enlisted staff's overall welfare, discipline, and training.
- Provided administrative, operational, and logistical support to the center's 10 wards.
- Administered accountability and material readiness for more than $14 million in organizational property.
- Coordinated training for 20 occupational specialties in support of the center's worldwide mission.
- Supervised and maintained enlisted barracks facilities housing 130 military personnel.

> Key Achievements:
> - Treated CIA special agents who were casualties of the War on Terrorism.
> - Oversaw the construction and control of the center's nuclear, biological, and chemical (NBC) room.
> - Developed an initiative to provide command experience for Navy nurse corps officers.

Continued

This resume would be equally at home in chapter 7, but we included it here because his specific focus is on medical facility management. Note how his relevant achievements are boxed for emphasis.

Edward James   Cell: (850) 650-2150

PROFESSIONAL EXPERIENCE
(Continued)

Headquarters, European Medical Command (EMC), Berlin, Germany (2003–2005)
Company Commander (2004–2005)

Served as an executive assistant to the senior officer and coordinator for all mission-readiness issues.

- Collaborated with dignitaries, senior officers, and surgeons general of several European countries.
- Managed schedules, itineraries, office communications, and logistical support.
- Monitored top-secret military briefings and ensured that the senior officer was kept informed.
- Supervised two officers and ensured accountability of equipment.
- Coordinated complex international missions in cooperation with affiliated services and organizations.

Health Facility Planner, Health Facilities Planning Unit (2003–2004)

Provided technical operations assistance to the EMC Commander/Commanding Surgeon and the 200-person staff of fixed and deployable medical, dental, and veterinary facilities.

- Identified necessary repairs and construction and assisted hospitals and clinics in maintaining regulatory compliance.

Key Achievements:
- Recognized among the top 1% of Navy Medical Department officers.
- Authored a synopsis of internship experiences as a resource for lieutenants new to health planning.
- Developed project approval packages for medical facility construction projects valued at $30 million.
- Coordinated with senior-level military officers to arrange treatment for recently released hostages.

MILITARY AWARDS AND HONORS

Meritorious Service Medal
Navy Commendation Medal
Navy Achievement Medal
National Defense Service Medal
Navy Service Ribbon
Overseas Service Ribbon

EDUCATION

BS, Mechanical Engineering, Tuskegee University, Tuskegee, AL, 2001
(Navy ROTC, Student Senate)

Combined Arms and Services Staff School
Navy Medical Department's Officer Basic and Advanced Courses
Honors Graduate, Nuclear, Biological and Chemical (NBC) School

Page 2

CHAPTER 11

Resumes for Careers in Law, Law Enforcement, Security, and Intelligence

- Paralegals

- Conservation Law Enforcement Officers

- Investigators

- Industrial Security Specialists

- Site (Security) Managers

- Security and Counterterrorism Consultants

- Security and Law Enforcement Professionals

- Emergency Preparedness Executives

The specialized areas of law enforcement, security, and intelligence are well represented in the military, and experience in these areas translates easily to civilian roles. In fact, having military experience and a high-level security clearance can give candidates a real edge. Each of the resumes that follow emphasizes relevant experience to paint a sharp picture of an experienced, well-trained professional.

TAMARA JOHNSON

7296 Matthews Avenue
Charleston, SC 29406

843.245.9001
tammyj126@roadrunner.com

OBJECTIVE

To enter the paralegal profession following an outstanding 14-year career in the U.S. Navy.

EDUCATION/TRAINING

THE PARALEGAL INSTITUTE, INC., PHOENIX, ARIZONA

Associate of Arts degree in Paralegal Studies
ABA-approved distance-learning program; current overall GPA 3.6

Expected Graduation
May 2010

Concentration: **Real Estate and Litigation Law**

Coursework included:
- ✓ The Professional Paralegal
- ✓ Substantive Law I and II
- ✓ Civil Litigation
- ✓ Criminal Law and Procedures
- ✓ Legal Research
- ✓ Legal Analysis and Writing

- ✓ Ethics and Professional Responsibility
- ✓ The Court System and Alternative Dispute Resolution
- ✓ Administrative Law and Governmental Regulation
- ✓ Trial Procedures
- ✓ Conducting Interviews and Investigations
- ✓ Computer-Assisted Legal Research

NAVY LEADER DEVELOPMENT PROGRAM (NAVLEAD) FOR LEADING PETTY OFFICERS

PROFESSIONAL AFFILIATIONS

- Student Member, National Association of Legal Assistants
- Student Member, National Paralegal Association

SKILLS & TRANSFERABLE EXPERIENCE

Administration/Organization
- Organized a large volume of paperwork and computerized files.
- Demonstrated computer proficiency with Microsoft Word and Excel programs.
- Coordinated, scheduled, and administered assignments.
- Extracted and summarized information and prepared reports.
- Established daily operating procedures.
- Trained and supervised personnel.

Communication
- Interacted with persons of diverse backgrounds.
- Conducted briefings and interviews.
- Provided assistance and information within scope of authority.
- Drafted written instructions and notices.
- Handled sensitive and confidential information with discretion.

Personal Attributes
- Cordial and well-mannered; positive attitude; strong work ethic; eager to learn and grow.
- Unrivaled in customer service; give 110% effort to satisfy client needs.
- Extremely dependable; take on additional tasks without hesitation.
- Confident, self-motivated, and resourceful in handling routine assignments as well as the demands of adverse situations.
- Highly organized, accurate, and efficient in meeting or exceeding production expectations and deadlines.
- Willing to travel and/or relocate.

(continued)

This individual is about to complete paralegal training and seeks a real career transition. Highlights from her military career show skills and experience that are highly transferable to the legal environment.

TAMARA JOHNSON   Page 2
843.245.9001 • tammyj126@roadrunner.com

PROFESSIONAL EXPERIENCE

UNITED STATES NAVY   1995 to Present

Educational Support Supervisor (2003 to present)
Naval Weapons Station, Charleston, South Carolina

Customer Services Supervisor (1999 to 2003)
Personnel Support Activity, Naples, Italy

Records Clerk (1995 to 1999)
USS *Shreveport* LPD12

Highlights of Accomplishments *(as noted from performance evaluations)*

- Selected as division training officer, a duty normally assigned to senior-level petty officers.
- Supervised up to 12 subordinates; directed their production and efficient performance of their administrative duties.
- Effectively counseled personnel in preparation for promotion exams, resulting in a 35% advancement rate.
- Restructured the division training format, achieving a 45% increase in personnel qualification.
- Skillfully managed a $7.5K training budget while ensuring a cost-effective means of attaining and enhancing required skill levels.
- Initiated new procedures to improve the tracking of personnel qualifications.
- Engineered an audit of personnel service records for more than 2,500 crewmembers.

HONORS

- Navy Achievement Medal, two-time recipient for outstanding professional achievement
- Three Good Conduct medals
- Numerous Letters of Appreciation

KEVIN REILLY

24 Raffia Road
Enfield, CT 06082

Telephone: (860) 763-8333
E-mail: kreilly@yahoo.com

CONSERVATION LAW ENFORCEMENT OFFICER
CONNECTICUT DEPARTMENT OF ENVIRONMENTAL PROTECTION

PROFILE

- Law enforcement specialist with six years of experience in military police and homeland security
- Familiar with group patrol and investigation methods, applicable laws, industry practices, due process, and criminal procedures
- Education in criminal justice and law enforcement
- Sharpshooter and expert marksman qualifications with both pistol and rifle

- Hunter safety, map and compass use, and outdoor survival skills
- Knowledge of search-and-rescue techniques, forest and structural fire control, and wildlife code inspections and violations
- Familiar with Connecticut fish, game, and habitat
- Recreational knowledge of Connecticut state parks and forests

EXPERIENCE

Military Police Officer   2003–Present
ARMY NATIONAL GUARD, 143rd Military Police Company, Hartford, Connecticut

Protect military personnel, safeguard military property, and assist in maintaining discipline through the enforcement of laws, orders, and regulations. Provide traffic control, conduct investigations, and prepare military police reports.

Squad Leader   2007–2009
OPERATION NOBLE EAGLE—HOMELAND SECURITY, throughout Connecticut

Provided law enforcement and airport security and supervised 18 military and civilian airport screeners. Trained and supervised 8–10 troops in proper procedures and bomb detection. Conducted inspections and communicated with the public and members of the press.

Lieutenant / Shift Supervisor   2002–2007
IRISH SECURITY SERVICES, LLC, Bradley International Airport, Windsor Locks, Connecticut

Supervised a crew of 6–10 security officers, made security rounds at Bradley International Airport, completed weekly payroll, processed reports, and prepared schedules. *Promoted from Security Guard in 2006.*

Security Guard   2000–2002
ROCKVILLE MEMORIAL HOSPITAL, Rockville, Connecticut

Protected personnel, safeguarded property, and assisted in maintaining discipline through the enforcement of laws, orders, and regulations. Conducted investigations and prepared daily security reports.

EDUCATION / TRAINING

Degree Program: B.S. Criminal Justice, University of Connecticut, anticipated completion June 2011
Basic Military Police / Basic Correction, U.S. Army Training Center, Fort Leonard Wood, Missouri
Connecticut River Sportsman's Training Program, Connecticut Department of Environmental Protection

AWARDS / HONORS / RECOGNITION

Overseas Service Ribbon (Peacekeeping Mission)
Red Cross First Aid and CPR Certified
Army Achievement Medal

State Emergency Service Ribbon
Expert (Rifle and Pistol) Badge
Leadership Ribbon Award

A chronological format shows progressive experience in the military that is highly relevant to this individual's new career goal.

KEVIN O'DONNELL
8529 North Whiting Street
St. Francis, Wisconsin 53235
kodonnell@wi.rr.com

414-489-1377 (h)   414-482-6495 (o)

INVESTIGATOR

Skilled in application of professional investigative skills and techniques to examine character, practices, and credentials. Knowledgeable about civil and administrative aspects of law, including laws of evidence, rules of criminal procedure, precedent court decisions, surveillance, and undercover work. Expert in decision-making relating to national security, subversive organizations and their methods of operation, security issues, and record-keeping. Proficient in evaluating reliability and credibility, gaining confidence and cooperation, and making positive decisions while distinguishing between conclusions and facts.

EDUCATION

Civilian
Cardinal Winters University, Mequon, WI
BACHELOR OF ARTS—MANAGEMENT (Dec. 2009)
- ❑ Business administration intensive; focus on research throughout curriculum; coursework included case studies, liberal arts writing, marketing, and business ethics and values.
- ❑ **Grade Point Average: 3.81**

Military
Community College of the Air Force, Luther Air Force Base, AL
ASSOCIATE DEGREE IN CRIMINAL JUSTICE (May 2008)
- ❑ Fundamentals of Ground Combat Skills, Law Enforcement and Marksmanship, Special Weapons and Tactics, Investigative Principles, and Support Weapons
- ❑ Air Force Specialty Internship (Journeyman—8.0 credits and Craftsman—4.0 credits)
- ❑ Medical Education (5 months), Emergency Medical Technician (EMT) (3 weeks)
- ❑ Security Forces Ground Combat (5 weeks)
- ❑ Honor Graduate of Security Forces Law Enforcement Academy course (2007)
- ❑ Detainee Operations and Movement Course (1 week)
- ❑ Air Force Journeyman Security Forces

AWARDS/HONORS

- ❑ Airman of the Quarter (2000)—Civilian Employee of the Quarter (2007)
- ❑ Ira L. Bong Award for Performance Excellence (2006)
- ❑ Lumbard Scholarship based on academics and essay about personal growth (2008)
- ❑ Honor Graduate, USAF Security Forces Ground Combat School and Academy (2003)
- ❑ Performance Awards annually (3 of 4 years)

MILITARY HISTORY

- ❑ Civilian Full-Time Employee for USAF, 220th Air Wing (Mar. 2005–Present)
- ❑ United States Air Force Reserve (May 2008–Present and 2003)
- ❑ Active Duty—Middle East (Nov. 2006–May 2008)
- ❑ United States Navy Reserve (1998–2002)
- ❑ United States Coast Guard Reserve (1996–1998)

Page 1 of 2

Detailed military experience is highly relevant to this individual's career goal of an investigator in the law enforcement industry.

Kevin O'Donnell
414-489-1377 (h)

Page 2 of 2
414-482-6495 (o)

MILITARY EXPERIENCE DETAILS

USAF, 220th Air Wing, Milwaukee, WI, 2005–Present
SUPERVISORY SECURITY GUARD/ASSISTANT SHIFT SUPERVISOR (third shift)
Responsible for safety and security of 11 aircraft, 30 buildings, property, and up to 2,000 personnel and armed patrols. Monitor and prevent suspicious activities, security breaches, and security deficiencies. Detain suspicious personnel and respond to calls for assistance. Employ Air Force and local policies on use of force and rules of engagement. Provide and proofread timely and accurate reports including incident reports (which may be used by government authorities). Coordinate materials and train base personnel.

AIR MARSHAL/FIRE TEAM MEMBER (6 trips between Nov. 2006 and May 2008)
Protected air crew, ensured order and restraint, and provided humanitarian care while transporting terrorist detainees from Afghanistan to Guantanamo Bay, Cuba. Handed over detainees to Marines and Army for confinement. Held full arrest powers over persons under the Uniform Code of Military Justice (UCMJ). Conducted interviews and "field interviews" with unidentified personnel. Assisted with training: use of force, use of expandable baton, CPR, and first aid. Generated and wrote accurate statements, accident reports, and incident reports.
- ❑ Recipient of multiple ribbon awards throughout the 18 months.
- ❑ Assisted with development of the first guidelines and procedures program.

CIVILIAN SAFETY/SECURITY

- ❑ **DEPUTY SHERIFF**—Ozaukee County Jail (2001–2003)
- ❑ **SECURITY**—hospitality industry (2001)
- ❑ **NIGHT SUPERVISOR**—various supermarkets (1993–1998)

EMERGENCY MEDICAL TECHNICIAN (EMT)

- ❑ Midwest Medstar EMS, Milton, WI (Jan. 2004–Mar. 2005)
- ❑ MedaCare Ambulance, Milwaukee, WI (1999–2000)

PERSONAL

Secret clearance—proficiency with Microsoft Office—Certified State of Wisconsin Time/NCIC (National Crime Information Center) Operator—Veterans' Preference: 5-point preference based on active duty in the U.S. Armed Forces—Highest Grade: GS-0085-06 (2006–Present)—Member of Veterans of Foreign Wars (VFW).

KSAs/References/Full Employment and Military History Available

RESUME 62: BY MELANIE NOONAN

Luis Colón

222 East 19th Avenue, Allentown, PA 18101 ■ ■ ■ ■ (484) 276-1265 ■ ■ ■ ■ lcolon@aol.com

GOAL   *Front Line Investigator* with the County Prosecutor's Office

PROFILE   Strong interest in the preservation of law and security from an early age, combined with active military duty concentrated in the police sciences. Extensive training and exposure to law enforcement techniques as well as the leadership of others.

Demonstrated skills in the following areas:

Civilian disturbance investigations—Instructor for all Eastern Pennsylvania Reserve Units in special assault tactics and survival skills in an urban and combative environment.

Narcotics detection—Trained to recognize and apprehend suspect persons and vehicles. Conducted searches with canine assistance. Applied forceful techniques and made one of the largest seizures of marijuana on the base.

Firearms and weapons handling—Classified as expert or sharpshooter in the use of M92F 9mm Beretta pistol, M1911 .45 caliber pistol, and M6A1 and A2 rifles. Skilled in the use of explosive grenades, chemical agents, and pain-inflicting weapons for riot control.

Self-defense—Well-developed "street smarts" from having grown up in a crime-ridden neighborhood, plus almost 10 years of martial arts training to earn First Class Black Belt in karate.

Physical fitness—Held record for 3 years at Fort Knox, KY, for fastest completion of the obstacle course, requiring top strength and endurance.

Emergency medical techniques—Knowledge of basic life-support systems, first aid, CPR, and underwater rescue. Passed EMT certification requirements at age 17, the first in the area to qualify at such a young age.

Defensive and offensive driving—Selected for bodyguard duties and transport of high-ranking military officers.

Leadership and communication—Advanced in status quickly by displaying ability to act decisively without intimidation, uphold the highest standards, and instruct others by example. Fluent in Spanish.

EXPERIENCE

UNITED STATES ARMY   2005–Present
Military Policeman, Fort Knox, KY, and Fort Dix, NJ

■ Attained rank of Corporal, honorably discharged from active duty in 2009.
■ Selected for rank of Sergeant while continuing military service in the Army Reserves.

AWARDS & CITATIONS

■ **Soldier of the Year,** 2007: Selected for this honor out of 150 soldiers in the unit for highest standards of physical fitness, dress, behavior, verbal communications, preparation for inspections, marksmanship, protection of officers, and involvement with the community.

■ **Army Commendation Medal** for getting prompt medical attention that saved the life of another soldier who was injured during training.

■ **Recruiters Award** for encouraging Army enlistment as a career direction for 36 urban youths following their high school graduation.

Continued

The strategy for this resume was to create a strong profile demonstrating how this individual's natural street survival instincts, enhanced by the disciplines of military service, make him a perfect choice for a front-line criminal investigator position.

Luis Colón ■■■■■■■■■■■■■■■■■■■■■■■■■■■■■■■■■ Page 2

COMMUNITY SERVICE

ALLENTOWN CORPS OF CADETS   2008–Present
Co-Founder
- With Army colleague, conceived and organized a co-ed program for urban youth, ages 12 to 17, based on military disciplines.
- Developed in these adolescents a sense of self-esteem, respect for authority, better study habits, awareness of the dangers of substance abuse, and the importance of keeping physically fit.
- Secured initial funding through the National Guard, and as program expanded from original 6 participants to currently more than 180, solicited support from local police department, fire marshal, educators, merchants, and family service agencies.
- Received commendations from both city mayor and state governor.

EDUCATION

LEHIGH COUNTY COMMUNITY COLLEGE   2009–Present
- Major: Criminal Justice, specializing in law and order
- Minor: Emergency Medical Technology

DEPARTMENT OF BASIC MILITARY POLICE TRAINING, Fort Knox, KY   2007
- Concentration in Military Police and Military Law

RESUME 63: BY ANDY BETHURUM, CPRW, CEIP

TERRY STEELE
134 Queen Anne Boulevard | Seattle, WA 98109 | (206) 538-6366 | terrysteele2346@hotmail.com

INDUSTRIAL SECURITY SPECIALIST
Assessing, improving, and administering security policies and procedures.

- ▸ Decorated U.S. Army intelligence analyst with a 22-year military career specializing in physical and personnel security.
- ▸ 19 years with Top Secret/SCI (SSBI) clearance, including 18 years in international leadership roles.
- ▸ Capable of writing, implementing, and inspecting policies for physical, personnel, and document security.
- ▸ Expert in complying with complex laws and regulations from U.S. Department of Defense and local government.
- ▸ Skilled at fostering strong communication at all levels of government, management, staff, and clientele.

KEY STRENGTHS

Physical, Personnel & Operational Security	Inspections	Security Support
Budget & Personnel Management	Training & Instruction	Point/Discussion Papers
Database Management & Computer Programs	Special Intelligence Reports	Special Access Programs

MILITARY CAREER HISTORY

U.S. ARMY **1988–2010**

Intelligence Analyst (2009–2010)
Evaluated battle damage. Interpreted foreign documents and briefings.

- ▪ First noncommissioned officer to brief foreign officers on intelligence-related material.
- ▪ Recognized for outstanding communication of U.S. Army tactics and doctrine to foreign countries to develop NATO's first rapid deployment unit.

Battalion S2 NC Officer in Charge (NCOIC) (2003–2009)
Presided over office administration, supply procurement, and vehicle maintenance. Managed 11 officers, NCOs, and junior-enlisted soldiers. Oversaw unit programs: Physical Security, Crime Prevention, Information Security, Personnel Security, Key Control, Map Custodian, and Inspection for adherence to security regulations dictated by DoD, U.S. Army, and local law enforcement. Managed intelligence products for 750-person unit.

- ▪ Developed new doctrine for Stryker Brigade Combat Team. Evaluated new computer systems and intrabrigade connectivity.
- ▪ Served in sergeant major position during deployment exercises (two grades above rank held).
- ▪ Selected among all senior-enlisted soldiers as NCOIC of forward-support element, in support of an armored cavalry battalion deployed to Qatar. Provided all training on and security for arms and supporting ammunition.
- ▪ Received commendable rating during inspections of unit programs by outside agencies.
- ▪ Recognized for superior leadership by senior observers/controllers during two deployments to the Army's National Training Center. Turned section into cohesive and capable unit, which directly contributed to brigade's success during two deployments.

Political-Military Analyst (2000–2003)
Served as political-military analyst for Malaysia, Taipei, and several South Pacific island nations. Inventoried 3,000 classified documents. Led and supervised political-military branch of 30-person joint service division. Produced in-depth assessments and daily briefings on regional developments for seven countries. Managed daily briefings to U.S. commander-in-chief of Pacific forces. Delivered country briefings to ambassadors, commanders, and incoming defense attachés. Liaised with national and theatre-level intelligence agencies to ensure accurate intelligence analysis.

- ▪ Received personal recognition from national and theatre-level intelligence agencies for intelligence briefings and political-military analysis.

Continued on next page...

This individual selected his most relevant military experience to position himself as a security professional for large corporations.

TERRY STEELE (Page 2)
134 Queen Anne Boulevard | Seattle, WA 98109 | (206) 538-6366 | terrysteele2346@hotmail.com

MILITARY CAREER HISTORY (continued)

Instructor/Writer (1997–2000)
Trained 300 initial-entry soldiers to become technically and tactically proficient with ability to function as intelligence analysts anywhere in the world. Served as faculty advisor for 30 students. Reviewed/edited reserve-component and U.S. Army correspondence and instructional material.

- Taught 900+ hours. In charge of lesson plans, examinations, and reference materials.
- Recognized by instructors and students for excellence in teaching.

Operations Sergeant (1995–1997)
Administered officer-training company that trained approximately 1,250 students annually. Oversaw individual and group classes completing leadership development and obstacle courses as well as end-of-course field-training exercises.

- Recognized by every class for outstanding support during training.

Intelligence Analyst/Section NCOIC (1992–1995)
Intelligence Analyst Trainee (1988–1992)
Served as senior intelligence analyst (three grades ahead of schedule). In charge of office administration, supply procurement, maintenance of three vehicles, and management of five subordinates. Collected, analyzed, prepared, and disseminated intelligence products for 1,200-person unit, with three subordinate units.

- Rewrote and implemented new inspection checklist for all seven unit programs.
- Received praise from outside agencies conducting inspections.
- Led section's continued success throughout training.
- Participated in two joint military exercises between 1992 and 1995 in Germany.
- Authored/implemented new operating procedures to process and administrate rotating company of 250+.

AWARDS & MEDALS

- Legion of Merit Award
- Meritorious Service Medal
- Two Joint Service Commendation Medals
- Six Army Commendation Medals
- Four Army Achievement Medals

CERTIFICATIONS & TRAINING

- Security Manager (2009)
- Interviewing Top Secret Clearance Applicants training (2008)
- Special Compartmented Information Facility (2007)
- Anti-Terrorism/Force Protection Level II (Army 2000, Air Force 2007)
- Advanced Reid Technique of Interviewing and Interrogation training (2007)
- National Intelligence Familiarization (2005)
- Emergency Management Techniques: Medical Evacuations, Mass Casualty Exercises, and Vehicle Recovery training (2005)

RESUME 64: BY LOUISE GARVER, JCTC, MCDP, CPRW, CEIP, CMP

ELAINE ERICKSON

Box 9004
APO AE 09220
011-972-4499-3267
elaine_erickson@net.com

CAPABILITIES OFFERED AS SITE MANAGER

Offering B.A. in Criminal Justice and 4 years of progressive experience in the U.S. military in protective services and security operations in hostile environments. Hold Secret Security Clearance—Protective Services Qualified.

- ✓ Solid qualifications in supervision and personnel training, contributing to operational readiness/success.
- ✓ U.S. citizen; born and raised in Russia; Russian linguist; scored 4/4 on Defense Language Proficiency Test.
- ✓ Recognized by supervisors as a highly self-motivated, efficient professional who delivers outstanding results through problem-solving, communications, and interpersonal strengths.
- ✓ Personal qualities include reliability, trustworthiness, sound judgment, and strong work ethic.

EXPERIENCE

U.S. NAVY COMMANDER FLEET, U.S. NAVAL CENTRAL COMMAND   2008 to Present
Protective Service Agent

Handpicked as the first woman to represent Naval support activity as a Protective Service Agent in the Persian Gulf. Conducted more than 100 VIP movements without any incidents.

- Plan, coordinate, and provide security, administrative, and logistics support to the Commander of the U.S. Fifth Fleet and visiting dignitaries who are high-risk targets of terrorism.

- Entrusted to coordinate monthly motorcade operations detail for the Commanders of Joint Chiefs of Staff and U.S. Naval Central Command.

- Range of experience includes protective service tactics, antiambush operations, countersurveillance operations, evasive driving techniques, and physical security.

- Execute and monitor force protection level training for the Command with an emphasis on crime prevention, port security, public relations, and language instruction.

- Train security staff in force protection, antiterrorism, threat collection, information security, crisis management, terrorist and weapons of mass destruction response, mass casualty, and physical security planning.

Accomplishments & Awards

- Liaised with numerous U.S. protection agencies and host nations, playing a key role in the successful protection of the Vice Admiral, 20+ visiting Flag Officers, and dignitaries.
- Recognized for successful results in planning and coordinating physical fitness assessment program for 50 Central Command personnel.
- Earned the National Defense Service Medal, 2009; Armed Forces Expeditionary Medal, 2009; Navy and Marine Corps Achievement Medal, 2008; and Meritorious Unit Commendation, 2008.

Supervisor's Evaluation Comments: *"Elaine is a key member of the Commander's Executive Protection Detail. One of the go-to sailors when things need to get done. A self-starter who rapidly established herself as a leader in the work center; both junior and senior personnel look to her for direction. Her knowledge and drive have reinvigorated the Executive Protection Detail. She is essential to its success."*

• continued •

This individual successfully transitioned from the military to a corporate security management position in the Middle East. Her highly relevant military experience was a key qualification, so it is included in some detail in her resume.

RESUME *64*, CONTINUED

ELAINE ERICKSON – PAGE 2

011-972-4499-3267   elaine_erickson@net.com

NAVAL SECURITY FORCE
Training Officer   2008

Promoted to Master-at-Arms Second Class and assigned to protective service detail in Bahrain.

- Planned and coordinated bimonthly training schedules for new security personnel in all aspects of force protection and security issues.
- Taught courses in security department operations and job duties, crime prevention, search and seizure, jurisdiction, public relations, uniform code of military justice, use of force, report writing, perimeter searches, interview and interrogation, crime scenes and preservation of evidence, and CPR.

Accomplishments

- Trained and ensured that all personnel were properly trained and qualified in search and seizure procedures, vehicle and personnel searches, and detention and apprehension of suspects.
- Initiated the Naval Security Force Bahrain CPR Program, certifying more than 150 security personnel and maintaining 300 records.

Patrol Officer/Training Coordinator   2006 to 2008

Supervised a team of 15 personnel during quarterly military exercises. Scheduled work assignments/rotations and acted as liaison between military and local authorities.

- Evaluated daily operations of force protection and physical security. Analyzed and reviewed complex security issues. Recommended action steps to ensure appropriate implementation of security measures in response to threat assessment and intelligence.
- Acted as a liaison for the Naval security department with Marine support units and the Coast Guard for safeguarding the live impact area during exercise operations.
- Ensured that security force personnel were properly equipped and briefed on threat level during protests.
- Performed additional responsibilities as Dispatcher, Incident Report Writer, DWI Patrol Officer, Security and Riot Support, Protective Service Volunteer, Range Support, and Base Security.

Accomplishments

- Developed and coordinated security policy and procedures for assigned security programs.
- Trained more than 300 Naval security force personnel on all aspects of law enforcement and force protection, ensuring their qualification in search and seizure procedures, vehicle and personnel searches, detention and apprehension of suspects, CPR, and weapons.
- Prepared and implemented automated presentations in classroom settings during the Department of Defense Joint Service Integrate Vulnerability Assessment briefings.
- Assisted in the safe removal of 16 anti-Navy protestors, enabling joint forces and U.S. Naval battle groups to maintain operational readiness.

EDUCATION

B.A. in Criminal Justice, emphasis in Policing, Excelsior College (military distance-learning program), 2009
Courses included: Criminal Investigation, Corrections, Deviant Behavior, Juvenile Delinquency, Forensic Science

MILITARY TRAINING

Naval Security Force Field Training Officer Academy, Protective Training and Antiterrorism Evasive Driver Course, Protective Service Detail School, Executive Protection Driver School, Naval Criminal Investigative Service Surveillance Course, Executive Protective Services, Emergency Medical Technician, and Law Enforcement Apprentice Course.

Thomas K. Salt

3500 Trident Avenue • Coronado, CA 92115
(619) 340-1265 • tksalt@hotmail.com

SUMMARY

Excellent qualifications relating to **Personal Security and Force Protection Consulting, Counterterrorism, and Security Operations** developed through extensive Naval Special Warfare experience and advanced training.

- Subject matter expert on Force Protection and Special Operations. Level II Force Protection Officer; conduct route analysis, escape & evasion planning, and tactical studies in advance of deployments. Consult with Navy SEAL Teams, Special Boat Units, Army and Air Force Special Operations, DEA, CIA, and Coast Guard on all aspects of mission planning, special operations, and clandestine operations.
- Expert knowledge of land-based and special warfare combatant craft (SWCC) operations, including threat assessment, strategic and tactical planning, situational analysis, combatant craft tactics, small boat handling, seamanship, navigation, engineering, weapons proficiency, and boarding procedures.
- Combat-tested leadership, judgment, teaching, and team-building abilities. Possess the initiative, adaptability, and motivation to meet any challenge; able to instill these qualities in others as an instructor and leader.
- Outstanding initiative and decision-making skills; proven ability to take effective action in rapidly changing, chaotic situations.
- Innovative. Credited with equipment modifications that **saved billions in development costs** and with new training programs that significantly improved readiness and survivability of United States Armed Forces.
- Consulted by private-industry engineers and elite military personnel about technical aspects of special warfare operations.
- Quick to learn new skills and new technologies. Committed to ongoing professional development.
- Conversant in Spanish (level 2+2) and Thai (1+0) as well as English. Highly effective liaison with senior military and civilian officials, including personnel from countries throughout South America and the Pacific.
- Secret security clearance.

PROFESSIONAL EXPERIENCE

United States Navy (2002 to Present)
   Awards. 2 Navy and Marine Corps Commendation Medals, Navy and Marine Corps Achievement Medal, Combat Action Ribbon, Navy Unit Commendation Medal, 2 Global War on Terrorism Medals, and Good Conduct Medal.

Special Warfare Combatant Crewman, Advanced (E-5)
Special Boat Units 11 and 23

   Elite combat units of Naval Special Warfare organized, trained, and equipped to conduct a variety of missions, including unconventional warfare, direct action, special reconnaissance, foreign internal defense, and counterterrorism. Specialized in supporting operations in maritime and riverine environments. Deployed worldwide, including South America and Pacific regions. Firsthand experience with direct action in Colombia, Ecuador, Peru, Bolivia, Panama, Singapore, Malaysia, and Thailand.

   Boat Captain with weapons release authority during operations. Primary Boarding Officer; in charge of boarding crew, inspections, and weapons release authority during VBSS (visit, board, search, and seizure) operations. Chief Engineer with total responsibility for maintenance and repair of assault craft, including 26-foot and 28-foot CAC (Coastal Assault Craft), SOC/R, and PBLs. Designated Coxswain (driver) for mission-critical operations, including high-speed and clandestine maneuvering.

   - Demonstrated expert knowledge of Naval Special Warfare operations, logistics, and host nation customs and protocol while conducting riverine counterterrorism and drug interdiction operations throughout South America.

(continued)

Important elements of this resume are the comprehensive summary and an extensive training section that frame the relevant security and protection experience.

Thomas K. Salt   Page 2
(619) 340-1265 • tksalt@hotmail.com

Mission Planning and Logistics. Instrumental in developing and implementing complete mission plans within as little as 5 hours of initial notification—including delivering initial briefings, defining objectives, identifying needed resources and equipment, creating precise timelines, and conducting in-depth review and contingency planning. In charge of preparing vehicles, equipment, and supplies for deployments, including safe storage and packaging of hazardous materials and compliance with USAF regulations for air transport.

Liaison to development teams and contractors for Special Operations Command.

- **Credited with saving billions of dollars in development costs** for SOC/R craft, introducing modification to bow design that enabled development teams to meet production deadlines.
- Developed modification to twin-.50 cal gun mount, significantly reducing reload time; **this design will replace all gun mounts throughout the United States Armed Forces.**

Training and Organizational Development. Primary instructor for force protection, convoy training for land and riverine/maritime operations, counterterrorism/countersurveillance, foreign internal defense (FID), counterdrug operations and interdiction, VBSS, and HRST/CAST (fast-rope and helicopter insertion).

- In charge of weapons and tactical training for Special Warfare Combatant Crewmen. Range Safety Officer (RSO) for small arms, heavy weapons, demolition, and both static and dynamic fire exercises.
- Created comprehensive survival training program for Landing Craft Command; developed lesson plans and conducted train-the-trainer courses, increasing survivability of boat crews.
- Author of some 15 training program improvements adopted by instructors and commanding officers in Special Warfare Combatant Crewman programs.

Conduct foreign internal defense exercises—joint training with foreign units designed to assess and critique allied nations' capabilities. Train foreign military personnel throughout South America and the Pacific in a wide variety of counterterrorism and special operations skills, from intelligence gathering and mission planning to land/air/sea operations. Develop mutual respect and teamwork between United States and foreign military personnel, as well as firsthand knowledge of equipment, training, and capabilities of other nations.

TRAINING AND EDUCATION

Naval Special Warfare training, United States Navy
    Force Protection Officer Level 2
    CQD (Close Quarters Defense) SWCC Level 1
    SERE (Survival Evasion Resistance and Escape)
    PDAS (Peacetime Detention and Antiterrorist School)
    Jungle and Desert Environment Survival Training
    Wilderness Skills and Survival Course
    Small Arms Instructor School
    RSO (Range Safety Officer) designations for Static Fire, Dynamic Fire, Small Arms, Heavy Weapons, and Demolitions
    Helicopter Cast Master
    HRST (Helicopter Rope Suspension Training)

    Qualified Navy Diver • Naval Diving and Salvage Training Center
    NAUI SCUBA Rescue Diver
    NAUI Master SCUBA Diver

    Qualified Small Boat Operator
    Certified SEATEK Diesel Engine Mechanic • Innovation Marine Corporation
    Certified Outboard Motor Technician
    Small Arms Weapons and Mounts, Enhanced Organizational-Level Maintenance

    Combat Trauma Medical Corps
    National Registry Emergency Medical Technician

STEVEN LEEDS

201 Dunnston • White Sands Missile Range, NM 88002
505.678.0001 (H) • 505.678.4300 (W) • sleeds@aol.com

SECURITY & LAW ENFORCEMENT PROFESSIONAL

- Practiced in safeguarding personnel; facilities; and sensitive, restricted areas.
- Accomplished in training staff in weapons, physical fitness, restraint, chemical defense, and facilities security. Served as Master Fitness Trainer for 2 military police (MP) companies.
- Strong supervisory skills; managed teams for 4 years and developed staff skills to achieve highest levels of performance.
- Consistent top performer and recipient of numerous medals and commendations.

PROFESSIONAL EXPERIENCE

UNITED STATES ARMY   Jan 2003–Present

6+ years of progressive leadership positions in security and law enforcement.

TRAINING SUPERVISOR ❖ WHITE SANDS MISSILE RANGE, NM ❖ APR 2006–PRESENT

Accountable for all company training including weapons qualifications, physical fitness, common task testing, and compliance with quarterly/annual requirements. Oversee training for 75 MPs in weapons, physical fitness, restraint, chemical defense, and facilities security. Direct staff of 3 and additionally manage squad of 9 MPs.
- Control use and maintenance of intrusion detection systems for safeguarding weapons.
- Provide physical security for nuclear reactor, checking personnel passes and clearances.
- Passed the Inspector General inspection with 2 minor inconsistencies that were corrected on the spot. First time in 3 years that inspection was passed.
- Increased frequency of MP training, resulting in higher qualified personnel.
- Armorer qualified, indicating ability to troubleshoot and repair weapons.

SECURITY SUPERVISOR AND SQUAD LEADER ❖ PUEBLO CHEMICAL DEPOT, CO ❖ JUN 2005–MAR 2006

Ensured physical security of chemical demilitarization site with 2,000 civilians and 400 soldiers. Maintained highest level of security, ensuring proper clearances. Directed squad of 9.
- Responded to weekly alarms, donned chemical protective masks, cleared building, and directed personnel to washing stations.
- Monitored numerous cameras and alarms and conducted hourly checks of the area.
- Provided security for transportation of sensitive chemicals, enabling all vehicles to reach their destination safely and securely.
- Trained staff in weapons qualification (rifles, pistols, and grenade launchers) and chemical emergency response.
- Assigned as Hazardous Materials Coordinator, conducted inspections to verify safe handling and storage of dangerous chemicals. Demonstrated knowledge in environmental compliance and hazardous material safety.

POLICE DESK SUPERVISOR ❖ FORT BENNING, GA ❖ NOV 2004–MAY 2005

As Desk Sergeant, received nonemergency calls, took reports, and dispatched personnel as needed.
- Collaborated with local law enforcement, fire, and ambulance units.
- Advised military police at crime sites to ensure procedures were correctly followed and that crime scene was appropriately secured.
- Trained in assault tactics, hostage negotiations, specialized weapons, and dive certification for Special Reaction Team (SWAT equivalent).
- Assisted in responding to demonstration and helped process 3,700 demonstrators for trespassing.

Page 1 of 2

Military language has been translated to civilian terms to help this individual position himself appropriately for corporate security positions.

STEVEN LEEDS   Page 2 of 2
505.678.0001 (H) • 505.678.4300 (W) • sleeds@aol.com

POLICE OFFICER ❖ FORT BENNING, GA ❖ JAN 2003–APR 2004

Protected personal and government property.
- Investigated security and safety violations. Wrote detailed reports for various crimes.
- Helped defuse conflicts in a public environment with regard to public safety.
- Trained in riot control tactics.

EDUCATION & TRAINING

University of Arizona ❖ Bachelor of Science in Agriculture, 2002 ❖ Major: Veterinary Science

SCUBA Certified ❖ 2005–2007

Armorer Orientation Course	2010	Certificate of Training
Environmental Compliance Officer	2009	Certification
Physical Fitness School	2008	Certified Personal Trainer
Primary Leadership Development	2004	Diploma and Promotion
MP5 Instructor Course	2004	Certified Instructor
Airborne Course	2004	Diploma
Military Police School	2003	Diploma

COMMENDATIONS

Training Non-Commissioned Officer	Present	Army Achievement Medal
Armory Non-Commissioned Officer	06/06–04/07	Army Commendation Medal
Squad Leader	04/06–05/07	Excellent Evaluation Report
Squad Leader/Fitness Trainer	06/05–03/06	Army Commendation Medal
Desk Sergeant	11/04–05/05	Army Commendation Medal
Fort Benning Special Reaction Team	05/04–05/05	Army Achievement Medal

RESUME 67: BY DIANE BURNS, CPRW, CCM, IJCTC, FJST, CCMC, CEIP

3850 Watchlight Court
Elkridge, MD 21046

GREG NICHOLS

410.998.3899
gregnic@aol.com

COUNTERINTELLIGENCE DISCIPLINE
Operations Manager · Investigator · Instructor · Special Operations Support

~ PROFESSIONAL & PERSONAL VALUE OFFERED ~

· Instruction/Training/Briefing	· Physical Surveillance	· Analysis	· Threat Assessments
· Operations Management	· Project Management	· Innovation	· Liaison
· Troubleshooting/Problem Resolution	· Investigations	· Supervision	· Administration

- *Gregarious leader, able to make team members comfortable. Assemble and motivate cohesive working teams. Exude a highly professional demeanor. Maintain high ethical values.*
- *Skilled and respected operations leader. Create quality, "customer service first" environments. Act as a liaison in international and national venues and spark collaborative relationships.*
- *Progressive record of accomplishment for analyzing in-place operations, identifying problems, determining solutions, and reworking processes. Skilled analyst and keen investigator. Create and implement strategic approaches.*
- *Experienced operations manager. Conduct the full cycle of CI operations, including investigations, interviewing, analysis, threat assessments, training, reconnaissance, and follow-up. Develop training programs, instructional materials, and exercise scenarios. Act as a role-player.*
- *Taught 2 100-series/level courses for Howard Community College: "Investigations" and "Introduction to Law," 2008 (2 8-week courses concurrently).*
- *TS/SCI (PR, Summer 2007).*
- *CI Scope Polygraph (completed March 2007).*

~ EXPERIENCE ~

Chief, Operations Support Branch (Geographic Section)   **2004–Present**
U.S. Army, Joint Field Support Center, Defense Intelligence Agency, Fort Belvoir, Virginia
Supervise a team of 4, providing secure administrative and operational support to 1,350 personnel assigned to sensitive military intelligence operations worldwide. Review and conduct quality control of documents. Draft weekly reports for 5 offices. Train new personnel in policies and procedures. Counterintelligence (CI) subject matter expert and consultant. Promoted from Senior Project Officer.

- Point of contact and liaison between offices and headquarters. Analyze and resolve CI issues, answer questions, and guide individual offices in CI procedures.
- Masterminded, researched, and implemented a database reconciliation and reconstruction system for optimum use of various departments accessing an information database.
- Manage an off-line secure database, supervise the maintenance of databases, and ensure the accountability of thousands of classified documents.

Operations Support Officer, U.S. Army, Iraq   **2006**
Chief, Operational Control Element, Iraq   **2004**
Deployed to Iraq for 2 separate assignments, 1 year each.

- Directed administrative, financial, logistical, and operations support, including technical planning, for a 20-person office.
- Constructed the FY06 budget for the headquarters and 5 subordinate elements. Maintained 100% accountability for $195,000 in contingency money. Procured housing, vehicles, and supplies.
- Supervised 12 personnel in the conduct of vulnerability/threat assessments and CI operations to support force protection.
- Analyzed investigative activity, monitored collection efforts, supplied quality assurance reviews, and drafted reports. Advised senior management regarding CI issues or threats at hand.

Continued on page 2

This resume highlights expertise in a narrow range of counterintelligence, special operations, and investigations to take advantage of the current high demand for these skills in both corporate and government positions.

410.998.3899   Greg Nichols, page 2   gregnic@aol.com

Chief, Operations Team/Instructor   **2001–2004**
U.S. Army, Counterintelligence Support Detachment, Germany
Planned and conducted large-scale operational CI activities in support of special operations forces. Managed administrative requirements, reviewed budget and HR estimations, and analyzed and determined costs and benefits for all projects. Developed performance standards, wrote ratings, and counseled subordinates. Drafted detailed reports.

- Instructed CI Special Agents and other intelligence personnel in surveillance and interrogation techniques. Trained various levels of personnel to work as a cohesive team. Evaluated performance of students at various CI courses.
- Developed training plans and exercise scenarios. Led training activities in cities nationwide, up to 17 days per month. Conducted risk analysis and security assessments.

Special Agent in Charge, Resident Field Office, Italy   **1998–2001**
Supervised 8 personnel in the conduct of CI operations and investigations. Investigated alleged/actual security violations and practices and incidents of espionage directed against the Army. Conducted Personnel Security Investigations (PSIs). Provided advice and guidance to security managers. Managed administrative requirements.

- Developed and administered security education programs.
- Built rapport and acted as liaison with foreign national and U.S. law enforcement agencies.
- Performed operations security evaluations and courtesy inspections.

Special Agent in Charge, Hawaii Resident Office   **1993–1998**
Conducted CI investigations and provided security support to the Strategic Defense Command. Acted as a liaison with law enforcement and security agencies. Conducted threat and security briefings.

- Involved in the planning and execution of a successful Joint U.S. Army Intelligence/FBI surveillance of known hostile intelligence operative. Performed extensive area reconnaissance and discreet foot and vehicular surveillance.
- Individually accomplished the difficult task of opening a new resident office. Developed all requirements necessary to provide superior CI support to the headquarters.
- Constructed a first-ever comprehensive surveillance training program and taught surveillance techniques to 42 personnel. Developed instruction materials and exercise scenarios.

Prior Positions:
Counterintelligence Agent (3 years, 9 months)
Military Police (2 years, 10 months)

~ EDUCATION & PROFESSIONAL DEVELOPMENT ~

- BS in Political Science, University of Virginia, 1993
- Federal Bureau of Investigation National Academy, 2005 (11 weeks and 15 undergraduate credit hours)
- Warrant Officer Advanced Course (Leadership and Administration), 2004
- Strategic Debriefer Course, Arizona, 2004 (4 weeks)
- Counternarcotics Training Course, Georgia, 2002 (2 weeks)
- Advanced Surveillance Course, Maryland, 2001 (4 weeks)
- Advanced Foreign Counterintelligence Training Center (AFCITC), 1995 (15 weeks)

ANNE EARHART

1937 Howland Road
Los Angeles, CA 90005

anneearhart@msn.com

Home: 562-925-3211
Cell: 562-369-4758

EMERGENCY PREPAREDNESS EXECUTIVE

Highly motivated, goal-oriented executive with more than 10 years of experience building and leading integrated operations in an emergency preparedness and shifting mission/threat environment. An experienced pilot with more than 17 years of comprehensive experience encompassing positions in management, safety, logistics, maintenance, and business operations.

Extremely knowledgeable in worldwide aviation operations, preparedness planning, emergency and disaster management, standardization, training, logistics, and administration. Consistently successful in managing and directing multidisciplinary operations, including all facets of community affairs; public relations; marketing; personnel; and collaboration with federal agencies, other organizations, and client services.

EXPERIENCE

Chief Financial Officer   Coast Guard Air Station, San Francisco, CA   2008–Present
- Develop, prioritize, and administer $700K annual budget; supervise supply staff handling myriad purchases and maintenance contracts. Maintain property accounts worth $40M.
- Created activity-based spreadsheets to assist departments in tracking funds, prioritizing purchases, and developing account history to successfully compete for future funding.

Chief Operations Officer   Coast Guard Air Station, San Francisco, CA   2001–2005, 2007–2008
- Directed and managed unit operations with 4 helicopters, 19 pilots, 15 flight mechanics, 5 EMTs, 20 watchstanders, and 2,680 annual flight hours to conduct 24/7 flight operations. Major mission areas included search and rescue, anti-terrorism/threat response, law enforcement, and pollution response. Oversaw pilot proficiency and unit training, flight services, communications, flight scheduling, law enforcement, Coast Guard Auxiliary, and public affairs programs. In 2008, crews flew 115% of programmed flight hours, more than any other West Coast unit.
- Planned and implemented first-ever West Coast "Sea Marshal" Vertical Delivery training program to increase anti-terrorism capabilities with regard to inbound merchant ships. Program has since expanded to train strike teams (chemical, biological, and radiological first responders) and marine safety and security teams. Developed concepts, budgets, and procedures to mobilize security, safety, and relief services. Wrote policies and published policy/training manual.
- Implemented squadron concept for Coast Guard Air Auxiliary (civilian volunteer pilots and aircraft) in northern and central California. Partnered Air Auxiliary pilots with active duty counterparts to improve training, safety, flight scheduling, and standardization. Used Air Auxiliary as a force multiplier, coordinating Auxiliary flights and active duty patrols to provide more effective area coverage in support of Homeland Security. Use of Air Auxiliary reduced mission costs by 90%.
- As lead investigator following Coast Guard helicopter crash resulting in 4 fatalities and loss of airframe, completed comprehensive year-long inquiry into cause of accident: interviewed eyewitness, inspected wreckage, reviewed helicopter maintenance and crew records, evaluated air station management practices, and assembled subject matter experts to analyze flight computer and digital engine data.

Chief Operations Officer   Aviation Training Center, Mobile, AL   2005–2007
- Supervised 12 officers, 56 mechanics, 4 helicopters, and equipment worth $57.4M to support Arctic and Antarctic deployments in excess of 800 annual helicopter days at sea.
- Planned and implemented rapid Polar Operations Division growth. Ahead of schedule, created detailed plans for additional personnel, budget, offices, helicopters, ramp space, and hangar construction. Prior to arrival of new personnel and aviation resources, developed sophisticated scheduling matrix, instrumental in meeting 152% of programmed deployment days, while accommodating scheduled transfers for 63% of pilots and 33% of mechanics.
- Developed plans for doubling size of Coast Guard aviation detachments in McMurdo Station, Antarctica, to include construction of additional helipad, improved fuel-handling procedures, enhanced maintenance facilities, office space, and parts storage; redesigned work schedules to eliminate inefficiencies. Plans currently being implemented.

Page 1 of 2

Culling only relevant experience from a lengthy military career was the challenge for this resume.

anneeearhart@msn.com • 562-925-3211   *Anne Earhart—Page 2*

Chief Operations Officer   McMurdo Station, Antarctica   2005–2007
- Responsible for planning and safe mission execution during 2 separate 7-month Antarctic deployments. Ensured aircrews were equipped and icebreakers were aviation certified to operate in foreign territories and varied climactic conditions for Coast Guard, National Science Foundation, Air Force, Air National Guard, and foreign science missions.
- Planned and executed first-ever installation of multiple weather stations on immense Antarctic iceberg; mission required detailed contingency planning, constantly changing load calculations, and flexible work schedules throughout.
- Developed complex plans for transport and multiday support of 7 divers and 55K pounds of equipment in successful completion of underwater repairs on 2 icebreakers.

Chief Operations Officer   Pacific Area Command Center, Alameda, CA   1996–2001
- Supervised 9 search-and-rescue (SAR) coordinators. Managed day-to-day planning and execution for fisheries enforcement, drug interdiction, illegal migration, pollution response, vessel safety, and myriad other operations.
- Initiated multiple Coast Guard directives accepted by the International Maritime Organization (IMO) to improve SAR response, reduce false alarms worldwide, improve quality of and access to international shipping databases, and correct flaws in automated distress alerting technology. Established Coast Guard–wide standard wording for distress broadcasts to improve comprehension by non-English-speaking mariners.
- Participated in development of aviation contingency plans to stem illegal migration.
- Oversaw first successful installation of Navy tactical computer systems at Coast Guard command.
- Overhauled outdated SAR training program, developing "SAR Lab" concept using realistic scenarios and exercises to train subordinate units.
- Routinely briefed senior Coast Guard leadership and U.S. and foreign dignitaries.
- Headed team administering Command Center merger w/ subordinate RCC. Advance preparations—including updating operating procedures, SAR plan, tsunami response, space shuttle support procedures, training, and personnel qualification plans—ensured seamless transition.

Law Enforcement Officer/Helicopter Pilot   Coast Guard Air Station, Brooklyn, NY   1991–1996
- Oversaw installation of secure communications equipment in unit helicopters and designed appropriate communications procedures. Totally responsible for upgrading nonsecure space to fully functional classified Operations Center with multiple monitoring and alarm systems, state-of-the-art privacy features, and formal entry procedures.
- As law enforcement officer, coordinated unit involvement in myriad law enforcement activities. Revised and published offshore aviation patrol routes to more accurately reflect likely areas of illegal operations. Liaised among multiple federal, state, and local law enforcement agencies to coordinate operations and eliminate redundancies.
- As military readiness officer, updated unit readiness plans; trained and prepared unit for participation in military exercises. Updated unit's war plans and prepared for possible unit mobilization.

EDUCATION AND TRAINING
MBA: Saint Mary's College of California, Moraga, CA
BA, History: Rhodes College, Memphis, TN

ICS (Incident Command System) Certification
Cockpit Resource Management Training, Continental Airlines
U.S. Navy Flight Training, Whiting Field NAS, Pensacola, FL

PILOT LICENSES
Airline Transport Pilot; Rotorcraft-Helicopter; Commercial Airplane; Single-Engine Land and Instrument Airplane.

SECURITY CLEARANCE
Issued Top Secret clearance based on SSBI (Single Scope Background Investigation) in 2000.

COMPUTER PROFICIENCY
Microsoft Office, Outlook, Explorer, Project; ALMIS (Aviation Logistics Management Information System), PFPS (Portable Flight Planning Software).

CHAPTER **12**

Resumes for Careers in Skilled Trades

- Heavy Vehicle Mechanics
- Biomedical Equipment Repair Technicians
- Maintenance Technicians
- Avionics/Aerospace Maintenance Personnel
- Aircraft Maintenance Engineers
- Power Plant Operators
- Maintenance Managers
- Aircraft Engine Mechanics
- Helicopter Pilots

Extensive training and hands-on experience are the hallmarks of a military career. This knowledge and expertise is highly valuable in the civilian sector, and the resumes that follow do a good job of highlighting the appropriate skills and experience using language that is easily understood by nonmilitary readers.

Jason T. O'Brien

12453 Indian Trail
Eugene, Oregon 97405
541.295.8747
jtob@aol.com

HEAVY VEHICLE MECHANIC

More than 4 years of experience as a **Construction Equipment Mechanic.** Strong supervisory and leadership skills. HAZMAT training and certification. Exceptional reliability and strong work ethic; well-disciplined, self-motivated, and career-minded.

PROFESSIONAL EXPERIENCE SUMMARY

- Maintained more than 80 pieces of equipment at 95% operational rating for 3 years—5% above the Army standard.

- Performed inspections and repaired construction equipment to include bulldozers, bucket loaders, scrapers, and road graders.

- Inspected and repaired light vehicles, including 2½-ton cargo trucks, 5-ton tractors, dump trucks, cargo trucks, and trailers.

- Coordinated and scheduled routine vehicle and equipment services.

- Replaced hydraulic hoses, throttle linkages, turbochargers, radiators, alternators, and starters.

- Repaired, replaced, rebuilt, and adjusted air and hydraulic brakes; suspension steering; and hydraulic, drive train, and electrical systems.

- Supervised up to 10 mechanics in a shop setting.

- Performed monthly accountability inventories on tools and equipment worth more than $227,000. Achieved/maintained no inventory losses.

- Drove more than 25,000 accident-free miles.

WORK EXPERIENCE

Senior Foreman / Mechanic, U.S. Army, Hanau, Germany, 2005–Present

EDUCATION AND TRAINING

Certificate, Maintenance Supervisor Course, 2 weeks, Vilseck, Germany, 2008
Diploma, Primary Leadership Course, 4 weeks, Fort Bragg, North Carolina, 2007
Certificate, Diesel Mechanic Course, 13 weeks, Fort Leonard Wood, Missouri, 2005
Diploma, Eugene High School, Eugene, Oregon, 2005

A strong experience summary makes the most of military experience that is highly transferable to the civilian world.

Mary Withers

606 West Main
Waukon, Iowa 52172

biomed500@hotmail.com
319.505.5590

MY VALUE TO **MAYO ROCHESTER** AS YOUR NEWEST **BIOMEDICAL EQUIPMENT REPAIR TECHNICIAN:**

✓ The **experience** to find and fix the right problem the first time.

✓ The **dedication** to do what it takes to support the mission.

✓ The **knowledge** to "build in" cost savings.

WORK HISTORY WITH SELECTED EXAMPLES OF SUCCESS:

- Six years as a **Biomedical Equipment Maintenance Specialist** with the U.S. Air Force, 2004–2010.

  ✓ Chosen over more senior technicians to manage contractor's relocation and setup of 10,000 pieces of medical equipment valued at $3.5 million. *Payoffs:* **New hospital ready for operations three months earlier** than planned.

  ✓ Set operating standards for hospital oxygen system. Found, checked, and supervised purging all 850 outlets—even though some were "hidden" in blueprints. *Payoffs:* Finished **two days early** and **on budget.**

  ✓ Volunteered to fix inaccurate medical equipment inventory system that had lost track of 15,000 components. Tracked every item in the 1,500-bed hospital single-handedly. *Payoffs:* Returned equipment to use that had been "lost" for half a year. **Cut work orders by 1,300 in only six months.**

  ✓ Called on to fix a remote medical facility's only panoramic dental x-ray unit—a 20-year-old machine for which no one made parts. *Payoffs:* Machine calibrated and running well **in just four hours.**

  ✓ Reorganized the system of testing and calibrating the hospital's equipment. Got 385 pieces of test equipment up to spec in two weeks. Found better way to schedule preventative maintenance. *Payoffs:* **The ability to test more equipment** and do it **better than ever.**

  ✓ Chosen over six more-experienced people to help meet tough compliance and engineering standards for pre-procurement survey. *Payoffs:* Management approved my plan without change. Project done in **half the allotted time.**

  ✓ **Corrected** a low battery voltage **problem** that affected 30 defibrillators after **other techs told me it couldn't be fixed.** Built and installed a part needed to trigger gamma counter. *Payoffs:* **Mission supported.**

  ✓ Transformed 5,000 disorganized pages of repair manuals into a structured system. *Payoffs:* 20 technicians, from novice to expert, found my system easy to use. **Countless staff hours saved.**

  ✓ Recognized for my work in repairing isokinetic exercise apparatus equipment after others had tried and failed to fix the problems. *Payoffs:* **Patients avoided four-week delays.**

COMPUTER CAPABILITIES

- Expert: MedLog (Air Force proprietary software that tracks equipment records, controls inventory, and maintains **calibration and compliance records**)
- Working knowledge: Windows XP, Vista, and 7; Fortran

TRAINING

- "X-ray Preprocurement and Acceptance," 40 hours, 2009
- "Repairing A-DEC Dental Chairs," 16 hours, 2008
- "Biomedical Equipment Repair," 1,682 hours, 2007
- "Total Quality Management," 16 hours, 2005

EDUCATION

- B.S., **Physical Science,** Auburn University Montgomery, Montgomery, Alabama, 2004. *Dean's List.*
- Undergraduate work in **anatomy, physiology, and calculus,** Iowa State University, 1992–2001.

This resume includes nine "examples of success" that highlight contributions to organizational efficiency, productivity, and cost control as well as strong skills in this individual's primary function of equipment repair.

RESUME 71: BY LOUISE GARVER, JCTC, MCDP, CPRW, CEIP, CMP

LAWRENCE P. WILLIAMS

34 Sullivan Avenue   ☎ 703.878.2299
Fairfax, VA 22313   ⌨ williams@net.com

MAINTENANCE TECHNICIAN

Ten years of experience in the maintenance, repair, troubleshooting, and operation of highly complex electronics equipment. Technical skills include maintaining hydraulic, pneumatic, mechanical, electrical, and electronic systems. Proficient in repairing hydraulic cylinders and motors, water breaks, sealing devices, O and V rings, gaskets, valves, and filters, and in using inside/outside micrometers and tools. Demonstrated ability to train and lead others to perform productively. Comfortable in fast-paced, high-stress environments requiring attention to detail, ability to meet deadlines, and quick adaptation to constantly changing priorities.

ACCOMPLISHMENTS

➢ Completed and achieved the highest number of technical qualifications out of 22 people within division.
➢ Selected by senior management as Employee of the Quarter twice in the last year for "superior performance, dedication, professionalism, and positive attitude."
➢ Recognized as a team player who requires minimum supervision, is motivated to the highest performance standards, and is committed to excellence.
➢ Displayed "unequaled troubleshooting skills in maintenance activities," resulting in the flawless execution of 50+ critical maintenance actions for the safe launch of 10,000+ aircraft.

EMPLOYMENT HISTORY

UNITED STATES NAVY   1999 to Present
Aircraft Equipment Maintenance Technician

Advanced through increasingly responsible positions in aviation equipment operation, maintenance, quality assurance, and safety. Selected by supervisor out of 22 technicians to handle one of the most complex assignments in the entire division.

Equipment Repair & Maintenance

- Experienced in the operation and maintenance of multimillion-dollar aircraft launching and recovery equipment.
- Performed troubleshooting and/or repair of electrical, electronic, hydraulic, pneumatic, and mechanical systems.
- Ensured and documented safe equipment operation and work practices within work center; oversaw proper handling, storage, and disposal of hazardous materials to meet compliance standards.

Quality Assurance & Inspection

- Accurately calibrated and installed 70+ precision-measurement tools valued at more than $250,000.
- Accountable for quality assurance of all tools, parts, and materials to maximize safety of all personnel and equipment.
- Supervised all maintenance checks to monitor accuracy and adherence to precise procedures.

continued...

An accomplishment focus and standard (nonmilitary and nonaviation-specific) language make this person's skills applicable to just about any industry.

LAWRENCE P. WILLIAMS • Page 2

34 Sullivan Avenue
Fairfax, VA 22313

☎ 703.878.2299
🖳 williams@net.com

EMPLOYMENT HISTORY, *continued...*

<u>Training & Team Leadership</u>

- Trained and oversaw 40-member work center in the operation, maintenance, and repair of various equipment.
- Trained and advanced the skills of new personnel, quickly advancing the qualifications of more than 15 team members who subsequently contributed to 15,000+ safe, error-free aircraft operations.
- Coordinated technical reference manuals on electrical and hydraulic systems and mechanical operations of equipment to update staff on new parts, materials, and maintenance procedures.

EDUCATIONAL TRAINING

Successfully completed specialized training programs in Maintenance Equipment and Operations, Aircraft Firefighting, Catapult Hydraulics, Arresting Gear Hydraulics, Quality Assurance, and Damage Control.

MICHAEL DEMERCHANT

1515 Gull Way
Middletown, RI 02842

(401) 555-1212

Avionics / Aerospace Management / Supervision

Maintenance Manager, U.S. Air Force, 6/96–12/09

EDUCATION / TRAINING

Master of Aeronautical Science, Specializing in Management
Embry-Riddle Aeronautical University, **GPA: 4.0**   2007
Bachelor of Science in Professional Aeronautics
Embry-Riddle Aeronautical University, **GPA: 3.73**   2003

Equal Opportunity and Treatment	2010	Flight Management System	2008
Operational Risk Management	2010	Inertial Navigation	2007
Avionics Guidance and Control Supervisor	2009	Compass Calibration	2006
Aircraft Maintenance Trainer / Supervisor	2009	High Reliability Soldering	2006
Airman Leadership School	2009	Micro-Miniature Soldering	2005
Total Quality Management	2008	ASQ-141 Flight Director	2005

MANAGEMENT / SUPERVISION

➤ Supervised shop of 15 avionics technicians responsible for maintaining 12 aircraft.

➤ Created duty schedules and prioritized shop tasks and qualification schedules.

➤ Monitored, counseled, and rated subordinates. Wrote performance reports.

➤ Identified and plotted career progression for subordinate career development.

➤ Forecasted, scheduled, and directly supervised implementation and control of assigned aircraft avionics systems upgrades and modifications.

➤ Primary on-the-job trainer for avionics technician qualifications and upgrades.

➤ Performed supervisory quality assurance inspections of accomplished work and aircraft documentation.

➤ Created, maintained, and tracked training documents for each avionics technician.

➤ Collected, analyzed, and presented performance data to superiors for their review.

▪ *Designated keynote speaker and master of ceremonies at organizational assemblies and functions.*

▪ *Designed and utilized a qualifications tracking system, reducing upgrade time by 20%.*

TECHNICAL

➤ Performed on- and off-equipment inspections and repairs of avionics systems, including

Fuel Quantity Indication	Pilot-Static	Engine Indication
Flight Management	Inertial Navigation	Color Weather Radar
Flight Control Augmentation	Flight Director	Digital Autopilot
Digital Interphone	Global Positioning	Traffic Collision Avoidance
Flight Data Recorder	Magnetic Compass	Turbine Engine Management

➤ Utilized wiring diagrams, schematics, handbooks, and technical data to perform in-depth troubleshooting, fault isolation, and maintenance on electrical and avionics systems.

➤ Intimately familiar with operation and use of all types of electrical and avionics test equipment.

➤ Performed rewire and modification of aircraft electrical and avionics systems.

▪ *Selected to head research team to correct elusive, recurring system malfunctions.*

▪ *Handpicked as the #1 Avionics Technician at MacDill Air Force Base. Competed at the worldwide aircraft operations competition, "RODEO 2005." MacDill AFB won the top overall prize.*

This resume emphasizes three strong components of qualifications: advanced education, management experience, and hands-on technical skills.

Shawn Michael Roy

1729 Hunter's Run Drive
Sweet Water, Virginia 22151
Home: 808-635-7741 ♦ E-mail: smroy@hotmail.com

AIRCRAFT MAINTENANCE ENGINEER—MECHANICAL
Superior technical acumen utilized to ensure operational readiness of all aircraft.

Specialist with more than 24 years as an aviation technician, demonstrating outstanding mechanical performance. Proven hands-on experience coupled with comprehensive aircraft knowledge base. Consistently elevated efficiency, quality of service, and productivity while ensuring excellent safety record. Hardworking, goal-oriented professional, demonstrating honesty and integrity across all life experiences. Competencies include

- Military Training & Experience
- Aircraft Electronic Knowledge
- Explosive Ordinance Disposal (EOD)
- Fixed Wing & Rotary Experience
- Technical Inspection & Quality Assurance

- Aircraft Fluid Handling
- WHIMIS & HAZMAT
- Hot / Closed Circuit Refuelling Certified
- Hydraulic, Fuel, Brake, & De-icing Systems
- Aircraft Life-Support Equipment

Disciplined professional exemplifying high standards of professional conduct.

HIGHLIGHTS OF ACCOMPLISHMENTS

AVIATION KNOWLEDGE AND EXPERTISE

✓ Thorough knowledge of both CC130 aircraft and Bell helicopters, including propulsion, airframe, and electrical, as well as life-support systems and components.

✓ Chosen to instruct pilots and air crew on process and safety implementations of emergency procedures, including deployment of pyrotechnical equipment.

✓ Performed quality assurance checks and aircraft handling tasks that included parking, towing, marshalling, starting, refuelling, cleaning, and de-icing.

ANALYTICAL / DECISION-MAKING ACUMEN

✓ Track record for recognizing complex problems and resourcefully developing and implementing creative solutions, resulting in increased productivity.

✓ Superior problem solving demonstrated through quick resolution of aviation system defects or anomalies.

✓ Utilized natural talent for quickly reacting to immediate emergencies and making fast, responsive judgements and decisions, both independently and as part of a team.

TECHNICAL AND EDUCATIONAL CERTIFICATIONS

✓ Possesses various aviation industry courses / certifications, including

Aircraft Maintenance Support Equipment ♦ Aviation Technician Conversion ♦ Hot End Inspection Course PT6 Engines ♦ Aero Engine & Airframe First and Second Line Maintenance, Bell 212 & 206 ♦ WHIMIS ♦ Confined Space/Fuel Tank Egress ♦ Basic Electronics ♦ Aircraft Battle Damage Repair ♦ Emergency Response Training ♦ Occupational Health and Safety Briefings ♦ Red Cross Disaster Responder ♦ D-MAT HI-(1) Incident Response to Terrorist Bombings ♦ D-MAT HI-(1) Incident Command System ♦ Phase 1 and 2 International EOD ♦ UXO Refresher Training Phase 1 & 2 ♦ First Aid and CPR ♦ Defensive Driving ♦ Ontario Airbrake System

Page 1 of 2

Splitting the experience into rotary and fixed-wing aircraft allows a quick look at exactly what this individual can bring to a civilian company.

Shawn Michael Roy

808-635-7741	Page 2	smroy@hotmail.com

RELATED WORK EXPERIENCE

AIRCRAFT / MILITARY EXPERIENCE

FIXED-WING AIRCRAFT

Canadian Forces Base Winnipeg, *Winnipeg, Manitoba*　　　　　2001–2010

Aviation Technician—12th Aircraft Maintenance Squadron

Assigned to perform 1st and 2nd line maintenance on CC130 (Hercules) aircraft within operational unit maintaining flyability of more than 40 planes. Vital member of team responsible for two UN deployments to Sudan and Haiti. Performed all relevant aircraft maintenance including load and unload duties of chaff / flare.

> ➤ Instrumental in performing periodic and special inspections by checking all systems for abnormalities, security of attachment, servicing, leakage, foreign material, clearances, and proper safeties.
> ➤ Demonstrated working knowledge of aircraft maintenance forms, records, and reports to meet aviation standards as prescribed by industry regulations.
> ➤ Designated as instructor and mentor of industry-specific training to peers and subordinates involving aircraft maintenance and safety.
> ➤ Completed International Explosive Ordnance Disposal (Phase 1 & 2).
> ➤ As unit safety representative, ensured highest standard of all issues, including upkeep of equipment and vehicles, staff protection, and WHIMIS compliance.

ROTARY AIRCRAFT

Canadian Forces Base Gagetown, *Gagetown, New Brunswick*　　　　1994–2001

Aviation Technician—430 Tactical Helicopter Squadron

Assigned upon completion of Aviation Tech Conversion Course (Canadian Forces School of Aerospace Technology) to team responsible for operational readiness of more than 47 rotary aircraft. Performed line maintenance with full inspection and pass-rating signing authority.

> ➤ Spearheaded creation of innovative method requiring convoy team to complete hot / closed circuit refueling for helicopters and troop planes during missions.
> ➤ Achieved cross-functional training of aero engine / airframe, assisting in installation, modification, and repair of aircraft or associated ground equipment.

Canadian Forces Base Valcartier, *Valcartier, Quebec*　　　　　1986–1994

Aviation Technician—421 Tactical Helicopter Squadron

Advanced through series of successive appointments within the squadron, beginning with entry-level roles and gaining appointments based on solid achievements. Designated operation of equipment in various technical and aviation projects.

COMMUNITY INVOLVEMENT

- Canadian Red Cross, New Brunswick Region, member of Disaster Assistance Team
- Qualified PADI Divemaster (including CPR and First Aid), completing Boat Ops and possessing PADI Medic Training and DAN Oxygen Qualification

MARK J. MCCALLA

2122 Greenport Lane
Toledo, Ohio 43612
(419) 268-4823
mjmccal@hotmail.com

<table>
<tr><td>PROFILE</td></tr>
<tr><td>Power plant operator with 6 years of experience and expertise in supervision, safety, and maintenance of plant operating procedures, systems, machinery, and auxiliary equipment.</td></tr>
</table>

EXPERIENCE

United States Navy   October 2003 to April 2010
LEAD POWER PLANT MECHANIC / TECHNICIAN

❖ **Power Plant Operations:**

- Supervised operation, installation/connection, inspections, testing, performance analysis and diagnostics, calibrations, preventive maintenance routines, troubleshooting, and repair of $2 million of equipment. Wrote classified reports and maintained records.
- Monitored operation of systems for continuity, regulated/controlled output, and functioning; initiated plans of action for outages and restoration of power; immediately responded to emergencies and initiated corrective action to minimize effects of malfunctioning equipment.
- Coordinated safety assurance for high-pressure and high-temperature steam and water; chemicals; rotating machinery; and energized, high-voltage equipment.

❖ **Machinery / Equipment:**

- Gas turbine engines and components, combustion turbines, main propulsion machinery, boilers, steam turbines, pumps, fans, and heat exchangers.
- Mechanical, hydraulic, pneumatic, and electrical propulsion control systems and signals.
- Precision instrumentation and controls.
- Electrical: solid-state logic circuitry, ladder logic, and function-block programming.
- Systems/technology: station-level computer systems and network interfaces, Intellution, ConCept, PLCs (Programmable Logic Controllers), DCS (Distributed Control System) Controllers, and SCADA (Supervisory Control and Data Acquisition).

❖ **Superintendent:**

- Mapped staffing needs for daily operations and special projects. Scheduled, directed, and evaluated 11 plant operators and technicians. Provided team leadership, technical advisement, information, and problem solving.
- Conducted hands-on training in all aspects of plant operation and system repair.

❖ **Accomplishments / Contributions:**

- Devised and implemented well-defined system operating standards and processes. Wrote procedural manuals for staff education and referencing.
- Managed 10 months of continuous plant operation with no downtime.
- Maintained an injury-free workplace for 13 consecutive months.

EDUCATION

❖ **Bachelor of Science Degree, Engineering** (2002), *University of Virginia, Alexandria, Virginia*

❖ **Boiler Technician / Machinist Certificate** (1997), *United States Navy Technical Training School*

This achievement-based resume clearly communicates transferable skills, scope of responsibility, and knowledge. It is well organized, using bold subheadings to capture attention.

RESUME 75: BY LOUISE GARVER, JCTC, MCDP, CPRW, CEIP, CMP

ROBERT MURRAY

(333) 222-4331   3345 Main Street • Fort Meade, MD 20311   robertmurray@net.com

PROFILE

Maintenance Management professional experienced in leading efficient, cost-effective maintenance and repair functions through strong planning and organizational skills. Earned the trust and respect of senior management, associates, and subordinates. Strong supervisory skills evident in building cohesive team spirit and developing staff to perform at peak levels. Proven ability to increase productivity, analyze problems, and implement solutions that turn challenges into results and enhance organizational effectiveness.

EXPERIENCE

AIR NATIONAL GUARD—Field Maintenance Division
Recipient of 17 awards for exemplary performance, leadership, and dedication.
Aircraft Systems Maintenance Supervisor   2001 to Present
Aircraft Maintenance Lead   1993 to 2001

Manage aircraft maintenance operations and inspections with accountability for strategic and financial planning, recruitment, training and development, purchasing, ground equipment, and resources. Manage team of 6 supervisors, 50 technicians, and 100 weekend Air Guard personnel. Plan and administer $800,000 annual budget to support operations. Instrumental member of continuous improvement and other initiatives impacting daily operations.

Accomplishments

▸ Significantly improved staff performance and skills by revamping the training and development program; passing rate on courses jumped from 74% over prior years to 94%.

▸ Consistently led unit to achieve top ratings from Air Force inspection team and increased division output 10% by introducing a quality assessment program.

▸ Increased efficiency in aircraft inspection preparation process by restructuring workflow, cutting prep time from 60 days to 8 days. Commended as the "best seen to date" by inspection team.

▸ Enforced unit's adherence to stringent safety regulatory requirements and cited for having "the best safety program in the state."

▸ Created an evaluation rating system resulting in the selection of top-tier employees; program was adopted by other supervisors with similar positive results in candidate quality.

▸ Ensured smooth, day-to-day operating continuity by creating comprehensive operations and procedures manual for all unit functions that was adopted throughout Air Force.

▸ Maintained perfect record for no labor union grievances throughout 18-year management career by empowering staff and promoting positive morale through open communications.

Previously as Lead, managed 180 personnel and 15 different maintenance shops for aircraft systems such as hydraulics, electrical, sheet metal, machine, welding, and others.

EDUCATION / TRAINING / CERTIFICATIONS

Completed Instrument Ground School, Flight School, Air Service School, Airmotive School, Senior Non-Commissioned Officer Academy, Management for Air Force Supervisors, and U.S. Air Force Air University Extension Institute.

Special Training: ANG Chief Master Sergeant Executive Course, Senior Leader Awareness Course, Middle Management Course, Personnel Management for Managers, Hazardous Waste Management, Mediation Training, and Aircraft Hydraulic Systems

Certifications: Aircraft Electrical Repair Technician, Maintenance Technician, and Aerospace Ground Equipment Repair Technician

This resume focuses on results, using language and job titles that are easily understandable to a civilian audience.

ANDREW M. BENSSICA

4211 Megan Blvd. • Nicholasville, OH 45088 • andrewbens@servenet.com
Home: (513) 555-0928 • Cellular: (513) 555-8846

Profile

Expert aircraft engine mechanic with outstanding record of accomplishment and proven ability to produce superior results in a fast-paced environment. Skilled troubleshooter; tenacious, resourceful problem solver. Quality-driven and diligent with a "do it right the first time" approach. Clear, concise communicator with the ability to teach, lead, and motivate others to exceptional performance levels. Experienced instructor and supervisor. Well-organized and attentive to detail; efficient in prioritizing, delegating, and managing multiple simultaneous projects. Hands-on experience in complete engine repair and maintenance of rotary and fixed-wing aircraft, power plants, and related systems. Superb technical knowledge and ability to use technical publications, the Internet, and other resources for research and sourcing parts. Working knowledge of aviation safety programs.

Professional Experience

UNITED STATES NAVY   1990–2010

Advanced rapidly through increasingly responsible positions involving aircraft maintenance, crew supervision, and training. Achieved rank of chief petty officer. Performed organizational maintenance on Sikorsky SH/HH-60F/H Seahawk helicopters and Grumman A6E/KA6D Intruder power plants and related systems, including in-flight refueling systems. Performed complete engine repair, including test cell operation, on J-52 and TF-30 engines. Proven war veteran; provided leadership and mechanical expertise during Gulf and Iraq wars.

Senior Instructor

Developed and taught Aviation Machinist Mate course. Trained new crew members in basic jet engine mechanics, aviation fundamentals, and jet engine theory and principles. Taught platform maintenance techniques on helicopters, jets, and turboprops. Class sizes ranged from 24 to 35. Planned and supervised instructor activities; coordinated student administration. (2005–2010)

- Designed and presented traditional classroom training as well as hands-on instruction in the hangar, in the field, and onboard ships. Developed computer-based training to facilitate learning at the student's own pace. One of only 2 master training specialists out of 20 instructors.

- Instructed classes consisting of military recruits, foreign nationals, and civilian students. Successfully maintained 92% overall class GPA with an unprecedented zero attrition rate.

- Organized and led 18 instructors in flawless transition into new course curriculum with zero downtime.

- Quickly became resident expert for Student Training Activity System (within 2 weeks of starting in the position). Reduced backlog and ensured timely progression of students through instructional pipeline. Tracked progress of 200+ new students weekly.

- Recognized as turbojet and helicopter strand course subject matter expert.

- Performed a wide range of administrative duties: prepared reports, scheduled and coordinated maintenance activities, controlled budgets (up to $9,000), ordered parts, and maintained inventory valued at up to $8 million. One of only 3 open purchase credit card holders in the department.

- Played a key role in one of the division's most successful fund-raising drives in history. As combined federal campaign coordinator, raised contributions for the needy totaling 3 times the targeted goal (more than $500,000).

Continued...

This detail-rich resume is enhanced by powerful testimonials that are a focal point on page 2.

ANDREW M. BENSSICA   Page 2

(513) 555-0928 • andrewbens@servenet.com

Power Plants Supervisor/Command Vibration Analysis Program Manager—Directed the activities of 10 crew members in performing scheduled and unscheduled maintenance on 5 SH-60F and 2 HH-60H aircraft. Maintained all recorded ground and in-flight vibration data for trend analysis. Trained mechanics in vibration test/analysis operations and performing trim tab adjustments. Monitored oil consumption, fuel surveillance, phase maintenance programs, and support equipment license qualifications. (2000–2005)

> *"Absolutely superior aviation maintenance technician ... always demonstrates total commitment to quality and production goals ... outstanding ability to make the right decisions in the field and quickly expedite repairs ... friendly personality and team-oriented approach fosters positive communications and good work center morale ... extremely reliable ... sustained superior performer ... phenomenal instructor, leader, and mentor ... exceptional professional knowledge and technical expertise ... Continually sets the standard for others to follow ... "*
>
> **Excerpts from performance evaluations**

- Was recognized for "superb technical and leadership skills" and credited with helping work center earn "Outstanding" ratings on 2 consecutive quarterly quality assurance audits.

- Earned Commendation Letter for "outstanding performance as shift supervisor."

Crew Leader—Supervised a team of 4 in complete engine repair, afterburner assembly maintenance, test cell operations, and troubleshooting on TF30 engines. (1999–2000)

- Commended for volunteering off-duty hours to work on engine maintenance during periods of high inductions.

Power Plants Shift Supervisor—Supervised team of 8 in performing scheduled and unscheduled maintenance on 20 A6E/TRAM aircraft. Removed, tested, troubleshot, and installed auxiliary fuel and in-flight refueling systems. (1997–1999)

Work Center Technician/Phase Maintenance Crew Supervisor—Supported wartime as flight deck troubleshooter, aviation mechanic, and crew supervisor aboard the USS *Apex*. Supervised 10 mechanics in phase maintenance work center. As power plants mechanic, maintained 16 aircraft. (1992–1997)

Mechanic, Aviation Intermediate Maintenance—Performed complete engine repair, including tear-down and reassembly, test cell operation, and troubleshooting. Overhauled in-flight refueling stores. (1990–1992)

Selected Achievements

Earned 3 Navy and Marine Corps Achievement Medals: First medal awarded for "...technical expertise and persistence toward maintaining the highest standards ensured proper and expeditious maintenance during a demanding post-deployment turnaround center."

Gold Star in lieu of second award for "exceptional technical knowledge and troubleshooting ability [that] enabled the command to achieve a 99.8% sortie completion rate during 2 deployments to the Arabian Gulf."

Gold Star in lieu of third award for "professional achievement in the education and training of aviation maintenance technicians."

Education

EMBRY-RIDDLE UNIVERSITY, Pensacola, FL   **Bachelor of Science, Professional Aeronautics**, 2005

Military Leadership/Instructor Training: Instructor Training Course (techniques, methods, group-paced instruction, evaluating course material, curriculum development), Quality Assurance Management, Naval Leadership Continuum Training, Naval Leadership Development Program.

Technical Training: Aviation Maintenance Work Center Management; Power Plant, Rotors, and Related Systems; Organizational Maintenance; Nondestructive/Dye-Penetrate Inspection; Corrosion Control; Air Refueling; J-52-P-6/8/408 Intermediate Level Repair; and others. Comprehensive listing furnished upon request.

JOHN DAVID TROTT

970-389-5505   3507 Bradford Road, Loveland, Colorado 80537   johndt@rdx.net

— Career Focus: Helicopter Pilot with Rocky Mountain National Park —
"a helicopter pilot who doesn't presume — or assume — anything when it comes to safety, accuracy, and professionalism, from liftoff to landing."

QUALIFICATIONS

- Military background of 17+ years in aviation with more than 3,200 accident-free hours.
- Proficiency in executing responsibilities and assignments; leadership skills; decisiveness.
- Ability to make wise choices and accurate judgments under intense pressure.
- Strong teamwork skills — reliability, stability, and trustworthiness.
- Consistent record of high performance in both military and corporate environments.

LICENSES AND RATINGS

- Commercial Pilot: Rotorcraft-Helicopter Instrument Helicopter
- Private Privileges: Airplane Single-Engine Land Instrument Airplane
- FAA Class I Medical (No Restrictions) Issued September 28, 2005
- Restricted Radiotelephone Operator's Permit
- Current U.S. Passport
- Currently pursuing FW rating to obtain Commercial Multi-engine Land
- Currently pursuing Airline Transport pilot ratings in both FW and helicopter

FLIGHT TIMES   Total Hours: 3,291

Pilot in Command:	1,251	Helicopter:	2,345
Second in Command:	1,142	Last 6 Months:	1,015
Instructor:	1,783	Actual Instruments:	1,001
Single Engine FW:	1,019	Simulator/Simulated Instrument:	1,008
Multiengine FW:	1,002	Night:	1,234

FLIGHT EXPERIENCE

Colorado National Guard — Detachment 3, Company A 101st Aviation Battalion
Longmont, Colorado, December 2002–Present
- CH47H Pilot. Skilled in operating aircraft during all types of meteorological conditions, during day and night. Perform aircraft operations, including rescue hoists, air assaults, aerial mine and flare deliveries, internal/external loads, and para-drop/rappelling procedures; may perform aerial reconnaissance and may be used to transport passengers or cargo.

United States Army Reserve / Task Force Med-Dispatch
Germany, November 2001–November 2002
- Med-Dispatch Officer-in-Charge. Established Med-Dispatch section, including standard operating procedures and protocols for the task force. Scheduled crew and aircraft to ensure 24-hour coverage of patient care and transfer. Serve as liaison between task force, medical community, and host country.

• continued •

This candidate prepared his resume for a very precise job target. First he researched the organization; then he included the specific information he knew would be valuable to that organization.

JOHN DAVID TROTT

970-389-5505   **Page Two**   johndt@rdx.net

FLIGHT EXPERIENCE

United States Army Reserve / 883rd Medical Detachment (Air Ambulance)
Denver, Colorado, October 1992–October 2001
- Standardization Instructor Pilot. Trained and evaluated aviators in accordance with Army doctrine. Encompassed VFR and IFR flight, night-vision goggles, tactical and aero-medical operations, and high-performance hoist operations.

EDUCATION

B.B.A.   University of Denver, Denver, Colorado, 2005
-         Major: Business—Minor: Spanish

A.O.S.   Associate in Occupational Studies in Aviation Degree
            University of Texas, Austin, Texas, 1997

Specialized / Flight Training:
- CH47H Aviator Qualification Course, Fort Lewis, Durango, Colorado, 2002
- Emergency Medical Technician—A Level, Denver, Colorado, 1995
- Aeromedical Evacuation Officer Course, Fort Benning, Georgia, 1994
- UH-1H Instructor Pilot Course, Fort Benning, Georgia, 1991
- U.S. Army Aviation Life Support Equipment Course, Fort Benning, Georgia, 1990
- U.S. Army Rotary Wing Aviator Course, Fort Lee, Virginia, 1989
- U.S. Army Petroleum Supply Specialist Course, Fort Lee, Virginia, 1987

EMPLOYMENT BACKGROUND

Flumepro Corporation, Durango, Colorado, January 1992–Present
Corporate Helicopter Pilot

Key Contributions:

- Helicopter Pilot with responsibility for providing safe and secure travel for key management team and employees during trips to various plant sites in Colorado, Wyoming, and Utah.
- Consistently demonstrate stability, reliability, and dependability.
- Earned a distinguished record of job performance as the corporation's senior Helicopter Pilot.
- Continually involved in ongoing training to maximize productivity, safety, and security.
- Utilize leadership skills on a daily basis to ensure highest standards of performance.

> **"John possesses a mental toughness, self-assuredness, and unflappable steadiness in both good and challenging times."—Julian A. Mandilin, Lieutenant Colonel, Colorado National Guard**

CHAPTER 13

Resumes for Continued Career Advancement After Successful Military Transition

- Electricians/Project Managers/Facilities Maintenance Experts
- Security Services Managers
- Trainers/Human Resources Professionals
- Project Analysts
- Supply Chain Managers
- Distribution/Logistics/Transportation Managers
- Operations and Logistics Executives
- Project Managers
- General Managers/Chief Operating Officers
- Operations and Business Development Executives

The resumes in this chapter were written for people who have made the successful transition from the military to civilian or government jobs and now want to move to a new career challenge. In each resume the military experience remains important, but the most current position takes center stage.

RESUME 78: BY LOUISE KURSMARK, MRW, CPRW, JCTC, CEIP, CCM

Derek Simms

2981 Abel Drive, Cincinnati, OH 45241 • 513-772-1249 • dsimms@cinci.rr.com

Electrician / Project Manager / Facilities Maintenance Expert

Expertise   Electrical & Control Systems • Building & Facility Maintenance • Mechanical, Plumbing & HVAC Systems

Strengths
- Planning, organizing, and prioritizing complex and multiple job requirements
- Troubleshooting a wide range of equipment and facilities, applying vast technical knowledge and firsthand experience with all major equipment brands and creatively problem-solving to achieve results
- Maintaining meticulous and detailed records
- Quickly learning new equipment, facilities, and operations

Attributes
- Initiative, leadership, and a strong work ethic consistently recognized during 17-year career in U.S. Air Force
- Versatility, proven performance, and a history of rising to new challenges

Experience

MEDIGLOBE TECHNOLOGIES, Cincinnati, Ohio • 2008–2010
Lead Plant Electrical Technician

Provided comprehensive electrical and building support services as the facility's sole electrician. Coordinated electrical work done by contractors. Installed power supply circuits for manufacturing equipment (water filtration pumps, HVAC system, plant air dryer systems). Methodically completed preventive maintenance procedures to ensure proper functioning of equipment and power delivery devices. Installed and maintained fire alarm and intrusion alarm systems, including control panels.

Highlights
- Repaired and maintained control systems for complex drug manufacturing equipment.
- As a member of the Hazardous Response Team, remained on call for facility evacuation and response to fire, chemical leaks, or natural disasters.

UNITED STATES AIR FORCE • 1991–2008
Project Manager / Staff Sergeant, Andrews Air Force Base, Maryland, 2002–2008

Technical and project leader for SABER military construction contracts. Managed multiple commercial construction projects, including estimating and drafting proposals, negotiating contracts, preparing budgets and monitoring costs, issuing documents to general contractor, purchasing, conducting job inspections, and preparing reports.

Highlights
- Project manager for $12 million project for Air Force One Hangar that enabled power and communications connections for use by press covering the President.
- Led team of 5 electricians in extensive reconstruction project in the Philippines, providing complete electrical services from power source to lighting fixtures.

Postmaster, Florennes Air Base, Belgium, 2000–2002

Ensured efficient operation of Air Post Office handling 1,200 pounds of outgoing mail and 1,400 pounds of inbound mail daily. Maintained excellent customer relationships through effective communication. Meticulously accounted for annual sales of $500K in money orders and stamps. Supervised 3-person mail-handling staff.

Highlights
- Rapidly learned and became effective in totally new environment (postal operation).
- Effectively managed operations during physical relocation of the post office and organizational realignment of staff operations.

continued...

> "Derek's character, work ethic, communication skills and sense of humor make him an ideal work leader as well as a team player."
> —Stanley Owens, Director of Manufacturing, MediGlobe Technologies

> "SSgt. Simms has done it again.... These projects were of a highly technical nature, which normally would have required design by a professional engineer—no problem for Sgt. Simms. His evaluations of contractor proposals are second to none and saved $500K from estimated project costs."—T.J. Edwards, TSgt., USAF

> "A superior performer. While turmoil abounded, he held on to one important perspective: Keep the mail moving and do it with style. His efforts have produced a high quality service to the base population."
> —Diane T. Evans, Lt. Col., USAF

Strong endorsements (both military and civilian) support all of the skills and achievements that are featured in this resume for a facilities management professional.

Derek Simms • Page 2   513-772-1249 • dsimms@cinci.rr.com

Electrical Planning Technician, Goodfellow AFB, Texas, 1996–2000

> Estimated the resources needed to accomplish work requirements; prepared detailed plans, specifications, and drawings; and coordinated requirements with logistics management personnel.

Highlights   • Participated as part of the forward civil engineering team to lay out and build military bases in Saudi Arabia, Bahrain, and Kuwait (housing, communications systems, roads, utilities, plumbing, water, kitchens, mobile hospitals, supply tents, runways, helicopter pads). Supervised 5 electricians.

Electrician Specialist, Osan Air Base, Korea, 1995–1996
Electrician, Wright-Patterson AFB, Ohio, 1992–1995
Apprentice Electrician, Hill AFB, Utah, 1991–1992

> **"...positive attitude and self-motivation make him virtually unafraid to tackle any assignment."**
> —John L. Cowens, TSgt., USAF

> **"...a prime example of what happens when a well-motivated, quick learner faces a challenge—success!"**
> Henry B. Smith, Col., USAF

Education and Training

ONGOING PROFESSIONAL DEVELOPMENT: Numerous training courses through U.S. Air Force.
COMPUTER SKILLS: Familiar with a variety of business applications including word processing and spreadsheets.
COMMUNITY COLLEGE OF THE AIR FORCE: Electrical Technician major, Management minor: Completed 2+ years.

Barry W. Ellison

1111 American Way
Hartfield, CT 06010

Home: 860-555-0055
bwellison1111@sbmc.com

PROFILE

Ten years of exemplary experience in **security,** including four years of active duty in U.S. Marine Corps. Trained to be exceptionally observant, attentive to detail, highly disciplined, and self-reliant. Analytical problem-solver with excellent interpersonal and negotiation skills; able to defuse tense situations. **Held Secret security clearance.**

Certifications: Emergency Medical Technician – Basic, American Heart Association Healthcare Provider, Basic Security Guard Certification, U.S. Marine Corps Security Force Battalion, Forklift Operator

PROFESSIONAL EXPERIENCE

MOUNT HARTFIELD AMUSEMENT PARK, South Hartfield, CT 4/05–Present
Services Manager (5/08–Present)
Advanced rapidly through increasingly responsible positions from Security Supervisor, through Security Manager, to Services Manager.
Budgetary, supervisory, and operational responsibility for Public Service / Security department, as well as oversight of First Aid, Housekeeping, Parking Lot, and Risk Management divisions (85 employees overall). Supervise approximately 25 security personnel throughout park to maintain park safety, control losses, and assist park guests. Respond to all emergency medical calls and security problems. Provide documentation and follow-up concerning accidents on park grounds; manage insurance claims and settlements. Schedule / coordinate employee orientation / training. Developed evacuation plan for park rides. Redesigned parking lot roadways to improve efficiency. Serve as liaison between local hospital and park; negotiate annual contract for first aid services.

- Serve as head of special security detail for all celebrity visits.
- Created and implemented integrated reporting and follow-up procedure for park incidents / accidents.
- Selected to chaperone / safeguard 42 European students through 10-week park employment.
- Through meticulous management of human resources, remained under budget every month since inception of job. Eliminated overtime in Housekeeping and Parking departments while maintaining positive employee relations.
- Implemented checkpoint policy; policy reduced internal losses 50% in first year and has remained effective.
- Commended for leadership ability and effective interpersonal skills.

U.S. MARINE CORPS 1/00–12/04
Security Force
Advanced rapidly to team leader, directing up to 10 personnel. Provided training, scheduling, and oversight of activities. **Held Secret security clearance.** Selected to serve as Custodian of Armory: Responsible for maintenance, repair, and distribution of more than $1 million in arms inventory.

- Analyzed / revised inspection procedure. Reduced monthly armory inspection time by 75%.
- In four years, only member of company to earn two Navy Achievement Medals.

EDUCATION / CONTINUING EDUCATION

Mount Hartfield Community College, Hartfield, CT Ongoing
More than 50 credit hours. Courses have included Introduction to Criminal Justice, Forensics, Psychology, Business Management, Financial Accounting, Managerial Accounting, Business Ethics, Business Law (I and II), Marketing, English, and Sociology.

Additional:
Mount Hartfield Park: Management of Aggressive Behavior (4/08). Coaches (Supervisory) Training (10/07).
U.S. Marine Corps: Non-Commissioned Officer Training (8/03). Machine Gun Training (6/00).

The current position takes up nearly one-third of the page because it is directly related to this candidate's career goal. Military experience, training, and certifications are also mentioned but are less prominent.

PAUL W. SMITH

444 E. Main Street, Lexington, Kentucky 40507 / Home: (859) 555-6262 / smith244@yahoo.com

PROFILE:	• Training/Performance Improvement • Team Leadership & Supervision • Planning & Budgeting • Project Management • Resource Administration
QUALIFICATIONS:	• Conducted in-house training for up to 1,110 associates. • 20 years of experience in supervision and management. • Assembled, equipped, managed, and maintained large fleets. • Managed staff teams of 40 to 150: Production, training, & clerical. • Computer utilization: database, publishing, financial, & scheduling.

ACHIEVEMENTS

Turnaround Specialist: Assigned to rebuild a major logistics center characterized by low morale and unacceptable performance levels. Identified mission, set goals, established priorities, and enlisted team support by reengineering operations into integrated work teams. ***Results:*** Received commendation for dramatically improving operations and morale: Selected as "Best Support Unit" out of 12 major logistics facilities in 2002.

Project Manager: Grew a flight operations unit from 1 refueling team to 5: Performed strategic planning in cooperation with senior management, secured equipment from worldwide sources, evaluated and trained more than 40 new staff members and molded them into a team. ***Results:*** Had the entire team of 53 operations-ready in less than 1 year.

Systems Designer & Implementer: Tasked with developing specifications for layout and design of new support facility for a global logistics organization. Analyzed needs in the existing undersized facility; drafted proposals for a new 26,000-sq.-ft. structure with state-of-the-art warehousing and logistics automation. ***Results:*** Architects accepted the great majority of my proposals; the new structure and equipment valued at $3.6 million is in operation today.

Project Expeditor: Assigned task of implementing new safety compliance standard by installing and implementing new emergency equipment. Spearheaded retrofit of 52 transport aircraft to accommodate both manufacturer's standards and employer's needs. ***Results:*** Completed project well within budget and 4 weeks ahead of schedule; equipment was used successfully in an aircraft emergency within weeks of installation.

PROFESSIONAL EXPERIENCE

WORKFORCE EDUCATION SPECIALIST   **2004–2010**
Cumberland County Tech Center, *Fayetteville, North Carolina*
Inaugurated a new program designing and implementing adult workforce education programs, including pre-employment skills, technology training (in Microsoft Office and application software), and customized OSHA safety programs. Provided on-site training at industrial facilities throughout the state: developing jobs for adult clients, assisting in job searches and resume writing, and serving as liaison with the North Carolina Employment Security Commission.

- **Recognized Subject Matter Expert:** Served as regional trainer/coordinator supporting the state Department of Education as it set up the federal National Reporting System (NRS); supported 27 local instructors at 13 training sites across central North Carolina.
- **Multifunctional Trainer:** Designed and provided technology training and staff development training for more than 600 private- and public-sector students in 80+ classes for all competency levels; received 98% student satisfaction rating.
- **Served as liaison** with and trainer for the local chamber of commerce.   *(continued)*

This resume was written to position the individual for roles in human resources, training, or operations management. Military experience is highlighted both in the strong achievements section on page 1 and in the career history on page 2.

PAUL W. SMITH
Page 2

(859) 555-6262 / smith244@yahoo.com

PROFESSIONAL EXPERIENCE—*continued*

SUPERINTENDENT, AIRCREW SUPPORT UNIT   2001–2004

Operations Support Unit, *Fort Bragg, North Carolina*

Managed logistical resources (warehouses, operations/manufacturing facility, fleet, equipment, and clerical support staff) valued at $7 million with 43 team members and an operational budget of more than $600,000. The team constructed, inspected, repaired, and maintained life-sustaining equipment in a light industrial setting for flight personnel and passengers. Kept current with 10,000+ time-critical inspection items supporting up to 53 cargo-transport aircraft.

- **Designed, scheduled, and conducted on-the-job technical training** for 43 team members; coordinated initial and recurring safety and survival training for 1,300+ students annually in 7 different locations.
- **Supervised and evaluated performance** of team members and equipment.
- **Streamlined procedures** for issuing personal flight equipment; reduced issue time by 80%.
- **Received commendation:** Best Support Unit in the U.S. Air Mobility Command, 2002.

QUALITY & RESOURCE ADVISOR   2000–2001

Operations Support Unit, *Fort Campbell, Kentucky*

Functioned as unit controller, implementing the U.S. Defense Department's "Total Quality Management" continuous improvement program and reporting directly to local executives. Managed a $333,000 unit budget for subcontracts and travel. Set up new personnel training program, doubling participation within 3 months.

- **Facilitated planning and implementation** to set up unit's initial strategic plan.
- **Determined training needs** for 150 individuals; scheduled training as required.
- **Facilitated the process improvement program** for the entire team's work activities.

SUPERINTENDENT, AIRCREW LIFE SUPPORT   1999–2000

Operations Support Unit, *Fort Lewis, Washington*

Managed a team of 50 technical and supervisory personnel at 5 locations, coordinating and implementing the training program for 750 to 1,000 pilots and aircrew members and 60 refueling aircraft. Planned and implemented budget for equipment, training, inspection, and maintenance of resources valued at more than $3.5 million.

- **Supervised and evaluated** the combat capabilities of assigned personnel and equipment.
- **Managed training programs** for 5 distinct on-the-job certification goals.

EDUCATION

Recent continuing education experiences have included

- **Instructor Training,** OSHA General Industry Outreach Program, 2005
- **Certified Health & Safety Manager,** HAZMAT, OSHA, & state compliance expert
- **Postgraduate military education,** Senior Officers Academy, 2001
- **Career Development Facilitator** certification course at The Citadel, offered by NCDA (National Career Development Association)

B.S. in Workforce Education & Development, Southern Illinois University at Carbondale, 2008
A.A.S. in Personnel Administration, Community College of the Air Force, 1997
A.A.S. in Criminal Justice, Community College of the Air Force, 1992

Lisa O'Neill

17 Mishantucket Trail, Ledyard, CT 06339
860-572-1194   lisaon@sbc.com

PROFILE

Training / HR / management professional with diverse background and a history of meaningful contributions in
- Counseling and advising students, staff, and training program participants
- Organizing, managing, and administering complex and detailed programs
- Leading and motivating teams to high levels of participation and performance

Key skills / strengths include *researching, editing, planning, coordinating, communicating, problem-solving, and troubleshooting…* using diverse background and broad knowledge base to overcome obstacles.

Consistently recognized for *leadership, initiative, teamwork, goal orientation, and results that exceed expectations.*

EDUCATION AND TRAINING

BA in History and Social Science, May 2010
Eastern Connecticut State University, Willimantic, Connecticut
>   Areas of concentration: 19th-Century American History, 20th-Century China
>   Additional coursework in geography, anthropology, sociology, English, environmental science, and math.

Extensive professional training includes

U.S. Navy electronics and computer training	Equal Employment Opportunity Counselor
Sexual Harassment: What It Is and What It Isn't	Financial Counselor
Alcohol and Drug Abuse	

Computer Skills
>   Proficient in a wide variety of business applications, including Windows-based word processing, spreadsheets, databases, and utilities. Skilled at Internet research and communications. Experienced with installing and troubleshooting both hardware and software.

EXPERIENCE

EASTERN CONNECTICUT STATE UNIVERSITY, Willimantic, Connecticut — 2008 to 2010
Peer Advisor for the Academic Advisement Center

Counseled and advised students on course selection, graduation requirements, school policies, and grade standards.
- Interpreted the course catalog and helped students utilize it to their best advantage.
- Created a newsletter for the center that was distributed to students and their mentors.

UNITED STATES NAVY— 1988 to 2008

Demonstrated leadership and organizational, interpersonal, and technical skills in a variety of challenging assignments for the U.S. Navy. Consistently promoted a strong teamwork environment and achieved outstanding staff retention (frequently 100%). Top Secret security clearance. Honorably discharged.

Relevant assignments included

Training Officer
- Handpicked by commanding officer to assume additional duties as Training Officer / Facilitator.
- Coordinated training schedules for active-duty and reserve personnel; managed logistics of billeting, transportation, training schedules, and obtaining reservists to fill critical roles.
- Taught 16-hour Navy Rights and Responsibilities workshops. Topics covered included cultural differences, language barriers, sexual harassment awareness, and changes in naval regulations.
- Revamped monthly training report, creating an effective management / decision-making tool.

…continued

After exiting the Navy, this individual went to school full-time and also held a part-time position that is relevant to her goals. Her military experience is summarized under functional headings to highlight her related expertise.

Lisa O'Neill

860-572-1194 • lisaon@sbc.com

UNITED STATES NAVY

Training Officer (continued)
- Coordinated the administration of more than 300 advancement exams; processed more than 600 correspondence courses.
- Managed a classified lending library of 1,160 publications and magnetic media without loss or compromise.
- Independently developed assessment survey and created information-tracking charts to report results.

Manager and Supervisor
- Supervised 35 technicians in preparing, installing, and maintaining electronics equipment suites on board submarines. Coordinated and scheduled timely project completion, communicating effectively via phone and e-mail with the ship's personnel and upper-level Navy commands.
- Prepared and transported classified material to deploying units. Maintained an electronic database that ensured accountability with 100% accuracy.
- Consistently achieved 100% participation in initiatives such as voter registration and charitable contributions through effective communication and meticulous follow-through.

Cryptologic Maintenance Technician
- Skilled electronic technician trained and experienced in installing and maintaining software and hardware.

Automatic Data Processing Special Security Officer
- Installed and set up software on networks and stand-alone PCs. Reduced user-related ADP trouble reporting by 50% through effective instruction in software operation and system intricacies.

HONORS AND AWARDS
- **Navy Commendation Medal** for Meritorious Service, 2006–2008; as Assistant Command Career Counselor, "directly contributed to 100% retention rate" and selection of this command for the 2008 Silver Anchor Award for retention excellence.
- **Navy Achievement Medal** for professional achievement, 2002–2006.
- **Letter of Commendation,** 1998, for outstanding results as Keyperson for Combined Federal Campaign (charitable fund-raising); achieved 100% contact and 101% of goals.
- **Navy Achievement Medal** for superior performance of duties, 1995–2001.

ADDITIONAL INFORMATION

Member, Connecticut Genealogy Society
Skilled researcher through libraries, Internet, and other information sources.

Focus Group Member, Ledyard Public Schools, 2007
Contributed to new strategic planning process.

James B. Calandro

245-D Middlesex Avenue • Metuchen, NJ 08840 • 732.207.1876 • jbcalandro@aol.com

PROJECT MANAGER / ANALYST

Operations ~ Life Cycle Engineering ~ Business Management
~ Delivered strong and sustainable revenue and profit gains in highly competitive markets ~

Results-driven and well-organized *project manager* combining a 12-year work history with a unique blend of experience in military leadership and management with additional qualifications in finance. Strong general management skills, as well as consistent success in identifying and capitalizing on opportunities to accelerate production, increase revenues, and improve operational efficiency profit contributions.

Expertise in production management that includes scheduling, procedures, quality assurance, P&L, and workflow, with additional experience in project management. Successful in maximizing resources and overall quality, while cutting costs and increasing production revenues. Specialize in start-up, turnaround, and acquisition of manufacturing businesses.

Excellent leadership, team-building, and communication skills. Possess the vision necessary to develop and implement successful action plans, with demonstrated proficiency across diverse product lines and organizations.

Computer skills include Microsoft Office Suite (Word, PowerPoint, Access, and Excel), Internet, e-mail, and various word-processing software programs.

Competencies Include

- Business Management
- Staff Training / Motivation / Development
- Human Resources Management
- Strategic Business Planning
- Process & Performance Optimization
- Organizational & Project Management
- Quality & Systems Improvement
- Supervision & Management

- P & L Responsibility
- Acquisitions / Restructuring / Reengineering
- Team Building / Leadership
- Operations / Materials Management
- Contract Negotiations / Vendor Relations
- Supply Chain Management
- Competitive Market Positioning
- Sales & Business Development

Professional Experience

UniCom, *Piscataway, NJ (July 2005–December 2009)*
UniCom is one of the world's top telecommunications companies, specializing in data and voice network solutions.

Implementation Project Manager ~ Life Cycle Engineering

- Managed the life cycle engineering processes, which entailed completing an order from an initial request to completion of installation, for up to 30 projects simultaneously.
- Processed customer network-building requests by determining the number of end users and the type of equipment required, as well as serving as liaison with the network design engineer to ensure proper setup.
- Arranged for circuit provisioning and delivery to enable a new company site's connection to the Wide Area Network (WAN).

Continued

Skills as a project manager were earned both in the military and in one post-military position. An extensive summary mentions both.

Page Two   **JAMES B. CALANDRO**
                          732.207.1876 • JBCALANDRO@AOL.COM

Professional Experience *(Continued)*

- Arranged for the dispatch of a field service engineer to install and test the circuit and all equipment, such as router, modem, channel service unit, and additional auxiliary equipment.
- Moderated conference calls, at the time of installation, between the field service engineer, network design engineer, circuit engineer, and a customer representative performing application tests at the new site.
- Directed, coordinated, and executed the implementation / modification of global projects involving more than 500 frame relay network sites for two of UniCom's top customers, to include planning, documenting, scheduling, monitoring, and controlling projects.
- Responsibilities included bid reconciliation, hosting internal / external meetings, tracking equipment / circuit order status, and real-time control of circuit turn-ups.

OFFICE OF NAVAL INTELLIGENCE, *Washington, DC*
Senior Analyst, January 2003–January 2005
- Provided cogent analysis of Iranian and Iraqi naval capabilities. Worked closely with Washington-area intelligence agencies and acquisition communities, resulting in more than 100 ONI and joint intelligence production efforts that directly impacted national policy decisions.
- Briefed more than 40 afloat / shore-based commands on foreign naval tactics in support of Persian Gulf operations.

AMPHIBIOUS SQUADRON 3, *San Diego, CA*
Amphibious Operations Officer, April 2001–December 2002
- Trained and qualified three staff tactical watch officers as well as five staff duty officers.
- Participated in every underway watch officer qualification board because of overall watch knowledge and experience.
- Prepared and presented USS *Tarawa* Amphibious Ready Group / Thirteenth Marine Expeditionary Unit post-deployment briefings to Commander in Chief Pacific Fleet, Headquarters Marine Corps, and the Secretary of the Navy.

USS OGDEN, *San Diego, CA*
Surface Warfare Officer, February 1998–February 2001
- Tracked more than 300 depot-level and 112 intermediate-level jobs throughout a four-month shipyard overhaul period in which repairs exceeded $14 million.
- Led and supervised 45 electricians, machinists, and mechanics, and maintained more than $30 million in equipment in 38 ship compartments throughout an arduous six-month overseas deployment, resulting in zero discrepancies.

Education

MBA ~ Finance, *NEW YORK UNIVERSITY*, New York, NY *(class of 2010)*

BS ~ Political Science, *UNITED STATES NAVAL ACADEMY*, Annapolis, MD

DOUGLAS R. SCOFIELD

16 Appletree Terrace, Denville, NJ 07834
Phone: (973) 435-1282
E-mail: drscofield@worldnet.com

SUPPLY CHAIN MANAGEMENT ⚞ PROCESS REENGINEERING ⚞ TECHNICAL PROJECT LEADERSHIP

PROFILE

♦ Versatile, highly motivated professional with 9+ years of combined business and military experience in cross-functional integration of marketing, sales, engineering, procurement, manufacturing, logistics, and finance to enhance performance and profitability.
♦ Solid track record of results based on a team approach to accomplishment, utilizing open communications and humor to successfully rally support for organizational changes.
♦ Greatest strength is the ability to structure simplified solutions to complex challenges.
♦ Offering a unique combination of business and technical expertise to a progressive company in need of a skilled strategist and tactician to bring its cutting-edge ideas into reality.

AREAS OF EXPERTISE

High-Profile Project Management
Supply Chain Operations
Change/Integration Leadership
Outsourcing Operations Management
Validation/QA/QC Production
Customer Service and Public Relations

Tactical/Logistical Business Planning
Organizational Analysis/Design
Crisis Management
Just-in-Time Inventory Procurement
Outsourcing and Returns
Credit and Accounts Receivable

SYSTEMS PROFICIENCIES

SAP
Microsoft Excel, Word, PowerPoint, Access, Project
MPS, MPR, AMAPS, Net Profit ABM
Monarch, Dunn & Bradstreet, Legacy
Primary/Secondary Data Analysis from Market Intelligence Reports
Internet: Best Practices Research, Benchmarking
Process Mapping: Visio, Process Charter, and ChangePro
Forecasting/Simulation Modeling: SIMUL8 and Visual Interactive Sensitivity Analysis (VISA)

PROFESSIONAL EXPERIENCE

PREMIERE ELECTRONICS GROUP, New York, NY   2004–2010

Customer Team Leader/Supply Chain Reengineering (3/09–5/10)
♦ Led customer team responsible for managing projects, defining objectives, and delivering results in support of overall CEO-sponsored corporate supply chain initiative.
♦ Optimized entire order fulfillment process through the design and implementation of a process-focused order fulfillment organization, integrating the functions of customer service, distribution, credit/accounts receivable, and returns.
♦ Revamped the $60 million returns business that resulted in actual savings of $20 million and a measurable process that can be utilized from a market intelligence perspective.
♦ Redesigned customer unidentified items (CUI) resolution process, resulting in reduction in CUIs from $8.5 million to $2 million, and put mechanism in place to sustain dollar reductions via continuous root cause analysis.
♦ Directed the credit/accounts receivable improvement project focused on detailed process mapping of key processes/activities. Project involved aligning the credit/accounts receivable area with the new order fulfillment organization, implementing process improvements targeted at work simplification, and developing/implementing a plan of action to clear the accounting trial balance of residual items over one year on the books.

(Continued)

Both regular Army and Army Reserves experience is included under the Military Background heading on page 2. Progression through three jobs is shown for the time since leaving the military.

DOUGLAS R. SCOFIELD   drscofield@worldnet.com   Page 2

PREMIERE ELECTRONICS GROUP (Continued)
Business Process Leader (10/06–3/09)
- Participated in cross-functional continuous quality improvement team, reporting directly to CEO. Achieved reduction of supply chain costs of 30% and increase in service levels to 99%.
- Developed recommendations that were subsequently used as a basis for downsizing technical operations, resulting in savings of $10 million.
- Completed a cycle-time reduction project to manufacture a $500 million product. Recommended and implemented actions that reduced cycle time from 30 weeks to 8 weeks.
- Elected by CFO to participate in a special project to identify opportunities that would align and optimize organizational effectiveness with the integrated process focus of SAP.

Project Manager/Principal Engineer (10/04–10/06)
- Led multidisciplinary engineering and design team from conceptual design through construction of new production facility in Morristown, NJ. Prepared bid documents and negotiated/awarded bids.
- Maintained costs within a $5 million budget, despite unforeseen delays.

MILITARY BACKGROUND

UNITED STATES ARMY RESERVES, Picatinny Arsenal, Dover, NJ   2004–Present

Supply and Services Manager (2/07–Present)
- Instructed all (state) National Guard units on proper security procedures for munitions.
- Under direction of adjutant general, investigated equipment losses and prepared complete and accurate quarterly reports to the National Guard Bureau in Washington, DC.
- Closed more than 50 outstanding claims, leading to recovery of approximately $100,000 in government funds.

Logistics Officer (9/04–2/07)
- Held accountability for storage and movement of all equipment in a unit with more than 300 members.
- Ensured vehicles, weapons, and other military apparatus were maintained and serviced.
- Coordinated logistical requirements for training and operations with outside entities.

UNITED STATES ARMY, Munich, Germany   2000–2004

Captain, Automation Officer (7/02–8/04)   Honorable Discharge, 8/04
- Served as government network administrator for more than 60 computer users.
- Created and implemented an internal work order program to prioritize the repair of automation equipment.
- Planned and executed logistical support for 3 deployments of a 400-member unit.
- Arranged funding and installation with commercial vendors for 36 additional network drops.

First Lieutenant, Platoon Leader (5/01–7/02)
- Led a 33-member tactical signal platoon that maintained and provided voice and data communications over a $6 million system.
- Initiated the integration of Cisco routers and new multiplexing technology into the tactical network.

Second Lieutenant, Communications Officer (8/00–5/01)
- Designated the primary advisor to the unit commander for all communications requirements.
- Maintained a yearly budget of $100,000 for user training and technology upgrades.

EDUCATION

FAIRLEIGH DICKINSON UNIVERSITY, MADISON, NJ
Master of Business Administration with emphasis in Supply Chain Logistics   2010

STEVENS INSTITUTE OF TECHNOLOGY, HOBOKEN, NJ
Bachelor of Science *magna cum laude* in Mechanical Engineering   2000
Received Army ROTC Scholarship

PHILIP BURNS

9536 Walker Drive ✧ Dallas, TX 76036 ✧ (214) 816-5300 ✧ pburns2001@aol.com

DISTRIBUTION / LOGISTICS / TRANSPORTATION

Accomplished manager with extensive background in supply management and automated distribution facilities with high-volume throughput. Experienced in all areas of transportation, logistics, and distribution, including shipping, receiving, invoicing, inventory control, returns, and loss prevention for multiple distribution centers ranging from 180,000 to 350,000 square feet. Equally strong in managing transportation fleets, including those with more than 1,000 vehicles. Consistently recognized for driving dramatic improvements in fill rates, service levels, on-time delivery rates, productivity, and profits. Areas of strength include

**Multiunit Operations & Logistics – Transportation Management – Budgeting & Forecasting
Supply Chain Management – Best Practices & Continuous Improvement – Computerized Systems
Contract Negotiations – Union & Labor Relations – Regulatory Requirements – Employee Development**

PROFESSIONAL EXPERIENCE

TRANSPO USA ✧ DALLAS, TX
Leading third-party logistics and distribution firm.

REGIONAL TRANSPORTATION & DISTRIBUTION MANAGER ✧ APR 2007–PRESENT

Recruited to manage Southwest region's warehousing, distribution, and delivery services centered on 4 main distribution centers in Philadelphia, Chicago, Dallas, and Las Vegas, totaling 630,000 square feet and housing more than $60M in inventory. Additionally, oversaw 8 satellite facilities nationwide, totaling an additional 480,000 square feet. Accountable for + 70,000 SKUs at any one facility representing $12M in inventory. Managed private fleet of 925 vehicles and 4 motor pool centers and refueling stations, as well as 20 private contractors used on an as-needed basis. Supervised 40 direct reports and approximately 500 indirect reports. Challenged to improve fulfillment rates, order turnaround time, inventory levels, direct replenishment programs, and forecasting accuracy.

- *Consistently ranked as #1 or #2 in division based on cost management, employee turnover, and fill rates.*
- *Grew fulfillment rate from low 70s to 98% in first 6 months on the job.*
- *Improved on-time delivery rate from 35% to a new high of 85%.*
- Evaluated staff competencies and reorganized personnel. Published and communicated job responsibilities and introduced employee training programs to improve skill sets and support succession planning. *Improved performance levels while reducing headcount 5%, resulting in approximately $575,000 of annual savings. Slashed staff turnover from 15% to less than 1%.*
- *Cut order turnaround time from 4 days to 1.*
- Consolidated 3 transportation groups and integrated private fleet into 1 transportation group, *reducing overhead by $500,000.*
- Championed the development of a transportation management system to support centralized load planning and tendering, resulting in *improved service levels and $1.7M in annual savings.*
- Analyzed inventory levels and historical trends and collaborated with plants to improve demand forecasting and delivery times. *Improved service level from 60% to 100% within 9 months, saving $120,000 in transportation and labor costs.*
- *Reduced out-of-stock conditions from 30% to less than 3%.*
- Managed RFP process to *outsource truck maintenance, resulting in headcount reduction of 32 and total savings of $880,000 annually.*

Page 1 of 2

This resume is loaded with accomplishments that include hard numbers and other specific results. No mention of military background is made until page 2.

RESUME 84, CONTINUED

PHILIP BURNS	pburns2001@aol.com	Page 2 of 2

U.S. MARINE CORPS. ✧ CAMP LEJEUNE, NC
One of the nation's busiest military bases, covering approximately 150 square miles of terrain, with facilities for more than 60,000 military and civilian personnel.

SUPPLY MANAGEMENT / WAREHOUSE / TRANSPORTATION CHIEF ✧ MAY 2004–MAR 2007

Held full charge of all supplies management, warehousing, and transportation operations. Managed 15 warehouses totaling 1.5M square feet that housed food, furniture, and supplies with approximately 20,000 SKUs at any one facility. Oversaw fleet of more than 1,000 trucks and equipment. Accountable for controlling operating and maintenance expenses and ensuring deployment readiness.

- Recognized for *cutting time for preparing a unit for deployment from 24 hours to 8.*
- *Developed operational productivity standards and training* for all functional areas, including packing, picking, receiving, replenishing, and shipping.
- *Supervised 80 Marines* in receiving and shipping inventory.
- Credited for *improving inventory/security controls and reducing shrinkage and shortage.*

ASSISTANT OPERATIONS MANAGER ✧ AUG 1999–APR 2004

Managed large-scale physical inventories and assisted in the management and operation of transportation activities for worldwide deployments.

- Performed audits on organizations returning from deployment.
- Coordinated with purchasing agents, ensuring all base supplies were replenished.
- Provided ongoing training and leadership to maximize readiness and support.
- Maintained records for more than 3,000 receipts received on a monthly basis.

EDUCATION

Bachelor of Science in Business Administration ✧ 1999
Almeda College and University ✧ Boise, Idaho

Supply Management, Distribution, Logistics, Facility Operations
Military Supply School ✧ Albany, Georgia

JOHN S. RAYMOND

48 Peachtree Way
Savannah, GA 30269   ◆ jackray@netscape.net ◆   Home (770) 624-6081
Cell (770) 618-2154

EXECUTIVE SUMMARY

Operations & Logistics Executive with extensive experience in directing full range of management responsibilities in international environments. Adept at directing large personnel groups and multimillion-dollar budgets. Excellent ability to implement process improvements, resulting in significant cost savings and bottom-line improvements, while facilitating cross-cultural relationships. High degree of proficiency in establishing, growing, and maintaining strong management teams. Proven skill to conceptualize, develop, and implement full range of projects. Dedicated to customer service excellence to ensure continued organizational success. Exceptional ability to develop and implement sustainable budgets and P&L. Outstanding problem-solving and interpersonal skills. Expertise in

◆ Leadership	◆ Professional Development	◆ Resource Development
◆ Staff Coordination	◆ Budgeting	◆ Logistics Planning
◆ Strategic Planning	◆ Financial Planning	◆ Diplomacy

PROFESSIONAL EXPERIENCE

SAVANNAH HOUSING DEVELOPMENT AUTHORITY   2004–2010
DIRECTOR OF SUPPORT SERVICES & QUALITY ASSURANCE INSPECTION
Federal Housing Assistance authority with 350 employees. Supervised 45 employees. Accountable for managing operations of 78,000-square-foot building, in addition to direct responsibility for overseeing inspection staff in timely inspections of more than 14,000 real estate properties. Developed strategic and long-term plans. Monitored contract administration and departmental budget of $2 million, ensuring expenditures were in accordance with established guidelines. Served as committee member of Landlord Advisory Board tasked with improving communications among landlords, residents, and housing authority staff. Supervised staff to ensure timely completion of tasks. Implemented and analyzed internal and external customer satisfaction feedback.

- Introduced and launched synchronized preventive maintenance checks and services schedule for all major mechanical systems—HVAC, Elevator, Fire Protection, and Electrical. This program resulted in no system failures for 2 years.
- Directed retrofit of building lighting system, which reduced energy consumption by 35%, resulting in annual savings of $20,000. Conducted monthly review of all utilities to minimize consumption and reduce cost.
- Developed and implemented customer service procedures for inspection staff, resulting in 40% complaint reduction.

UNITED STATES ARMY
DIRECTOR OF CURRENT OPERATIONS, Fort Shasta, GA   2000–2004
Accountable for 2,500 employees and 58 staff organizations located in 17 states. Administered and maintained communications and automated data-processing equipment valued at $2 million. Directed daily operations and provided leadership and guidance during emergencies and natural disasters. Designed, implemented, and conducted training programs and operational readiness exercises of Crisis Action Team in order to efficiently and rapidly respond to emergencies and natural disasters. Conducted monthly connectivity tests. Developed and monitored annual section budget.

- Functioned as lead liaison to local, state, and federal agencies to provide timely support during 17 federally declared disasters.
- Reengineered information flow and distribution to maximize the executive decision-making process.
- Performed as Operations Officer during 3 major exercises for Response Task Force–East.

◆ continued ◆

This executive resume helped the candidate advance to a civilian position more suitable for his deep experience and advanced level of responsibility in the military.

JOHN S. RAYMOND

PAGE 2

(770) 624-6081 ♦ jackray@netscape.net

PROFESSIONAL EXPERIENCE (CONTINUED)

DEPUTY DIRECTOR OF TRAINING, Jordan   1998–2000
Served as senior U.S. Advisor to commanding general of foreign National Guard comprised of more than 3,000 personnel. Administered 17 direct reports. Tasked with strengthening organization to secure stability in the Middle East. Conceptualized, developed, and implemented training and logistical support improvements. Assisted in development of brigade annual budget. Fostered excellent cross-cultural relationships and displayed superior diplomatic skills.

- ♦ Implemented business strategies that resulted in turnaround of company selection from worst to top performer for 2 consecutive years.
- ♦ Reengineered organizational structure composed of the Department of Defense personnel and government contractors to support training and logistical support requirements. This resulted in an initial savings of more than $3 million in operating costs.

Previous experience includes numerous rapid promotions during military career due to leadership abilities and technical expertise. Gained comprehensive operations and logistical experience. Served in Fort Bliss, Texas, and in Germany as **Director of Operations & Administration, Assistant Director of Logistics, Platoon Leader,** and **Company Executive Officer.** Directed activities of up to 1,000 personnel. Administered equipment inventory of more than $60 million and operating budget of up to $30 million. Accountable for maintenance, human resources, logistics, operations, and strategic and fiscal planning. Accomplishments include planning, prioritizing, and orchestrating upgrade and relocation of more than 5,000 armored vehicles from Germany to U.S., a task that had never previously been accomplished in Army history.

EDUCATION & PROFESSIONAL DEVELOPMENT

UNIVERSITY OF NOTRE DAME, South Bend, IN
Bachelor's Degree, Political Science

Command and General Staff College, Fort Covey, KS
Combined Arms Service Staff School, Fort Covey, KS
Armor Officers Advanced Course, Fort Knox, KY
Armor Officers Basic Course, Fort Knox, KY
Tank Commander Certification Course, Fort Knox, KY

Total Quality Management—Certificate
The 7 Habits of Highly Effective People—Certificate

PROFESSIONAL ASSOCIATIONS

Building Owners and Managers Association (BOMA)

PAUL A. ANDERSON

2184 Mockingbird Lane • Atlanta, GA 30306
Home: 770-435-1684 • Mobile: 770-292-5678 • panders66@236a.usna.com

PROJECT MANAGEMENT / BUSINESS DEVELOPMENT / STRATEGIC ALLIANCES

U.S. Naval Academy … MBA Degree … TS/SSBI Security Clearance

- Top performer with 14 years of leadership successes in demanding Naval and high-technology organizations.
- Project management expertise with exemplary track record of matrix-managing high-performance, cross-functional teams that collaborate as a focused unit to achieve aggressive business and technology goals.
- Proficiency in requirements definition, resource allocation, budget development / administration, contract negotiations, daily operations / scheduling, team building, and staff development.
- Proven ability to identify, establish, and manage strategic partnerships to leverage and generate key business opportunities that maximize revenues and contribute to bottom-line growth.
- Effective, tactful, and diplomatic communicator with excellent analytical, presentation, and negotiation skills.

Expertise in Aviation Surveillance, Communications, and Navigation Systems

**C4ISR • EO/IR • ISAR/SAR • ESM/ECM • ASW/USW • AGM-84D Harpoon Missile
AGM-84E SLAM • AGM-65 Maverick Missile • MK-46/50 Torpedoes**

CAREER HIGHLIGHTS—MILITARY

United States Navy—Lieutenant, Naval Flight Officer, **P-3C/UIII,** 1996–2003 (honorable discharge)
United States Naval Reserves—Lieutenant Commander, **P-3C/AIP,** Patrol Squadron 92, Ongoing

Project Management

- Led a cross-functional team of 40 multidisciplined engineers, technicians, and subcontractors in the installation, deployment, and integration of the Stand-Off Land Attack Missile (SLAM) on the P-3C aircraft.
- Spearheaded the research, evaluation, and deployment of a revolutionary night vision system employing low-light amplification for the P-3C aircraft, allowing for the first-ever night photography of vessels at sea by a maritime patrol aircrew. Awarded the *Navy Achievement Medal* for superior initiative and performance.

Mission Command

- Commanded U.S. ISR aircraft charged with detecting surface-to-air missile systems utilizing EO/IR, ESM, and ISAR technologies. Awarded the *Navy Air Medal* from the President of the United States for "meritorious achievement in aerial flight."
- Safely and successfully led a 12-person combat aircrew in 20+ tactical reconnaissance and surveillance missions in hostile fire zones.

Aviation Maintenance

- Directed a team of 3 officers, 5 senior enlisted, and 120 technicians and engineers in the maintenance, modification, and quality assurance of 28 surveillance aircraft in 3-shift, 24/7, 365-day multisite operations—the largest maintenance division in U.S. Naval Aviation. Developed and managed an annual budget of $15M.
- Key member of project team responsible for developing the new P-3C/AIP aircraft. Provided tactical and technical expertise and leadership in defining the capability and operation of this advanced ISR platform.

Operations

- Developed, executed, and managed the command master schedule supporting all operational requirements for 330 personnel on a weekly, monthly, and quarterly basis, consistently ensuring maximum combat readiness.
- Personally directed P-3C Update III aircraft transition training and maintenance for 11 combat aircrews.

(continued)

This resume is unusual because the military experience is highlighted, whereas a more recent position is downplayed on page 2. This individual was seeking a position with a government contractor where his strong military and program management experience would be highly valued. Functional headings make it easy to skim the resume for areas of greatest interest to the reader.

PAUL A. ANDERSON – RESUME   panders66@236a.usna.com   PAGE 2

CAREER HIGHLIGHTS—HIGH TECHNOLOGY

Calloway Technologies, Inc., Atlanta, GA, 2004–2010
Director, Business Development
Recruited to this start-up developer of search and navigation software to identify and develop strategic partner and system integrator relationships to expand market channels and drive revenue/profit growth.

- Defined joint value propositions and forged strong alliance partnerships with KPMG, Ciber, Niteo Partners, Deloitte, Digitas, and Sapient Technologies. Led negotiations, due diligence, and final transactions on all contracts and programs.
- Led prospecting and closing efforts with direct sales and alliance partners to capture key national accounts— Schwab.com, Yahoo!, TDWaterhouse, Johnson & Johnson, Mellon Bank, Deutsche Bank, and Bank of America.
- Liaised with iPhrase direct sales, engineering, marketing, and professional services teams to support alliance partners in defining application tools and deployment practices, establishing training curriculum, defining partner profiles and requirements, and creating co-selling / co-marketing plans.

EDUCATION

MBA, Georgetown University, McDonough School of Business, Washington, DC, 2005
Winner – Small Business Plan Competition ... Finalist – Diane Weiss Consulting Competition

BS, Economics, United States Naval Academy, Annapolis, MD, 1996

HONORS, AWARDS, AND MEDALS

Navy Air Medal ... Navy and Marine Corps Achievement Medal ... Joint Meritorious Unit Award
Navy "E" Ribbon (2) ... Humanitarian Service Medal ... National Defense Service Medal (2)
Navy Meritorious Unit Commendation ... Armed Forces Expeditionary Medal

OTHER

Former FRS Instructor
NATOPS-qualified Mission Commander, Tactical Coordinator, and NAV/COMM in P-3C UIII & AIP Aircraft

ARTHUR YAO

Boxford, North Carolina 880.555.4444 (c) 880.777.9666 (h) e-mail: ayao@yahoo.com

EXECUTIVE PROFILE
GM ■ COO

HIGHLY ACCOMPLISHED EXECUTIVE LEADER with outstanding track record and history of 25 years of domestic and international manufacturing operations, with IBM Micro-Electronics division as well as with Eastern Associates. Demonstrated ability to create and deliver complete solutions in competitive markets. Expertise in international business, lean manufacturing, supply change management, global sales service, and P&L management. Laser-focused visionary with demonstrated communication skills and expertise with the tenacity to realize the vision (often in situations of high ambiguity).

Unique and proven ability to direct multisite operations, strategic planning of sales and marketing efforts, technology expansion, and divestitures. Exceptional ability to leverage operational expertise across an extensive spectrum of technologies to deliver compelling value propositions. Launched new products for IBM facilities in U.S.A., Italy, Germany, Singapore, Thailand, Japan, and Hungary. Demonstrated comprehensive knowledge of manufacturing operations, delivering targeted solutions to meet clients' international business needs. Knowledge of cultural nuances necessary to do business in Asia.

Areas of Expertise

■ Project Implementation ■ Change Management ■ Lean Manufacturing ■ Global Operations ■ Business Development	■ P&L Management ■ Start-up Ventures ■ Integrated Marketing ■ Program Management ■ Multisite Operations	■ Cross-Cultural Leadership ■ Product Life Cycle Management ■ Supply Chain Management ■ Sales and Marketing

PROFESSIONAL SUMMARY

SENIOR V.P./PRINCIPAL/COFOUNDER

Eastern Associates, Boxford, NC   2005–Present

Private consulting firm launched to assist small to midsized manufacturing companies establish operations in China or Vietnam. Process involves a detailed review of each firm's vision & strategy, followed by rigorous due diligence of each organization's business and financial plan and on-site project management. Created and implemented all EA consulting processes and methodologies.

➤ Developed business case for NY electronics firm to establish manufacturing presence in China.
  ➤ Status: Activity complete in 2005. Strategy implemented by client in 2006. Currently in production.

➤ Conducted due diligence on business case for women's apparel company. Developed project management process and conducted site selection activities in 13 cities in China.
  ➤ Status: Activity completed 2006. Factory in production in Ningbo, China.

➤ Performed due diligence on business case for heavy equipment manufacturing company (refuse trucks). Developed project management process and served as on-site project manager in Shanghai for 8 months. Became first General Manager. Hired replacement GM and turned completed facility over to new GM (2006).
  ➤ Status: Currently manufacturing refuse trucks for the Shanghai market.

➤ Developed a Vietnam business case (completed 2008) for client manufacturing flexible stainless steel hose.
  ➤ Status: Factory implementation begins 2009 in the Amata Development Zone, Ho Chi Minh City, Vietnam.

➤ Completed business case and alternative investment strategies for a California-based construction polymers company (plant to be located in Nanjing area).

Continued

Including military awards from early in this executive's career enhances his resume strategy of showcasing extensive global experience and notable achievements in order to capture international employment or consulting opportunities.

ARTHUR YAO

ayao@yahoo.com

Page 2 of 3

DIRECTOR—IBM GLOBAL STRATEGY TASK FORCE & RESOURCES PROJECT OFFICE
IBM HQ, Armonk, NY, and IBM Technology Group, East Fishkill, NY   2004–2005

➢ Served as Senior Executive Representative for the IBM Technology Group on the IBM international strategy task force. Leader in identifying global operations strategy for the next 10–15 years through in-depth analysis of global emerging economies, resulting in identification of favored locations for manufacturing, distribution, progressive development, and other high-technology applications.

➢ Led IBM technology task force in identifying/rebalancing human resources among various elements of worldwide workforce to achieve targeted labor savings and create flexibility for addressing innovative business opportunities.

➢ *Note:* Postinternational assignment while awaiting a manufacturing position in the U.S.

DIRECTOR of ASIAN OPERATIONS
IBM Microelectronics Division (China)   1994–2004
Line-management responsibility for 4 manufacturing companies licensed to do business in the People's Republic of China. China operations were "Greenfield" applications with complete end-to-end responsibility from initiation through partner negotiations, site selection, construction, recruitment, equipping, qualification, and ongoing operations (sales execution, sales delivery follow up, P&L, supply chain, H/R, etc.).

➢ Overall employee population exceeded 2,500. Major customer base included Nokia, Matrox, Minolta, Kyocera-Mita, Cannon, Ricoh, Xionics, IBM, and others in Asia, Europe, and North America.

➢ Supervised 2 general managers (for Shenzhen and Beijing EMS operations) and 1 location manager.

➢ Served as the acting General Manager of the Shanghai facility (IBM InPac) while directing sales, distribution, and customer fulfillment efforts for the overall organization.

➢ Implemented lean manufacturing facilities in Shenzhen and Beijing (EMS Operations) via focused customer/product teams. Maximized process value chain and simplified product flow with elimination of waste.

➢ Drove synergy among major EMS customers, internal manufacturing team, major suppliers, freight forwarders, customs clearance agents, and China customs to achieve world-class supply chain process.

Select Achievements

➢ **Grew revenue** to **$750M** a year through establishment of a local (Chinese) sales force. (EMS)

➢ **Achieved profit margins** above industry average. (EMS)

➢ **Attained profitability** in all facilities within 9 months of start up. (EMS)

➢ **Retired all long-term debt** within 1 year of establishment of facilities. (EMS)

➢ **Achieved ISO certifications** (14001 and 9001) and other industry-specific certifications. (EMS)

➢ **Implemented Six Sigma, FMEA,** quick changeover, and other continuous improvement techniques. (EMS)

➢ **Completed construction** of a 900K-sq.-ft. state-of-the-art organic substrate fabrication facility in Shanghai on budget and ahead of schedule; represented a total investment outlay of > $100M. (IBM InPac)

➢ **Maintained over 90% capacity utilization** through internal sales force and customer incentives. (EMS)

➢ **Averaged 70 inventory turns** a year in Shenzhen and 100+ in Beijing facility. (EMS)

➢ **Achieved cost-reduction targets and streamlined the new products development process.**

Attained highest levels of customer satisfaction with Nokia—#1 & 2 out of 5 suppliers in 1999–2001. (EMS)
Awarded Matrox Outstanding Program Management Award of the Year (1999). (EMS)
Received awards from IBM customer for highest quality and best on-time delivery (1997–1998). (EMS)

SALES AND MARKETING EXECUTIVE
IBM Microelectronics Sales, Marketing, and Customer Support Center, Charlotte, NC   1993–1994
Accountable for marketing, sales, and follow-on account management for all Charlotte EMS customers. Charlotte was one of the first IBM manufacturing sites to pursue a dedicated OEM sales force. Exceeded OEM revenue targets as well as overall after-sales customer satisfaction ratings. Introduced an external sales mentality into what had previously been an IBM-only business model.

ARTHUR YAO

ayao@yahoo.com

Page 3 of 3

BUSINESS UNIT EXECUTIVE
IBM Local Area Network Products, Charlotte, NC   1991–1993
Established latest vertical integrated manufacturing facility; focused on a specific IBM customer set (PC Co. and Network Hardware Division) modeled on customer value focused (lean) manufacturing philosophy.

Previous Titles with IBM
SENIOR SITE QUALITY EXECUTIVE, Charlotte, NC & Endicott, NY
ADVISORY SALES REPRESENTATIVE, Chicago, IL
EARLY CAREER POSITIONS (Product Engineering/Quality Assurance/Middle Management)

EDUCATION AND PROFESSIONAL DEVELOPMENT

M.S.—Chemical Engineering Major with a Minor in Business Administration/Accounting
Pennsylvania State University, State College, PA

B.S.—Chemistry Major with Minors in Math and Physics
University of Pittsburgh, Pittsburgh, PA

Professional development activity includes numerous IBM management and assessment courses.

UNITED STATES ARMY
Military Service, Honorable Discharge
Retired Lieutenant Colonel, U.S. Army Corps of Engineers, U.S. ARMY RESERVE

ONE YEAR ACTIVE DUTY IN DESERT SHIELD AND DESERT STORM—SAUDI ARABIA, 1990–1991.
AWARDED BRONZE STAR FOR ACTIONS DURING DESERT STORM.
MULTIPLE AWARDS OF ARMY COMMENDATION MEDAL AND MERITORIOUS SERVICE MEDAL.

BOARD of DIRECTORS
★ IBM InPac Company, Ltd.—Shanghai (1999–2003)
★ Beijing GKI Electronics Company (2000–2002)
★ Tianjin Advanced Information Products Co., Ltd. (1999–2003)
★ Shenzhen GKI Electronics Company (1995–2002)
★ Shenzhen Association for Enterprises with Foreign Investment (1995–1999)
★ Programs for Accessible Living (Handicapped Advocacy Group), Charlotte, NC (1991–1993)

MEMBER
★ Shanghai Chamber of Commerce (1999–2003)
★ Shenzhen Chamber of Commerce (1994–1999)
★ Charlotte Chamber of Commerce, IBM Representative (1991–1993)
★ International Who's Who of Professionals (1999)
★ Chairman of EMS Subcommittee—Shenzhen Electronics Industrial Association (1994–1999)
★ Volunteer with Habitat for Humanity Cabarrus County, Concord, NC (2003–Present)

RESUME 88: BY JACQUI BARRETT AND ELIZABETH AXNIX

BRIAN C. JACKSON

Certified Professional Manager / ICPM
3838 NW Fairview · Washington, DC 20004
202.555.5551 H · 202.555.5552 C · bcjackson@email.net

SENIOR OPERATIONS & BUSINESS DEVELOPMENT EXECUTIVE

FEDERAL GOVERNMENT VERTICAL, HIGH-TECH, CERTIFIED 8(A) & START-UP ENVIRONMENTS

Industries—Specialty Chemical / Commercial Marine / Nuclear Services / IT Services
Select Customers—GSA / DOE / FDIC / U.S. Navy / USAF / DOT / Royal Caribbean Cruise Lines

13+ years of P&L experience effecting organizational growth and maximizing federal market exposure:	
Secured extremely competitive U.S. Government R&D contract with a combined revenue potential of >$7.5M	President / CEO ChemTechnology, Inc.
Established accounts with USAF, Comptroller of the Currency, Department of Transportation, and FDIC valued at >$5M annually	Director, Business Development RP Global
Built $3.2M stand-alone profit center serving primarily Department of Energy customers	Program Director Beacon, Inc.

Visionary CEO with an exceptional entrepreneurial track record of making "possibilities into products" and "products into profits." Consistent record of maximizing limited capital, human resources, and time to the bottom-line benefit of stakeholders and federal government customers. Experience leading critical operational, business development, and R&D initiatives and managing business operations on a virtual basis. Adept in recruiting and retaining quality personnel in extremely competitive environments. Goal-oriented leader with a high degree of business acumen and ability to independently manage multiple functions simultaneously. Top producer in challenging situations compounded by a high level of ambiguity.

Critical Strengths & Executive Competencies:

Start-up, M&A, Growth & Turnaround Situations • Strategic Planning & Tactical Execution • P&L Operations Management
Fiduciary Oversight • Top Management & Corporate Board of Directors Reporting • Organizational Development
DCAA-approved Accounting Systems • Multimillion-dollar GSA Contract Administration • Complex Contract Negotiations
Intellectual Property Management • R&D Oversight • NSF/EPA/OSHA/MILSPEC Product Certification
Security Clearances (previously held)—Department of Defense (Secret/Top Secret) • Department of Energy (Levels L & Q)
National Security Agency (TS/SCI)

EXECUTIVE PERFORMANCE OVERVIEW

Intellectual Property Management / Technical Product R&D Oversight / Operations Turnaround

CHEMTECHNOLOGY, LLC (www.chemtechnology.com), Washington, D.C.   2000 to Present
Small, privately held, multifacility specialty chemical company serving the marine, nuclear, and industrial markets and utilizing various domestic contract manufacturers.

PRESIDENT & CHIEF OPERATING OFFICER

Organizational Challenge: *Transform unique chemical technology intellectual property rights into marketable product lines. Developed nebulous business concept into highly valued, fully operational, and profitable enterprise well equipped and positioned to successfully compete against multibillion-dollar multinational corporations for customers throughout the commercial marine, industrial, retail, transportation, and nuclear markets.*

Value-add Result: *Built company from ground up, attaining such amazing levels of growth and innovation as to be a nominated finalist in the Virginia Center for Innovative Technology's (CIT) Annual Commercialization Awards (2004).*

Hold fiduciary accountability for every asset possessed by company and complete responsibility to all equity holders for corporate performance, growth, and P&L position. Directly manage all sales and marketing efforts; negotiate, finalize, and execute all contracts and agreements; administer entire employment cycle, including compensation packages, of all employees; and oversee all administrative and back-office functions. Solicit new capital investment, raising >$1M in early-stage financing over course of tenure.

Single-handedly rewrote business plan, broadening focus and proposed market scope, to ensure operation's long-term viability. Mounted 1-man marketing campaign and navigated complex world of environmental (EPA), safety (OSHA, NSF), and military (MILSPEC) requirements to introduce products into unique marketplaces and secure exclusive commercial supply contracts, U.S. Navy R&D contracts, and multiyear / multimillion-dollar indefinite delivery / indefinite quantity General Services Administration (GSA) contracts. Developed intellectual property protections (e.g., registered patents, trademarks, product licensing agreements) and implemented Defense Contract Audit Agency (DCAA)-approved accounting system. Managed acquisition, operation, and maintenance of all corporate offices, laboratory facilities, and warehouse space.

This executive's substantial military career is detailed on page 3 to show the solid foundation for the technical and management skills he has continued to develop in more recent positions.

RESUME 88, CONTINUED

- **Directly accountable for 925% revenue increase between FY01 and FY04.** Oversaw development, marketing, and new product launch of environmentally safe teak deck cleaner for use on cruise ships, leading to an exclusive contract with Royal Caribbean Cruise Lines for its entire fleet. Negotiated package of contracts with U.S. Navy totaling $1.1M. Consistently outperformed key competitors (i.e., Barwil-Unitor, EcoLab, Ashland) to gain market share / visibility.

- **Delivered a series of major corporate transactions resulting in slashed R&D costs, guaranteed fixed production cost, and multimillion-dollar top-line revenue increases.** Developed strategic alliance with key market player to **achieve >65% decrease in R&D cost** and structured and executed teaming agreement with Envoy Systems to ensure annual revenue flow conservatively estimated at $2M per year.

- **Expanded corporate footprint and transitioned company from commercial products supplier to a bona fine government contractor.** Successfully pursued highly competitive U.S. Government R&D program contract. Authored winning proposal for U.S. Navy's Small Business Innovation Research (SBIR) Phase I, II, and III contract award, a first-time effort that beat out >95% of the respondents.

  - **Resulting corporate benefits: >$2M in direct Navy contract awards and additional government contracts with revenue potential of >$5.5M.**

- **Spearheaded several initiatives designed to strengthen productivity, suppress costs, and maximize results despite limited capital reserves.**
  - Employed new product development system, slashing product evaluation / market launch from 9 months to 90 days.
  - Developed virtual office structure to effectively manage geographically dispersed laboratory and scientific staff and off-site sales manager and support staff.
  - Eliminated slow-moving items from product offering; cut insurance cost 78%; and negotiated minimal upfront-cost, profit-sharing arrangement with an extremely high-dollar nuclear energy industry consultant.
  - Conducted low-cost PR campaign resulting in high-visibility articles in influential trade magazines and industry-related publications. Established world-class distribution chain.

RP GLOBAL, Sterling, Virginia (www.rpglobal.com)   1998 to 2000
High-growth "roll-up" of several specialized, IT-focused federal contractors.

DIRECTOR, BUSINESS DEVELOPMENT

Organizational Challenge: *Penetrate and exploit previously untapped segments of the federal market. Executed sales, marketing, and executive-level business development activities of newly formed "Learning Systems" business unit offering a comprehensive menu of services.*

Value-add Result: *Prototyped home-based officing model for all subsequent business development personnel to hold down costs and support 10-fold corporate growth during tenure.*

Functioned as Federal Accounts Sales Executive and met a series of aggressive sales goals using a consultative sales approach underpinned with specialized federal-sector experience. Prepared and executed tactical and strategic marketing plans, qualified sales leads, worked closely with all business unit directors, and developed and managed teaming relationships with *Fortune 500* companies and federal agencies. Reported directly to executive vice president for sales and marketing. Trained all business development managers in the marketing of instructional, learning management, and electronic performance systems. Assisted with sales personnel compensation plan development.

- **Built annual private-sector sales portfolio from zero accounts into $3M book of business** in 2 years. Established accounts with USAF, Comptroller of the Currency, Department of Transportation, and FDIC valued at >$5M per year.

- **Attained TS/SCI clearance** to establish lucrative account with National Security Agency (NSA)—an $800,000 annual revenue benefit.

BEACON, INC., Washington, D.C.   1994 to 1998
Start-up 8(a) federal contractor. Consistently listed on Washington Post's *Fast 50 (top 50 fastest growing companies in area).*

PROGRAM DIRECTOR (February 1995 to April 1998) / **PROGRAM ANALYST** (August 1994 to February 1995)

Organizational Challenge: *Expand corporate marketplace footprint into nuclear services. Within 15 months of hire, introduced and successfully demonstrated new nuclear decontamination technique (chelant-based decontamination chemistry) adopted and still in current use by several Department of Energy (DOE) facilities.*

Value-add Result: *Demonstrations led to establishment of new business unit generating more than $2.5M in annual revenue.*

Established 2 wholly new corporate divisions. Simultaneously functioned as profit centers' Program Director, managing divisional P&L (comprising 20% of corporate budget) and executing new business development, proposal preparation, and all aspects of Division staffing and personnel recruiting. Supervised and administered both commercial and government contracts, comprising task orders, firm fixed price, time & material, cost + fixed fee, cost + award fee, and GSA schedules.

Brian C. Jackson, Page 3 of 3   202.555.5551 H • 202.555.5552 C • bcjackson@email.net

- **Training Development Division**—Prepared computer-based and traditional technical and professional training development materials and delivery systems for customers (e.g., DOE, Federal Highway Administration, Department of the Navy). Managed staff of 10 featuring instruction design specialists, graphic artists, software designers, and instructors. **Stand-alone profit center's annual revenue: >$1.5M.**

- **Nuclear Services Division**—Leveraged Naval nuclear engineering training and supervisory experience to launch division providing new, innovative nuclear decontamination and remediation services to primarily DOE clients.
  - Recruited and managed 12 employees (engineers, health physicists, technicians, administrative personnel); ensured all appropriate staff received required OSHA, HAZWOPER (Hazardous Waste Operations and Emergency Response), and site-specific training; and maintained all records documenting security clearances and physical examinations.
  - Negotiated contracts for construction of complex decontamination equipment with small specialty manufacturing facilities and complex, high-dollar nuclear decontamination services contracts with companies such as Bechtel and Lockheed Martin Energy Services.
  - **Stand-alone profit center's annual revenue: >$3.2M.**

- **Salvaged extremely overbudget and significantly behind-schedule project.** Tackled personnel issues, overcame customer dissatisfaction, and worked onsite to direct all day-to-day efforts to bring project in on time and on budget. **Efforts resulted in additional contract with customer valued at >$1M.**

- **Saved key customer well over $3M.** Supervised design, construction, and use of prototypical and proprietary decontamination equipment used to conduct a complex project at the Oak Ridge National Lab.

- **Established performance-based bonus system within both divisions.** Reported regularly to president, COO, and board of directors on divisional performance and profit-center projections for each business unit and participated in senior management meetings.

MILITARY SERVICE • 1980 to 1994

United States Navy • Submarine Service

MASTER CHIEF PETTY OFFICER / E-9
Honorable Discharge—Comprehensive listing of commendations, medals, and duty ribbons available at interview.

NUCLEAR POWER PLANT TECHNICAL SUPERVISOR

- Qualified in submarines; supervised operation and maintenance of submarine nuclear propulsion plant and radiological controls. Held Secret security clearance.

CHIEF OF THE BOAT (COB) / COMMAND MASTER CHIEF

- Second highest senior enlisted officer (and 1 of the youngest ever) selected by admiral in charge to function as primary liaison and advisor among and between officers and noncommissioned personnel. Within 90 days of arrival onboard, effected dramatic turnaround in crew morale and operational performance as evidenced by battle readiness award and recognition for 1 of the highest personnel retention rates of any ship in the fleet.

NAVY RECRUITING ZONE SUPERVISOR

- Supervised 8 offices in 3 states in recruiting region that had never achieved its assigned recruiting goal. Within 3 months of assignment, region met or exceeded assigned sales goals each month during tenure. Recognized 2 consecutive years as 1 of the Navy's top salesmen.

GRADUATE / NAVY NUCLEAR POWER SCHOOL
- Completed highly selective academic program of U.S. Navy nuclear engineering school featuring an emphasis in math, nuclear physics, thermodynamics, reactor plant technology / theory, chemistry, materials engineering, and metallurgy.

EDUCATION / PROFESSIONAL DEVELOPMENT

MISSOURI UNIVERSITY, Columbia, Missouri
BACHELOR OF BUSINESS ADMINISTRATION

CERTIFICATION Certified Manager (CM) • Institute of Certified Professional Managers / James Madison University

CONTINUING PROFESSIONAL EDUCATION (RECENT): Sales training courses including week-long training program by Decision Dynamics, Inc. Professional training in presentation and lecture techniques presented by Dawnbreaker, Inc.

AFFILIATIONS: American Nuclear Society (Member) / Ocean Watch Council of Owners (President) / Mustang Owners Club of America (Member) / Fleet Reserve Association (Active Member) / American Legion (Member)

PART III

Cover Letters for Military-to-Civilian Transitions

CHAPTER 14

Writing a Winning Cover Letter

Now that your resume is written, you may think that you're all set to launch your job search. If it were only that easy! Just as critical to the effectiveness and success of your job search campaign is your cover letter. To begin our discussion of this vital element in your search, let's start with a concise definition:

> **Cover letter**: A document that accompanies your resume and highlights your specific skills, qualifications, competencies, achievements, and more that *relate directly to the position for which you are applying.*

That's right... the best cover letters are letters that are targeted to specific positions (for example, a supply chain management position with a local manufacturing company, a corporate training position with a Fortune 500 health care company, or a project engineering assignment with an international company). Targeted letters allow you to selectively include information about your past work experience (both military and civilian), training and education (both military and civilian), affiliations, professional activities, and more that directly support your candidacy for a particular position. In essence, you're taking everything about your career, laying it out on the table (so to speak), and then selecting only the information that is most important to your current job objective.

Here's an example of a wonderfully written cover letter that is targeted to this candidate's specific objective—a position in training and development.

1189 Denver Drive
Laurel, MD 21766

301-555-2290
MartyPorter@aol.com

Martin Porter

September 20, 2009

Dorothy Daniels, Human Resources Director
Raytheon
2100 Raytheon Drive, MS 1908
Baltimore, MD 21278

RE: Systems Engineer

Dear Ms. Daniels:

I am currently enrolled at the University of Baltimore to attain a **Master's Degree in Systems Engineering** to complement my **Bachelor's Degree in Electrical Engineering** that I earned while attending West Point and my 10 years of experience as a **Telecommunications Engineer.**

In 2007, I was recalled to active duty to lead troops in the Middle East, boosting my management and communications skills. Now that I have fulfilled that obligation and am nearing graduation, I am selectively applying for positions for which I believe I'm an excellent candidate. As you'll note, the enclosed resume highlights my Systems Engineering experience, both during my service with the U.S. Army and while working for HughesNet.

I meet and, in fact, exceed many of the requirements for your position of Systems Engineer:

- ❑ Experience with a number of telecommunication design and implementation projects—for both military and civilian applications—to create efficient, cost-effective, and replicable solutions.

- ❑ Outstanding team-building and team leadership skills, complemented by extensive experience working with major contractors and their technical/engineering teams.

- ❑ Technical knowledge of E3, SM, RF, EV, TOC, and M&S life cycle.

- ❑ Top Secret security clearance (required for your company).

I will contact your office in a few days to see if there is a convenient time to schedule an appointment to meet and further discuss this employment opportunity with your firm. I look forward to providing value and innovation to your projects and project teams.

Sincerely,

Martin Porter

Enclosure: Resume

A targeted cover letter (submitted by Diane Burns, CPCC, CPRW, CEIP, CLTMC, CCMC, FJST, CCM, JCTC).

All too often, job search candidates write what we refer to as general cover letters—letters that can be used to apply for any position with any type of organization. In essence, these letters simply summarize information that is already included on your resume and tend not to be nearly as effective as targeted cover letters that are customized to each position to which you apply. Because you do not have a specific position in mind when you write a general letter, you are not able to highlight information that would be most essential in a particular situation. As such, we strongly urge that you stay away from general letters and devote the time that is necessary to develop targeted cover letters that will sell you into your next position.

Another real advantage to targeted cover letters is that the recipient will notice that you have taken the time to write an individual letter to him or her; and, of course, that leaves a great impression. When you are able to integrate specific information into your letter about the company to which you are applying, it clearly demonstrates your interest in the position and the organization, before you've ever had the opportunity to speak with anyone there. Just think how impressed a prospective employer will be when he or she realizes that you've spent the time and energy necessary to research and get to know his or her organization. This, in and of itself, will give you a distinct advantage over the competition.

Six Steps to Writing Better Cover Letters

To help guide you in writing and designing your own winning cover letters, we've created a step-by-step process and structure that will allow you to quickly and easily write letters that will get you and your resume noticed, not passed over:

1. Identify your key selling points.
2. Preplan.
3. Write the opening paragraph.
4. Write the body.
5. Write the closing.
6. Polish, proofread, and finalize.

Now, we're going to explore each of these steps in detail to provide you with an action plan to write your letters with ease and confidence. Our most detailed discussion will be of the first step, which is the entire foundation for your cover letter.

STEP 1: IDENTIFY YOUR KEY SELLING POINTS

What qualifications, experiences, achievements, and skills do you bring to a company? It's time to evaluate and quantify what it is that makes you unique, valuable, and interesting to potential employers.

Know Your Objective

The best place to start is by clearly identifying *who* you are and what your job objective is. Are you a ship's engineer, a telecommunications engineer, an electrical engineer, or a weapons systems engineer? Are you a training officer, an intelligence security officer, or a logistics officer? Do you specialize in manpower planning and workforce training? Who are you? It is critical that you be able to clearly and accurately define who you are in an instant. Remember, an instant is all that you have to capture your reader's attention, encouraging him not only to read your cover letter in full, but also to read your resume and contact you for a personal interview.

Summarize Your Experience

Just as important, you must be able to clearly identify why an organization would be interested in interviewing and possibly hiring you. Is it because of the companies you've worked for? The positions you held? The promotions you earned? Your accomplishments? Your technical expertise? Your specific skills and qualifications? Your licenses and educational credentials? Your leadership skills? Your foreign-language skills and international experience? Why would someone be interested in you?

Sell Your Achievements

Your achievements are what set you apart from others with a similar background. They answer the reader's all-important question, "What can you do for me?" because they tell precisely what you have done for someone else. Cover letters and resumes without achievements are simply dry compilations of position titles and responsibilities. They don't sell your unique attributes, and they don't compel readers to pick up the phone and invite you in for an interview.

In thinking about your achievements, ask yourself how you've benefited the organizations where you've worked. In general terms, you can help an organization by

- **Saving money** (cost reductions, streamlining, automating, efficiency improvements, manpower reductions)

- **Creating new things** (systems, processes, technologies, methodologies, metrics, techniques, and more)

- **Improving existing things** (reengineering, redesigning, revitalizing, consolidating)

- **Improving personnel and/or organizational performance** (productivity, efficiency, quality, delivery, and customer service)

- **Winning honors, awards, and commendations**

- **Making money** (revenues, profits, and earnings—which, although remarkably important to companies, is not generally a function that people in the U.S. Armed Forces are responsible for or have any impact on)

In writing your achievements, think about the two key pieces of information you want to convey about each of your successes: what you did and how it benefited the organization. The combination of these components will make your achievements—and, in turn, you—shine.

Who you are, what you have achieved, and why an organization would want to hire you are critical questions you must ask yourself before you ever begin to write a cover letter. The answers to those questions will directly impact what you write in your cover letter and how you present that information. You must determine what you have to offer that relates to that organization's specific needs, what will be of interest to them, and what will entice them to read your resume and offer you the opportunity for an interview. That information then becomes the foundation for every cover letter that you write.

STEP 2: PREPLAN

Before you begin writing a single word of your cover letter, you must determine the appropriate strategy for that particular letter. You're not ready to write until you can clearly answer the following questions:

- **Why am I writing this letter?** Am I writing in response to a print or online advertisement, sending a cold-call letter to companies and/or government agencies, contacting someone in my network, writing to an organization at the recommendation of someone else, or writing a follow-up letter to a company to which I already sent a resume? The answer to this question will significantly impact the content of your cover letter—the introduction in particular.

- **Have I researched the organization and/or the position?** There will be instances where you know, or can find, information about an organization you are writing to, the services and products it offers, the positions that are open, the types of candidates it hires, the hiring requirements, and so much more. Do your research! The more you know about a company and the position, the more on-target you can write your letters, relating your experience to the company's identified needs. If you know a company is facing a serious budget crisis, focus on your success in cost-cutting and productivity improvement. If you know that the company is struggling with its technical support organization, focus on your success in building stronger help-desk operations and training technical support personnel. Your goal is to find common ground between you and the company and then leverage that to your advantage.

- **Do I have a contact name?** The fact is that if you write to the Human Resources department of a company, you'll never quite know where your letter and resume have landed. However, if you write to a particular individual in a particular department with particular contact information, you not only know who has your resume and cover letter, you also know who to follow up with. This is critical for job search success in today's competitive market! Make sure to double-check the spelling of the name and the person's job title and obtain the full mailing address or e-mail address.

STEP 3: WRITE THE OPENING PARAGRAPH

The opening paragraph of your cover letter is your hook, your sales pitch, that tells your reader who you are and why you are of value to that specific organization. It should entice the recipient to read your letter in its entirety and then take the time to closely review your resume. Because it is so critical, the opening paragraph is often the section that will take you the longest to write.

> **TIP:** If you're having trouble writing the opening paragraph of your cover letter, leave it for the time being and move on to the body of the letter. Once you've written the rest of the letter, the opening paragraph will usually flow much more smoothly and quickly.

There are three specific questions you must address in the opening paragraph of your cover letter:

1. Who are you?

2. Why are you writing?

3. What message are you communicating?

Your answers to these questions, combined with the specific reason you are writing (for example, in response to an advertisement, on recommendation from a network contact, or because of an Internet job lead), will almost always dictate the type of opening you select. Review the introductory paragraphs of the sample cover letters in chapter 15 to help you get started developing your own introduction.

STEP 4: WRITE THE BODY

Now you're ready to tackle the real task at hand: writing the body of your cover letter—the key qualifications, accomplishments, successes, technical expertise, and whatever other information you choose to highlight that will entice the reader to closely review your resume and offer you the opportunity for a personal interview.

In order to sell yourself (or any product) as "the answer," you must highlight the attractive *features* and *benefits* of that product. Put yourself in the shoes of the buyer (employer) and ask yourself:

- What will catch my attention?

- What's interesting about this candidate?

- What's innovative or unique about this candidate?

- Why is this candidate different from (or better than) other competitive candidates?

- Do I understand the value I'll get from this candidate?

- Do I need this candidate?

- Do I want this candidate?

Whether or not you're conscious of it, every time you buy something, you ask yourself these questions and others. It's the typical process that everyone goes through when deciding whether to make a purchase. It is imperative that you remember this as you begin to write your cover letters. Understand that you must clearly communicate the answers to these questions in order to get people to want to "buy" *you*.

> **TIP:** Your cover letter *should not* be written as "Here I am, give me a job," but *should be* written as, "Here I am; this is why I am so valuable; give me a

chance to solve your problems." Focusing on the value and benefits you have to offer is a good way to capture the reader's attention. Remember, the employer's most compelling question is "What can you do for me?"—not "What do you want?"

Your challenge, then, is to convey your value in a short and concise document—your cover letter. Unfortunately, there are no rules to guide you in determining what to include in each specific cover letter that you write. It is entirely a judgment call based on the specific situation at hand—the position, the organization, and the required qualifications and experience. What you include in your letter is not necessarily based on what you consider to be your most significant responsibilities and achievements from throughout your career, but rather what is *most relevant to the hiring company and its needs.*

Achievements, accomplishments, contributions, and successes are the cornerstone of any effective cover letter. It goes without saying that you want to demonstrate that you have the right skills, qualifications, and experience for a particular job. However, you do not want your letter to be a "job description"—a mere listing of job responsibilities. First of all, you've addressed a great deal of that information in the resume that you'll be sending along with your cover letter. You don't want your letter to simply reiterate what's in your resume. The challenge is to write a cover letter that complements the resume and brings the most notable information to the forefront.

Depending on the format of your letter, you can convey this information in a paragraph format, a bullet-point format, or a combination of both. Use whichever you feel is most appropriate to convey the particular information. If you decide to use full paragraphs, make sure that they are fairly short to promote readability. Edit and tighten your copy so that every word and phrase conveys information that relates to the employer's needs and your most relevant qualifications.

STEP 5: WRITE THE CLOSING

Now that you've written your introductory paragraph and the body of your cover letter, all you have left to do is the closing paragraph. This section of the cover letter is generally the easiest one to write. To get started, ask yourself these two simple questions:

- What style of closing paragraph do I want to use?

- Is there any specific personal or salary information I want to include that was requested in the advertisement to which I am responding?

Choosing a style for closing paragraphs is easy. There are basically only two styles—passive and assertive—and the distinction between the two styles is evident:

- **Passive:** A passive letter ends with a statement such as "I look forward to hearing from you." With this sentence, you are taking a passive approach, waiting for the hiring company or recruiter to contact you. We do *not* recommend this strategy.

- **Assertive:** An assertive letter ends with a statement such as "I look forward to interviewing with you and will follow up next week to schedule a convenient appointment." In this sentence, you are asserting yourself, telling the recipient that you will follow up, and asking for the interview!

We strongly recommend that you end your cover letters with an assertive closing paragraph. Remember, the only real objective of your cover letter is to get an interview, so *ask for it*! Furthermore, we also advise that you outline an agenda that communicates you will be expecting the employers' call and, if you don't hear from them, you will follow up. This approach puts you in the driver's seat and in control of your job search. It also demonstrates to a prospective employer that once you've initiated something, you follow it through to completion. This is a valuable trait for any professional.

Inevitably, there will be instances in your job search when you will not be able to follow up:

- If you are responding to a blind advertisement with a P.O. box, you won't know whom to call.

- If you are responding to an advertisement that states, "No Phone Calls," don't call.

- If you are sending out 1,000 letters to recruiters across the nation, don't waste your time calling them. If they're interested or have an opportunity for which you are suited, they'll call you.

- If you know that you'll never get the individual you want to speak with on the phone, don't waste your time or money.

The closing paragraph of your cover letter is also the preferred placement for any personal or salary information you will include. There are generally only two times you will want to include this type of information:

- **When it has been asked for in an advertisement.** Common requests include such things as salary history (what you have made in the past and are currently earning if you are employed), salary requirements (what your current salary objectives are), citizenship status, or geographic preference.

- **When you are writing "cold-call" letters to recruiters.** When contacting recruiters, we recommend that you at least minimally address your salary requirements (a range is fine) and any geographic preferences in the closing paragraph of your cover letter.

STEP 6: POLISH, PROOFREAD, AND FINALIZE

The process we recommend for writing your cover letters suggests that you first craft the opening, then the middle, and then the closing of each letter. Although the step-by-step process makes the task fairly quick and easy, you will probably find that your letters need final polishing, wordsmithing, and tweaking to ensure that each section "flows" into the next and that you have a cohesive-sounding whole.

Take the time to proofread your letter thoroughly and carefully. Read it for sense and flow; then read it again to check for spelling errors, punctuation mistakes, and grammatical inconsistencies. We cannot emphasize this point enough. The people who receive your cover letter and resume *do* judge your professionalism based on the quality and accuracy of these documents.

In fact, in a survey of hiring authorities we conducted for a prior book, *90 percent of respondents* mentioned quality and appearance factors (such as typos, misspellings, smudged print, and low-quality paper) as reasons for *immediately discarding a resume.* Don't take a chance that your carefully written letter and resume will end up in the circular file before your qualifications are even considered.

Here are a few things to look out for during the polishing phase:

- **Spelling:** Use your computer's spell-checker, but don't rely on it totally. The spell-checker won't flag an "it's" that should be "its" or a "there" that should be "their." Make triple-certain you've correctly spelled all names: people, organizations, and so on.

- **Grammar and punctuation:** If you're not confident about your grammar and punctuation skills, purchase an all-purpose reference guide and use it as often as you need to. Don't let your cover letter be discarded because of basic grammar and punctuation errors.

- **Interesting language:** As much as possible, avoid cliches and outdated language (such as "Enclosed please find my resume"). It's difficult to find new ways to express familiar sentiments (such as "I would appreciate the opportunity for an interview"), and it's certainly not necessary to come up with unique language for every phrase. But make sure that your cover letter doesn't sound like a cookie-cutter, one-size-fits-all letter that could have been written by any job seeker.

Authors' Best Tips for Writing Winning Cover Letters

Here's our most important cover-letter advice, gleaned from our experience writing thousands of cover letters, thank-you letters, and other job-search communications.

DON'T REINVENT THE WHEEL

A great amount of our discussion has focused on the fact that your cover letters should be written individually based on the specific situation. And that is quite true. The more focused your cover letters, the greater the impact and the more likely you are to get a response and opportunity to interview. However, you *do not* have to reinvent the wheel with each and every cover letter you write. If you're a jet engine mechanic writing in response to advertisements for other jet engine mechanic positions, you can very often use the same letter with just a few minor editorial changes to match each opportunity. Remember to use your word-processing program's "copy and paste" function. It's a great labor-saving tool!

SELL IT TO ME; DON'T TELL IT TO ME

Just like resume writing, cover letter writing is sales—pure and simple. You have a commodity to sell—yourself—and your challenge is to write a marketing communication that is powerful and pushes the reader to action. (You want him to call you for an interview!) Therefore, it is essential that when writing your letters you "sell" your achievements and don't just "tell" your responsibilities.

Here's a quick example. If you are recruiter for the U.S. Marine Corps, you could "tell" your reader that you're responsible for managing recruitment programs in Portland, Oregon. Great! Or you could "sell" the fact that you've recruited more than 200 new Marines in the past 16 months, 95% of whom are still serving with the Corps and 85% of whom have already earned at least one promotion. Which letter would capture your interest?

GET OVER WRITER'S BLOCK

Very often, the most difficult part of writing a cover letter is getting started. You can sit and look at that blank piece of paper or computer screen for hours, frustrated and wondering whether the whole world has such a hard time writing cover letters. If writing is part of your daily work responsibilities, the process might not be too arduous. However, if you do not have to write on a regular basis, cover letters can be an especially formidable task. That's why it is so important to follow the step-by-step process we have created. It is guaranteed to make cover letter writing faster, easier, and much less painful!

If you're still having trouble, consider this simple thought: **You do not have to start at the beginning.** Even after writing thousands and thousands of cover letters, we'll sit stumped, unable to come up with just the right opening paragraph. Instead of wasting time and brain power, and getting frustrated, we'll just leave it alone and move on to another section in the letter that we feel more confident writing. You'll find that once you get going, new ideas will pop into your head and the more difficult sections will come much more easily and confidently.

ANSWER THE EMPLOYER'S MOST IMPORTANT QUESTION: "WHAT CAN YOU DO FOR ME?"

A powerful cover letter can help you get what you want: a new, perhaps more advanced, and more satisfying position. It is certainly important that you understand what you want to do, the kind of organization you'd like to work for, and the environment in which you'll be most productive. Yet you must remember that employers aren't really interested in you. They're interested in *what you can do for them*. If you do not keep this thought in the forefront of your mind when writing your cover letters, you're likely to produce a self-centered-sounding "here I am" letter that probably won't do much to advance your job search.

When writing your cover letters, consider the employer's needs and make sure that you communicate that you can add value, solve problems, and deliver benefits for that employer. You can do this through a strong focus on accomplishments ("Ah, she did that for the U.S. Army's logistics command; she can do the same for me.") and through careful attention to the wording and tone of your letter so that you appear to be more interested in contributing to the organization than satisfying your own personal needs.

Review the Cover Letter Checklist that follows to be sure that your letters meet all of our requirements for style, appropriateness, quality of text, quality of presentation, and effectiveness. Follow our rules and we guarantee that your letters will open doors, generate interviews, and help you land your next great professional opportunity.

Cover Letter Checklist

Before mailing, faxing, or e-mailing each cover letter you prepare, complete the following checklist to be sure that you have met all the rules for cover letter writing. If you cannot answer "yes" to *all* of the questions, go back and edit your letter as necessary before mailing it. The only questions for which a "no" answer is acceptable are questions #5 and #6, which relate specifically to the organization to which you are writing. As we have stated previously, there will be instances when you can find this information, but there will also be instances (for example, when writing to a P.O. box) when you cannot.

		YES	NO
1.	Do I convey an immediate understanding of who I am in the first two sentences of my cover letter?	❑	❑
2.	Is my cover letter format unique, and does my letter stand out?	❑	❑
3.	Have I highlighted my most relevant qualifications?	❑	❑
4.	Have I highlighted my most relevant achievements?	❑	❑
5.	Have I included information I know about the company or the specific position for which I am applying?	❑	❑
6.	Have I highlighted why I want to work for this company?	❑	❑
7.	Is my letter neat, clean, and well-presented without being overdesigned?	❑	❑
8.	Is my letter error-free?	❑	❑
9.	Is my cover letter short and succinct, preferably no longer than one page?	❑	❑
10.	Do I ask for an interview in the letter?	❑	❑

CHAPTER 15

Sample Cover Letters

What follows are six more sample cover letters for your review. Look at them closely. Select opening paragraphs, closing paragraphs, formats, and styles that you like, and then model your own cover letters accordingly. You'll find that if you use these sample letters for hints, your letter-writing process will be much easier and faster. To see even more samples and get more help with writing your cover letters, see our book *Cover Letter Magic* (JIST Publishing), the industry's leading book on cover letter writing, now in its fourth edition.

GERALD G. ANDERSON

1142 Walker Road, Apt. 122 - Albuquerque, NM 55882
gerryanderson@hotmail.com
(505) 555-4567

October 12, 2009

Ms. Deborah Whitman
Vice President of Construction Operations
Ryland Homes, Inc.
777 East Hanover Street
Albuquerque, NM 55801

Dear Ms. Whitman:

I am writing in response to your advertisement for a Heavy Equipment Operator and have enclosed my resume for your review. Highlights of my experience include

- Nine years with the U.S. Air Force as a Heavy Equipment Operator and Mechanic.

- Hands-on skills in operating forklifts, tractors, loaders, backhoes, motor graders, track loaders, bulldozers, bobcat skid/steer loaders, and scrapers.

- Excellent technical and mechanical troubleshooting skills and qualifications.

- Certification as a Heavy Equipment Operator through Lackland Air Force Base.

I can read and interpret technical documents, drawings, maintenance manuals, repair instructions, and more. In addition, I have clearly demonstrated my ability to work independently, productively, and efficiently.

Working for Ryland Homes would be a great opportunity, and I am most interested in meeting with you as soon as your schedule allows. I will call Tuesday morning, October 20, so that we can coordinate a specific date and time for an interview. Thank you for your time and your consideration. I guarantee it will be worth it.

Sincerely,

Gerald G. Anderson

Enclosure

This well-targeted cover letter emphasizes a combination of hands-on equipment skills as well as related "office" skills. The closing paragraph includes a specific date for follow up (written by Wendy S. Enelow, CCM, MRW, JCTC, CPRW).

DANIEL GROSSMAN

2324 Lucy Boulevard
Smithtown, PA 19093

Phone: 601.555.0287
danielgr222@aol.com

June 10, 2010

Dennis Donovan
Senior Engineer
Oceanic Research Center, Inc.
1400 Seacoast Boulevard
San Diego, CA 98977

RE: Oceanographic Engineer & Research Technologist Position

Dear Mr. Donovan:

For the past 12 years, I have advanced through a series of increasingly responsible scientific and engineering positions with the U.S. Coast Guard Oceanographic Office. The opportunities have been tremendous, allowing me to work across a broad range of disciplines and providing me with outstanding qualifications in

- Planning and independently conducting scientific research and experimentation, from initial planning through experimental design, data collection, analysis, synthesis, and reporting.

- Managing oceanographic, seismic, geologic, electronic, and systems engineering projects.

- Coordinating project planning, staffing, and performance management, including direct supervisory responsibility for up to 20 engineers, scientists, and technologists.

- Developing advanced IT software and applications, as noted on the enclosed resume, with particular emphasis on digital imaging and signal-processing technologies.

- Controlling $4 million in scientific, engineering, and technology assets.

In addition, I have extensive technical/scientific writing and public presentation experience.

I am currently separating from active duty with the Coast Guard and am now exploring new professional opportunities that will allow me to continue to work in the field of oceanography. Your position appears to be ideal for a candidate with my qualifications, and, as such, I look forward to an interview. If I haven't heard from your office within a week, I'll call to schedule a convenient time. Thank you.

Sincerely,

Daniel Grossman

Enclosure

Well-targeted and easy to review, this letter highlights all of the relevant qualifications as stated in the advertisement and ends with an assertive close (written by Wendy S. Enelow, CCM, MRW, JCTC, CPRW).

MICHAEL LYNCH, JR.

2110 Maple Drive
Annapolis, Maryland 21401
(301) 555-0987
mikelynch@msn.com

April 7, 2010

Don Ryder
Vice President—Operations
Tyson Transportation, Inc.
1220 12th Street SE
Washington, DC 20090

Dear Mr. Ryder:

For the past nine years, I have managed large-scale, fully integrated logistics, warehousing, distribution, and transportation operations for the U.S. Army in locations worldwide. The focus of my career has been divided between coordinating start-up operations and facilitating productivity improvements to existing operations. In each situation, I have delivered strong and sustainable results in productivity, efficiency, and other performance metrics. Most notably, my team and I

* Led the successful and profitable turnaround of the Army's internal logistics system, implemented training and productivity improvement programs, and **improved efficiency by more than 200%.**

Currently, I am orchestrating a complete revitalization of our logistics operations in Baltimore. In less than nine months, my team and I have reengineered the organization, **reduced costs by better than 10%, and improved on-time shipments by 48%.** We are now positioned to continue our strong performance and achieve even greater improvements.

Although my years with the Army have been a wonderful experience, I am now ready to pursue new professional challenges in the private sector. As such, I would welcome the opportunity to interview for any upcoming logistics, transportation, and/or distribution management positions with Tyson Transportation.

Thank you for your consideration, and I look forward to talking with you about how I can improve productivity and efficiency at Tyson.

Sincerely,

Michael Lynch, Jr.

Enclosure

Showcasing some powerful percentages that support this candidate's claim of performance improvement, this letter also explains his interest in upcoming opportunities with the company (written by Wendy S. Enelow, CCM, MRW, JCTC, CPRW).

DONNA R. SIMPSON

7766 Delilah Avenue North
San Antonio, TX 77992

Phone: 601.555.9088
donnars@datastar.net

April 22, 2010

Loretta Algrove
Chief Technology Officer
Systems & Software Recruiters
8900 Washington Boulevard, Suite 1200
San Antonio, TX 77901

Dear Ms. Algrove:

I am writing and forwarding my resume in anticipation that you may be interested in a candidate with more than **10 years of experience in information technology, software design, and applications development**. Highlights of my career that may be of particular interest to you and your client companies include

- Pioneering innovative, next-generation GPS and GIS applications.

- Evaluating organizational and operating needs to determine appropriate technologies.

- Designing, testing, and implementing new software and new applications for a broad range of engineering, technical, business, administrative, analysis, and reporting needs.

- Training and supervising less experienced technical and design teams.

- Developing new uses and applications for existing technologies.

- Improving performance, productivity, and efficiency of operations through technological enhancement.

I am most proud of a particular IT project I managed: the development of the only tidal projection software in the U.S. Navy. This major initiative delivered a significant improvement in the Navy's ability to predict adverse tidal impact on land masses worldwide and, in turn, prevent catastrophic damage to people and property. Another notable project I orchestrated was the design of the back-end architecture for an asset management system now in use at Naval and Air Force installations worldwide.

In anticipation of my upcoming discharge at the end of this year, I'm contacting a few select recruiters who specialize in candidates with my experience. Of course, Systems & Software Recruiters is at the top of my list, and, as such, I'd welcome a phone call from you to learn more about your current and upcoming search assignments.

Note that I am open to relocation nationwide and anticipate annual compensation between $125,000 and $150,000. Thank you for your time and consideration.

Sincerely,

Donna R. Simpson

Enclosure

This is a typical recruiter letter with a three-part combination of (1) career overview, (2) significant skill sets and achievements, and (3) information about salary and relocation (written by Louise Kursmark, MRW, CPRW, JCTC, CEIP, CCM).

ANDREW MARTINSON

2209 Dulles Avenue
Littleton, CO 80943

Mobile: (303) 555-2209
andymartinson@msn.com

March 4, 2010

Dr. Angela Garner
South Denver Community College
One Community College Boulevard
Denver, CO 80909

Dear Dr. Garner:

Greg Farmer suggested I contact you directly. He and I have known each other for years, and he believes that I have precisely the qualifications you're seeking for your new Director of Workforce Planning, Development, and Leadership. What's even better is that I'm right in your backyard!

I bring to SDCC a unique blend of management qualifications that briefly include

- Directing workforce planning and management for 700,000 U.S. Army personnel.
- Leading headquarters-based personnel, training, and leadership development programs.
- Designing manpower planning and staffing models for worldwide implementation.
- Authoring, negotiating, and administering large-dollar training contracts (including RFP preparation).
- Developing and justifying funding requests from both government and private sectors.
- Managing partner development and multiorganizational linkages/liaison affairs.

In addition, I completed a 9-month consulting contract with SDCC, during which time I designed and implemented a complete workforce training program. As such, I am somewhat familiar with the college's administrative and outreach operations, and I have worked in cooperation with your personnel. I would be pleased to provide additional information regarding this engagement and the specific individuals at SDCC with whom I interfaced.

I would be delighted to have the opportunity for a personal interview and can, of course, be available at your convenience. I thank you in advance for your time and consideration and look forward to what I anticipate will be the first of many positive communications. I will follow up next week to schedule our interview.

Sincerely,

Andrew Martinson

Enclosure

This letter opens with a referral source and mentions the candidate's proximity to the college, and then follows with short and succinct highlights of relevant experiences. Of particular note is the way he's highlighted his short-term consulting engagement with the college to instantly position himself as an "insider" (written by Wendy S. Enelow, CCM, MRW, JCTC, CPRW).

Joe B. Maynard

4120 Harding St.
New York, New York 10010
Mobile (212) 345-5678 • Residence (212) 345-9012
jbmaynard@worldnet.com

SENIOR INFORMATION TECHNOLOGY & SYSTEMS EXECUTIVE

Architecture / Platforms / Software / Networks / Databases / Voice & Data Communications
Internet & Intranet Technologies / E-commerce Technologies / Conversion & Migration

Sophie Demarceux
Management Recruiters International
295 Madison Avenue
New York, New York 10017

IN RE: SENIOR INFORMATION TECHNOLOGY / SYSTEMS EXECUTIVE OPPORTUNITIES

Dear Ms. Demarceux,

I am a well-qualified **Information Technology and Systems Design Executive,** successful in identifying organizational needs and leading the development/implementation of emerging technologies. With extensive experience in both private and government sectors, I have been highly successful in the conceptualization of effective system design, as well as improving productivity, quality, and operating performance. Presently, I am focused on providing support for a 300,000-seat, multibillion-dollar IT infrastructure management project in conjunction with the U.S. Department of the Navy.

The scope of my responsibility transcends the entire project management life cycle, from initial needs assessment and technology evaluations through vendor selection, internal systems development, pilot testing, technical and user documentation, and full-scale implementation. Most notable are my strengths in facilitating cooperation among cross-functional project teams to ensure that all projects are delivered on time, within budget, and as per specifications. Highlights of my professional career include the following:

- Led the development of a streamlined e-commerce solution for the Navy/Marine Corps Intranet's (NMCI) Asset Management Process valued in excess of $6 billion.

- Responsible for data modeling, application development, and project management representing $82 million in new revenue.

- Received the *Hammer Award* for "Reinventing Government" and the USAG Surgeon General's *Coin of Excellence* for my work developing full life cycle software products.

- Earned the *Commander's Plaque* for setting up the Combat Ammunition System-Base Level (CAS-B) at Holloman Air Force Base while serving in the United States Air Force as a commissioned officer.

Secure in my current position, I am confidently exploring challenging new opportunities and am therefore enclosing my résumé for your review. My goal is a CTO, CIO, or CKO position where I can affect positive results for start-up, turnaround, or high-growth operations. My current compensation package exceeds $200K, and I am available for travel and/or domestic relocation.

If one or more of your clients is looking for a dynamic, aggressive leader, we should talk. I would welcome the opportunity to speak with you regarding your clients' needs, and appreciate both your time and consideration of my qualifications.

Sincerely,

Joe B. Maynard

The heading on this letter mirrors the resume and is a powerful statement of the executive's exper-tise and capability. The second-to-last paragraph includes personal and compensation information appropriate to its recruiter audience (written by Debbie Ellis, MRW, CPRW).

APPENDIX

Internet Career Resources

The Internet has changed job search forever. Information that used to take days or even weeks to find can now be accessed in just minutes. It truly is a revolution.

However, the pace of development and the number of new Internet sites that emerge every day make it impossible to provide a comprehensive list of *all* Web sites related to employment, careers, and job search. The following list includes some of our favorite sites, some of the largest sites, and some of the best sites.

This list is by no means comprehensive. We strongly suggest that you devote the time necessary to conduct your own independent Web-based research as applicable to your specific job search campaign and career path.

Dictionaries and Glossaries

These sites provide outstanding information on keywords and acronyms.

Acronym Finder	www.acronymfinder.com
ComputerUser Dictionary	www.computeruser.com/resources/dictionary
Dave VE7CNV's Truly Canadian Dictionary of Canadian Spelling	www.luther.ca/~dave7cnv/cdnspelling/cdnspelling.html
Duhaime's Legal Dictionary	www.duhaime.org
High-Tech Dictionary Chat Symbols	www.computeruser.com/resources/dictionary/chat.html
InvestorWords.com	www.investorwords.com
Law.com Legal Dictionary	www.dictionary.law.com
Legal Dictionary	www.nolo.com/lawcenter/dictionary/wordindex.cfm
Merriam-Webster Collegiate Dictionary & Thesaurus	www.m-w.com/home.htm

TechWeb TechEncyclopedia	www.techweb.com/encyclopedia/
Verizon Glossary of Telecom Terms	http://www22.verizon.com/wholesale/glossary/0,2624,P_Q,00.html
Washington Post Business Glossary	www.washingtonpost.com/wp-srv/business/longterm/glossary/index.htm
Webopedia: Online Dictionary for Computer and Internet Terms	www.webopedia.com
Whatis?com Technology Terms	http://whatis.techtarget.com
Wordsmyth: The Educational Dictionary/Thesaurus	www.wordsmyth.net
Yahoo! Babel Fish Text Translation	http://babelfish.yahoo.com/

Job Search Sites

You'll find thousands of current professional employment opportunities on these sites.

GENERAL SITES

6FigureJobs	www.6figurejobs.com
AllStar Jobs	www.allstarjobs.com
America's CareerInfoNet	www.acinet.org/acinet
BlackWorld Careers	www.blackworld.com/careers.htm
BlueCollar.com (Australia)	www.bluecollar.com.au
Canada WorkInfo Net	www.workinfonet.ca
CareerBuilder	www.careerbuilder.com
Career.com	www.career.com
CareerExposure	www.careerexposure.com
CareerJournal	www.careerjournal.com
Careermag.com	www.careermag.com
Career Services (New Zealand)	www.careers.govt.nz/
Contract Employment Weekly	www.ceweekly.com
EmploymentGuide.com	www.employmentguide.com
Excite	http://careers.excite.com
Futurestep	www.futurestep.com
Help Wanted	www.helpwanted.com

The Internet Job Locator	www.joblocator.com
JobBankUSA	www.jobbankusa.com
JobCircle	www.jobcircle.com
Job.com	www.job.com
JobHuntersBible.com	www.jobhuntersbible.com
Job-Hunt.org	www.job-hunt.org
Jobserve	www.jobserve.us
Monster.com	www.monster.com
NationJob Network	www.nationjob.com
Net Temps	www.net-temps.com
NowHiring.com	www.nowhiring.com
Online-Jobs.Com	www.online-jobs.com
The Riley Guide	www.rileyguide.com
Saludos Hispanos	www.saludos.com
Spherion	www.spherion.com
The Ladders	www.theladders.com
TrueCareers	www.truecareers.com
Vault	www.vault.com
Yahoo! HotJobs.com	http://hotjobs.yahoo.com
WorkTree	www.worktree.com

MILITARY TRANSITION SITES

About.com: Military Separation	http://usmilitary.about.com/library/weekly/aa082001a.htm
Absolute Portal	http://abportal.50megs.com/careers/military.html
Air Force Times	www.airforcetimes.com/careers/
Army Times	www.armytimes.com
Career Command Post	www.careercommandpost.com/
Corporate Gray	www.corporategray.com/
G.I. Jobs Magazine	www.gijobs.net
Hire Vets First	www.hirevetsfirst.gov
Key to Career Success	www.careeronestop.org/militarytransition/
Military.com	www.military.com/Careers/Home
Military Exits	www.militaryexits.com/

Military Hire.com	www.militaryhire.com
Military Money	www.militarymoney.com/resources/careers/
Military Resumes	www.militaryresumes.org/
Military-to-Civilian Interview Questions	www.job-interview.net/Bank/QMilitary.htm
Military Transition Links	www.militarytransitionlinks.com/
Navy Times	www.navytimes.com/careers/
The Riley Guide	www.rileyguide.com/vets.html
Transition Assistance Online	www.taonline.com/
USAJOBS	www.usajobs.gov/veteranscenter/
Washington Post: How to Switch from a Military to a Civilian Career	www.washingtonpost.com/ac2/wp-dyn?pagename=article&node=&contentId=A60971-2003Feb24&notFound=true

CAREER-SPECIFIC SITES

Accounting Careers

American Association of Finance and Accounting	www.aafa.com
Career Bank	www.careerbank.com
CFO.com	www.cfonet.com
CPAnet	www.CPAnet.com
SmartPros Accounting	www.accountingnet.com

Arts and Media Careers

Fashion Career Center	www.fashioncareercenter.com
Playbill (Theatre Jobs)	www.playbill.com/jobs/find/
TVJobs.com	www.tvjobs.com

Education Careers

Chronicle of Higher Education Career Network	www.chronicle.com/jobs
Council for Advancement and Support of Education	www.case.org
Educationjobs.com	www.educationjobs.com
Teaching Jobs	www.teaching-jobs.org
TopSchoolJobs.org	www.topschooljobs.org
UniversityJobs.com	www.universityjobs.com

Food Service Careers

Chefs Job Network	www.chefsjobnetwork.com
Escoffier On Line	http://escoffier.com
Foodservice.com	www.foodservice.com

Government Careers

Federal Jobs Net	www.federaljobs.net
FRS Federal Jobs Central	www.fedjobs.com
GetaGovJob.com	www.getagovjob.com
GovExec.com	www.govexec.com
HRS Federal Job Search	www.hrsjobs.com
USAJOBS	www.usajobs.gov

Health Care/Medical/Pharmaceutical Careers

Alliance of Medical Recruiters	www.physicianrecruiters.com
AlliedHealthCareers.com	www.alliedhealthcareers.com
HealthJobSite.com	www.healthjobsite.com
MedHunters.com	www.medhunters.com
Medzilla	www.medzilla.com
Monster Healthcare	http://healthcare.monster.com
Nurse.com	www.nurse.com
Pharmaceutical Company Database	www.coreynahman.com/pharmaceutical_company_database.html
RehabJobsOnline	www.rehabjobs.com
Rx Career Center	www.rxcareercenter.com

Human Resources Careers

HR Hub	www.hrhub.com
HRJobs.com	www.hrjobs.com
Human Resources and Skills Development Canada	http://www.hrsdc.gc.ca/en/home.shtml
Jobs4HR	www.jobs4hr.com
Society for Human Resource Management	www.shrm.org/jobs

International Careers

EscapeArtist.com	www.escapeartist.com
International Jobs Center	www.internationaljobs.org

LatPro	www.latpro.com
OverseasJobs.com	www.overseasjobs.com

Legal Careers

AttorneyJobs.com	www.attorneyjobs.com
Greedy Associates	www.greedyassociates.com

Sales and Marketing Careers

American Marketing Association	www.marketingpower.com/careers/
MarketingJobs.com	www.marketingjobs.com
NationJob	www.nationjob.com/marketing
SalesJobs.com	www.salesjobs.com
Sales Ladder	http://sales.theladders.com

Technology/Engineering Careers

American Institute of Architects	www.aia.org
American Society for Quality	www.asq.org
Chancellor & Chancellor Resources for Careers	www.chancellor.com/fr_careers.html
ComputerWork.com	www.computerwork.com
Computerworld Careers Knowledge Center	www.computerworld.com/ careertopics/careers?from=left
Dice	www.dice.com
IEEE-USA Job Service	www.ieeeusa.org
National Society of Professional Engineers	www.nspe.org
National Technical Employment Services	www.ntes.com

Sites for Miscellaneous Specific Fields

AG Careers/Farms.com	www.agcareers.com
American Public Works Association	www.apwa.net/WorkZone/
AutoCareers.com	www.autocareers.com
CEOExpress	www.ceoexpress.com
Environmentalcareer.com	www.environmental-jobs.com
Environmental Career Opportunities	www.ecojobs.com

Find a Pilot	www.findapilot.com
Logistics Jobs	www.jobsinlogistics.com
MBACareers.com	www.mbacareers.com
Social Work Jobs	www.socialservice.com

Company Information

These outstanding resources can be a great help when you are researching specific companies.

555-1212.com	www.555-1212.com
Brint.com	www.brint.com
EDGAR Online	www.edgar-online.com
Fortune Magazine	www.fortune.com
Hoover's Business Profiles	www.hoovers.com
infoUSA (small business information)	www.infousa.com
OneSource CorpTech	www.corptech.com
SuperPages.com	www.bigbook.com
U.S. Chamber of Commerce	www.uschamber.com/
Vault	www.vault.com

Interviewing Tips and Techniques

The expert guidance at these sites will help you sharpen and strengthen your interviewing skills.

About.com Interviewing	http://jobsearch.about.com/od/interviewsnetworking/
Bradley CVs Introduction to Job Interviews	www.bradleycvs.demon.co.uk/interview/index.htm
Job-Interview.net	www.job-interview.net
Northeastern University Career Services	http://careerservices.neu.edu/job_search/interviewing.php
Wendy Enelow	www.wendyenelow.com/articles/?page_id=11

Salary and Compensation Information

Learn from the experts to strengthen your negotiating skills and increase your salary.

Abbott, Langer & Associates	www.abbott-langer.com
Bureau of Labor Statistics	www.bls.gov/bls/wages.htm
CareerOneStop	www.careeronestop.org/SalariesBenefits/
Clayton Wallis Co.	www.ictcw.com/
Economic Research Institute	www.erieri.com
Janco Associates MIS Salary Survey	www.psrinc.com/salary.htm
JobStar	www.jobstar.org/tools/salary/
Monster.com Salary Info	salary.monster.com/
Salary.com	www.salary.com
Salary Expert	www.salaryexpert.com
WorldatWork: The Total Rewards Association	www.worldatwork.org

INDEX OF CONTRIBUTORS

The sample resumes and cover letters in this book were written by professional resume and cover letter writers. If you need help with your resume and job search correspondence, you can use the following list to locate a career professional who can help.

You will notice that most of the writers have one or more credentials listed after their names. In fact, some have half a dozen or more! The careers industry offers extensive opportunities for ongoing training, and most career professionals take advantage of these opportunities to build their skills and keep their knowledge current. If you are curious about what any one of these credentials means, we suggest that you contact the resume writer directly. He or she will be glad to discuss certifications and other qualifications as well as information about services that can help you in your career transition.

Michele Angello, CPRW
Advance Your Career Resume
19866 E. Dickenson Place
Aurora, CO 80013
Phone: (303) 537-3592
E-mail: michele@aycresume.com
www.aycresume.com

Doris Appelbaum, CEO
Appelbaum's Resume Professionals, Inc.
P.O. Box 804
Milwaukee, WI 53201
Phone: (414) 352-5994
Toll-free: (800) 619-9777
E-mail: dorisa@execpc.com
www.appelbaumresumes.com

Kerry Atkins
133 Raffia Road
Enfield, CT 06082
Phone: (860) 833-4521
E-mail: Kerry.Atkins@gmail.com

Elizabeth Axnix, CPRW, JCTC, CEIP
The Axnix Advantage
Riverside, IA
Toll-free: (800) 359-7822
E-mail: axnix@earthlink.net

Jacqui Barrett, MRW, CPRW, CEIP
Career Trend
3826 NW Barry Rd., Ste. A
Kansas City, MO 64154
Phone: (816) 584-1639
E-mail: jacqui@careertrend.net
www.careertrend.net

Beverly Baskin, Ed.S., MA, LPC, NCCC, CPRW
Mitchell Baskin, MMS, PE
BBCS Counseling Services
6 Alberta Dr.
Marlboro, NJ 07746
Also in Iselin and Freehold, NJ
Toll-free: (800) 300-4079
Fax: (732) 972-8846
E-mail: info@bbcscounseling.com
www.baskincareer.com

Janet Beckstrom, ACRW, CPRW
Word Crafter
1717 Montclair Ave.
Flint, MI 48503
Phone: (810) 232-9257
Fax: (810) 232-9257
E-mail: janet@wordcrafter.com

Laurie Berenson, CPRW
Sterling Career Concepts, LLC
P.O. Box 142
Park Ridge, NJ 07656
Phone: (201) 573-8282
E-mail: laurie@sterlingcareerconcepts.com
www.sterlingcareerconcepts.com

Andy Bethurum, CPRW, CEIP

Louri Boilard

Arnold G. Boldt, CPRW, JCTC
Arnold-Smith Associates
625 Panorama Trail, Building One, Ste. 120
Rochester, NY 14625
Phone: (585) 383-0350
Fax: (585) 387-0516
E-mail: Arnie@ResumeSOS.com
www.ResumeSOS.com

Ann Boyer, CCMC, ACRW
E-mail: aboyerconsult@aol.com

Diane Burns, CPRW, CPCC, CCM, IJCTC, FJST, CCMC, CEIP
Career Marketing Techniques
E-mail: diane@polishedresumes.com
www.polishedresumes.com

Catherine Childs, CPRW
133 N. Pompano Beach Blvd., Ste. 310
Pompano Beach, FL 33062
Phone: (954) 946-3953
E-mail: catherinechilds@bellsouth.net

Annemarie Cross, CPRW, CARW, CEIP, CECC, CCM, CWPP, CERW, CMRW, CPBS, COIS
Advanced Employment Concepts
P.O. Box 91
Hallam, Victoria 3803
Australia
Phone: +613 9708 6930
Fax: +613 9796 4479
E-mail: success@aresumewriter.net
www.aresumewriter.net

Robert A. Dagnall
ResumeGuru.com
4640 Campus Avenue
San Diego, CA 92116
Phone: (619) 297-0950
E-mail: Robert@ResumeGuru.com
www.ResumeGuru.com

Michael Davis, CPRW, GCDF
940 Ashcreek Dr.
Centerville, OH 45458-3333
Phone: (937) 438-5037
E-mail: msdavis49@hotmail.com

George Dutch, CFP, CCM, JCTC
JobJoy
900-275 Slater St.
Ottawa, ON K1R 5H9
Canada
Phone: (613) 563-0584
Toll-free: (800) 798-2696
E-mail: george@jobjoy.com
www.JobJoy.com

Debbie Ellis, MRW, CPRW
Phoenix Career Group
Toll-free: (800) 876-5506 (U.S. and Canada)
International: (281) 458-5040
E-mail: debbie@phoenixcareergroup.com
www.PhoenixCareerGroup.com

Dayna Feist, CPRW, JCTC, CEIP
Gatehouse Business Services
265 Charlotte St.
Asheville, NC 28801
Phone: (828) 254-7893
Fax: (828) 254-7894
E-mail: dayna@bestjobever.com
www.bestjobever.com

Art Frank, MBA
Resumes "R" Us
17 Green Meadow Court
Flat Rock, NC 28731
Phone: (828) 696-2975
E-mail: af97710@bellsouth.net
www.powerresumesandcoaching.com

Louise Garver, JCTC, MCDP, CPRW, CEIP, CMP , CCMC, CPBS, CLBF, CJSS, COIS, 2Young2Retire Facilitator
Career Directions, LLC
P.O. Box 587
Broad Brook, CT 06016
Phone: (860) 623-9476
E-mail: Louise@careerdirectionsllc.com
www.careerdirectionsllc.com

Don Goodman, CPRW, CCMC, CJSS
18 Eton Drive
North Caldwell, NJ 07006
Toll-free: (800) 909-0109
E-mail: DGoodman@GotTheJob.com
www.GotTheJob.com

Lee Anne Grundish

Loretta Heck
All Word Services
924 E. Old Willow Rd. #102
Prospect Heights, IL 60070
Phone: (847) 215-7517
Fax: (847) 215-7520
E-mail: Siegfried@ameritech.net

CJ Johnson, JCTC, CHRM, FJST, CCC, MSVA
Transition Manager
U.S. Coast Guard ISC Alameda
Worklife, Bldg. 16, Coast Guard Island
Alameda, CA 94501
Phone: (510) 437-5991
E-mail: cjohnson@d11.uscg.mil

Marcy Johnson, NCRW, CPRW, CEIP

Bill Kinser, MRW, CPRW, JCTC, CEIP, CCM
President, To The Point Resumes
Fairfax, VA
Phone: (571) 276-8342
E-mail: info@tothepointresumes.com
www.tothepointresumes.com

Jeanne Knight, JCTC, CCMC
Career and Job Search Coach
P.O. Box 162
Westford, MA 01886
Phone: (617) 968-7747
E-mail: jeanne@careerdesigns.biz
www.careerdesigns.biz

Bonnie Kurka, CPRW, CCMC, JCTC, FJST
Executive Career Suite
Portland, OR 97219
Phone: (918) 494-4630
E-mail: bonnie@executivecareersuite.com
www.executivecareersuite.com

Louise Kursmark, MRW, CPRW, JCTC, CEIP, CCM
President, Best Impression Career Services, Inc.
Founder, Resume Writing Academy
Phone: (781) 944-2471
E-mail: LK@yourbestimpression.com
www.yourbestimpression.com
www.resumewritingacademy.com

Brian Leeson, MSc
Vector Consultants Pty Ltd
P.O. Box 553
Echunga, South Australia 5153
Australia
Phone: +61 8 8388 8183
E-mail: brian@vectorconsultants.com.au
www.vectorconsultants.com.au

Abby Locke, MRW, NCRW, ACRW
Premier Writing Solutions, LLC
3289 Hardin Place NE
Washington DC 20018
Phone: (202) 635-2197
Toll-free fax: (866) 350-4220
E-mail: alocke@premierwriting.com
www.premierwriting.com

Peter S. Marx, JCTC
Tampa, FL 33611
Phone: (813) 832-5133
E-mail: marxps@aol.com

Nicole Miller, CCM, CRW, IJCTC, CECC
Mil-Roy Consultants
Ottawa, ON
Canada
Phone: (613) 834-2439
E-mail: resumes@milroyconsultants.com
www.milroyconsultants.com

Melanie Noonan
Peripheral Pro, LLC
560 Lackawanna Ave.
Woodland Park, NJ 07424
Phone: (973) 785-3011
Fax: (973) 256-2685
E-mail: PeriPro1@aol.com

Debra O'Reilly, CPRW, CEIP, JCTC, FRWC
A First Impression Resume Service/
ResumeWriter.com
Brandon, FL 33510
Phone: (813) 651-0408
Toll-free: (800) 340-5570
E-mail: debra@resumewriter.com
www.resumewriter.com

Don Orlando, MBA, CPRW, JCTC, CCM, CCMC
The McLean Group
640 S. McDonough St.
Montgomery, AL 36104
Phone: (334) 264-2020
E-mail: yourcareercoach@charterinternet.com

Julie Rains, CPRW
Executive Correspondents
P.O. Box 495
Clemmons, NC 27012
Phone: (336) 712-2390
E-mail: jr@workingtolive.com
www.WorkingToLive.com

Michelle Mastruserio Reitz, CPRW
Printed Pages
3985 Race Rd., Ste. 6
Cincinnati, OH 45211
Phone: (513) 598-9100
E-mail: michelle@printedpages.com
www.printedpages.com

Alan J. Rider, MA, MCDP
6969 Copper Mountain Ct.
Indianapolis, IN 46236
Phone: (765) 350-0030
E-mail: the_riders@hotmail.com

Edie Rische, NCRW, JCTC, ACCC, CPBS, CPBA
Lubbock, TX 79424
Phone: (806) 543-2388
E-mail: erische@suddenlink.net

Laura Scheible, CCMC, CJST, JCTC
Toll-free: (888) 685-3507
E-mail: laurascheible@earthlink.net

Marcella Schuyler, MSW

Robin Sherrod

Laura Smith-Proulx, CPRW, CCMC, CIC
An Expert Resume
Arvada, CO
Phone: (303) 805-4315
E-mail: laura@anexpertresume.com
www.AnExpertResume.com

Billie Sucher, MS, CTMS, CTSB, JCTC, CCM
Billie Sucher & Associates
7177 Hickman Rd., Ste. 10
Urbandale, IA 50322
Phone: (515) 276-0061
E-mail: billie@billiesucher.com
www.billiesucher.com

James Walker, MS
Counselor, ACAP Center
Bldg. 210, Rm. 006, Custer Ave.
Ft. Riley, KS 66442
Phone: (785) 239-2278
Fax: (785) 239-2251
E-mail: jwalker8199@yahoo.com

Beth Woodworth

INDEX

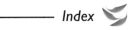